The Complete Guide to Business Risk Management

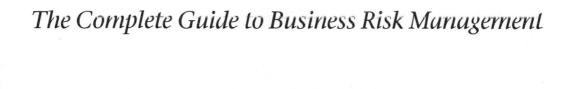

To Madeleine

The Complete Guide to Business Risk Management

Second Edition

KIT SADGROVE

GOWER

Published by
Gower Publishing Limited
Gower House
Croft Road
Aldershot
Hants GU11 3HR
England

Gower Publishing Company
Suite 420
101 Cherry Street
Burlington
VT 05401–4405
USA

Kit Sadgrove has asserted his right under the Copyright, Designs and Patents Act, 1988, to be identified as the author of this work.

British Library Cataloguing in Publication Data
Sadgrove, Kit
   The complete guide to business risk management
   1. Risk management
   I. Title
   658.1'55

   ISBN 0 566 08661 1

Library of Congress Cataloging-in-Publication Data
Sadgrove, Kit
   The complete guide to business risk manageement / by Kit Sadgrove.
      p. cm.
   Includes bibliographical references and index.
   ISBN: 0-566-08661-1
   1. Risk management. I. Title.
   HD61.S2 2005
   658.15'5--dc22

                                                                                    2005001195

Typeset by IML Typographers, Birkenhead, Merseyside and printed in Great Britain MPG Books Ltd, Bodmin

Contents

List of figures

List of tables

Preface

Any company that wants to be in business in ten years' time has to ask three questions:

1 What are the worst things that could happen to us?
2 How likely are they to happen?
3 Are we taking the right steps to prevent them?

This is the art of risk management, and the subject of this book.

The Complete Guide to Business Risk Management helps management identify risks, and prevent them from taking place. It then shows what steps should be taken in the event of a crisis.

Business is inherently risky. At any moment, a fire may engulf the premises. A competitor may launch a superior product. Or a government decision may tie the company in red tape. Businesses have to live with those uncertainties because no company and no product is risk-free.

There is no point in trying to avoid risk completely. 'Hide from risk and you hide from its rewards' says a sign in the New York dealing room of Bankers Trust Co. Inaction merely creates new risks. Lack of innovation creates stagnation, and ultimately failure. So this book does not warn companies against risk taking. Rather, it helps businesses understand their risks and manage them professionally. It emphasizes the really big risks such as being caught napping by a change of technology, a change in the business cycle, or being left behind by competitors' activity.

We start by asking the questions, 'What is risk?', 'How do we assess it?', and 'How can it be managed?' Each subsequent chapter covers a major area of risk, such as finance or the environment.

The book shows how the reader can audit the main areas of risk. It outlines the questions that need to be asked, and then helps the reader develop a risk management plan for each area. At the end of the book is a list of recommended reading and a glossary.

For your convenience, all the forms used in this book are available for free download at www.inst.org/risk/forms. It is a requirement of their use that you leave the copyright notice intact.

In addition, the online resources (to be found under 'Useful links' at the end of each chapter) will be updated twice a year at www.inst.org/risk/resources.

Remember that every company is different, and the comments made in this book may not apply to individual cases. Companies should seek qualified advice.

Kit Sadgrove
2005

Acknowledgements

I have drawn on information from many sources. They include the AIRMIC, ALARM, Amnesty International, AON, Arson Prevention Bureau, ASH, Bankruptcy Action, BBC, BizSites.com, Breaking News, Business Continuity Online, Business Report South Africa, ChannelMinds, Charted Institute of Management Accountants (CIMA), Clearly Business, *Computer Business Review*, *Computer Weekly*, *Computer World*, Control Risks Group, Coso, Council of European Municipalities and Regions, Cow & Gate, Department of Environment, Food and Rural Affairs (DEFRA), the Department of Industry, Dun and Bradstreet, Email-policy.com, *Entrepreneur* magazine, Epolicy.com, European Union, Financial Services Authority, *Financial Times*, the Fire Protection Association, Foresight.org, Green Party, *Guardian* newspaper, the Health and Safety Commission, HM Treasury, Hull University, Institute of Charted Accountants in England and Wales (ICAEW), *Inc.* magazine, Institute for Crisis Management, Institute of Internal Auditors, the Institute of Risk Management, Kable, Logitech, Law Society, LegalActionforWomen.org, the Loss Prevention Council, the Millennium Project, Mongabay.com, National Health Service (NHS), *Observer* newspaper, Office of Government Commerce, Procurement Strategy Council, *Purchasing* magazine, *Real Business* magazine, Reebok, RiskInfo, *Risk Management* magazine, RiskReports, Rits, Said Business School, Standards Australia, StoraEnso, *Sunday Business Post*, *Sunday Times*, Survive.com, SustainAbility, TalkLeft, *The Economist*, *The Scotsman*, *The Times*, UK Foreign Office, UK Home Office, UK RiskWorld, *Wall Street Journal*, *Whittaker's Almanac*, and Ziff Davis.

Statistics and survey data were also provided by AT Kearney, the Audit Commission, Aveco, Axa, British Retail Consortium, Carlsberg-Tetley, Chubb Fire, Contingency Planning Research, CyberSpace International, DataFort, Ernst and Young, Federation of European Risk Management Associations (FERMA), FM Global, Health and Safety Executive, IBM Business Recovery Services, Infoplan, International Coffee Organization, International Monetary Fund, KPMG, Marsh Inc., Ontrack, *PC* magazine, PricewaterhouseCoopers, Royal Academy of Engineering, RSM Robson Rhodes, Sedgwick, Transparency International, US Bureau of Labor Statistics, and the UK Patent Office.

I am grateful to my researcher Tom Gibbs, as well as all the individuals and organizations who have helped to create this book; but any errors are my responsibility alone.

1 Risk Management: A Powerful Tool

In this chapter we consider the following issues:

- *History of risk management*
- *What are business risks?*
- *What kinds of organizations are affected by risk?*
- *Which risks are important?*
- *The dangers of uncontrolled risk, and the benefits of managing risk*
- *Why risk management is growing in importance, and how it lacks maturity*
- *How much risk is acceptable, and how much should be spent on risk management?*
- *Steps to take.*

History of risk management

The earliest risk management record is from Babylon in the Code of Hammurabi, dating from around 2100 BC. This concerns 'bottomry', a form of naval insurance whereby the owner of the vessel can borrow money to buy cargo and does not have to pay the debt if the ship is lost at sea. The term 'bottomry' refers to pledging the bottom of your boat to the lender.

Until recently insurance was still the main way that companies managed risk. Thus in the 1960s and 1970s insurance companies sought to reduce their potential losses by encouraging businesses to make their premises safer. This was the *first age of risk management*, as shown in Figure 1.1. Businesses considered only non-entrepreneurial risk (such as security). They also used risk reactively, to see how much insurance they should buy.

In the 1970s and 1980s, businesses started to introduce quality assurance, to ensure that products conformed to their specifications. This was heralded by the British Standards Institution (BSI) launching the quality standard BS 5750 in 1979 (itself the successor to US military standard MIL-Q-9858 launched in 1959). In this, the *second age of risk management*, companies treated risk in a more proactive or preventative way.

Risk awareness was also fostered by government legislation that wanted businesses to think about the risks they posed to workers and customers. New concerns started to emerge in the 1980s about environmental risks.

In 1993, James Lam became the world's first chief risk officer, at the US financial services firm GE Capital.

The *third age of risk management* arrived in 1995 with the publishing by Standards Australia of the world's risk management standard, AS/NZS 4360:1995, which has now been

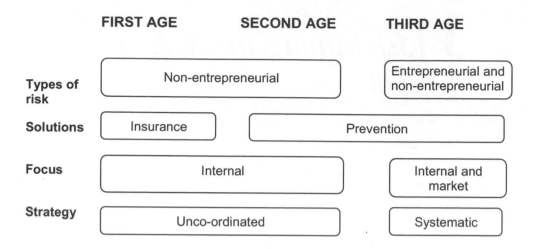

Figure 1 1   The three ages of risk management

updated three times. This was followed by the Canadian standard CAN/CSA-Q850-97. We discuss these and other standards in Chapter 17.

Reporting of risk in financial accounts became important in the late 1990s. In 1998 the UK's Department for Trade and Industry launched a review of company law aimed at developing a more modern framework for doing business in Britain in the twenty-first century. This led to the Operating and Financial Review in 2004 which required more extensive reporting of risk.

In 1999, the Institute of Chartered Accountants in England and Wales published the Turnbull Report. This called for stronger internal financial controls and better monitoring of risk. Also in 1999, the European Union decided to harmonize accounts across Europe, so that investors in one country could understand and trust annual reports from a company based in another country. This, the EU Accounts Modernization Directive, took effect in 2005. It requires, among other things, a report on 'environmental and employee matters'. From then on, company reports were to be broader in scope.

Meanwhile, corporate scandals in the early 2000s, such as Enron, led legislators around the world to define new standards for reporting company accounts, in an effort to ensure honest and transparent reports.

Risk management standards

Two risk management standards appeared in quick succession: in 2001, Japan launched a risk management system called JSI Q 2001:2001, which offered two advances: the formal definition of a risk management system, and the introduction of continuous improvement; and in 2002, the UK Institute of Risk Management introduced its risk management standard.

Meanwhile, the 9/11 disaster had taken place in 2001, and companies were beginning to think more about business continuity. Thus, in 2003, the BSI launched PAS 56, a specification for business continuity.

In 2004, the US Coso organization launched a document called 'Enterprise Risk Management – Integrated Framework'. This was developed partly in response to the Enron and Andersen scandals, and the need for good corporate governance.

The UK's Operating and Financial Review (OFR), published in 2004, required companies to publish, in their annual reports, information about the company's principal risks, as well as non-financial information about environmental and employee matters. This was partly in response to the EU Accounts Modernization Directive, described above.

Thus, in the third age of risk management, companies assess their entrepreneurial risk, and face much more stringent reporting requirements. They also treat risk as a positive force. By examining the risks in a new contract or market, businesses can reduce their chances of failure, beat the competition and increase their profit. Above all, such companies are managing risk as a system. A risk management system (RMS) ensures that the company manages its threats in a proactive, coordinated, cost-effective and prioritized way.

Risk management can be adapted to meet the needs of each business. It can be used to educate staff, and to give them a deeper understanding of the corporate risks. This turns managers into business people, and makes the business more effective.

What are business risks?

There are two types of business risk. The first and more traditional type is non entrepreneurial risk, found in fire, pollution or fraud. Companies used to protect themselves by buying insurance but, as we shall see, insurance is only one way to protect the company: there are many others.

The second type is entrepreneurial risk. This happens when a company builds a new plant, launches a new product or buys a company. If the company gets its forecasts wrong, it loses money. There are ways of reducing entrepreneurial risk, as will be discussed later.

Risk applies to any management decision that could have a good or bad outcome. It follows that most management projects and decisions contain risk. Most risks are not catastrophic but, as Table 1.1 shows, some can cause loss of life and great damage. Better risk management could have forestalled some of these crises.

Risk is also a future event that results from actions taken now. That is why managers should consider different options for any problem, and evaluate the consequences.

It is easy to focus on obvious risks, such as workplace accidents. Important though they are, the company must be alert to the big or unexpected risks. The company that is not expecting change is especially prone to suffer.

Risks often defy conventional thinking. For example, what is the most likely cause of death for a New York police officer? It is not being killed by a drug pusher's bullet, but by his own poor driving ability. In one year alone, 1230 officers of the NYPD (known as Not Yet Proficient Drivers!) were hurt in car crashes, compared with 20 who were wounded in shootings. The force now requires its officers to wear seat belts and take driving lessons, especially as the accidents cost the NYPD $3 m in sick pay.

Risk is also a positive thing. The book does not aim for the elimination of risk; risk is a necessary part of enterprise. It is a pre-condition for innovation; and without innovation the business will fail.

What kinds of organizations are affected?

All kinds of organizations face risk. Even those whose future is assured, such as government bodies, could be harmed by allegations of fraud.

Small companies are often more vulnerable to risk, since a disaster at a single-site company could leave the business with no production facilities. On the other hand, scale also brings its own problems. A multinational business will have more complex financial

Table 1.1   Some recent catastrophes

1980	The North Sea oil platform Alexander Keilland collapses	One leg of the rig snapped in heavy seas	123 crew members died
1983	South Korean airplane shot down over Kamchatka peninsula	Soviet Union fighter pilots shoot the plane down	269 passengers die, including 61 Americans
1984	Toxic gas released at the Union Carbide plant in Bhopal, India	Burst valve	3000–10 000 people die
1985	Fire sweeps Bradford football stadium	Match or cigarette dropped on to rubbish underneath the stadium	56 people die
1986	Challenger space shuttle exploded on take-off	Malfunctioning rocket seal	The three crew members die
1986	Nuclear reactor at Chernobyl explodes	Power surge causes the nuclear rods to disintegrate, causing overheating and explosion	250 000 people may have died, plus damage to agriculture and the environment
1986	Series of explosions on the Piper Alpha oil rig	Excessive flare from gas safety release led to fire	167 crew members die
1987	Herald of Free Enterprise ferry sinks in Zeebrugge harbour	Bow doors left open	193 people die
1988	Pan Am flight explodes over Lockerbie	Terrorist bomb	259 passengers die
1988	Iranian airplane shot down during Iran–Iraq conflict	US destroyer Vincennes mistook the airliner for a fighter plane	299 passengers die
1989	Hillsborough stadium disaster, Sheffield	Fans pushed to enter the stadium, where the match had started	95 people die
1990	Exxon Valdez shipwrecked off the Alaskan coast	Navigation error	Two million gallons of oil covered the coast; 2 000 sea birds and 300 otters die
1991	Iraqis set fire to Kuwait's oil wells	Economic sabotage at the end of the Gulf war	Environmental catastrophe
1994	Estonian ferry sinks in the Baltic	Faulty bow doors	900 people die
1995	Kobe earthquake	Earth movement	5500 people die, 300 000 made homeless, 180 000 buildings destroyed or badly damaged
2001	Foot and mouth disease on UK farms	Viral disease	£8 bn losses
2001	Two aircraft fly into the twin towers, New York	Terrorism	3000 die
2003	Nissan recalls 2.55 million cars	Faulty engine sensors may prevent the vehicles from starting	Costs of $140 m

2003	Space shuttle Columbia	Pieces broke off the craft on take-off	All crew die
2003	Power blackouts in Eastern USA and Canada	Power fluctuation and overload	80 million people affected, losses of $6 bn
2004	Madrid train bombing	Terrorism	191 people killed

arrangements and more processes, making it difficult for any individual to effectively manage risk.

The checklists at the end of each chapter help the reader identify the most important risks for their own business.

Risk management terms

There are many definitions of the words used in risk management, most of which are verbose. Here are a few that seek to combine clarity with brevity:

* *Hazard* – a source of potential harm (ISO/IEC Guide 51)
* *Risk* – the possibility that a hazard will cause loss or damage
* *Risk assessment* – defining what can go wrong
* *Risk management* – a discipline for dealing with uncertainty (Kloman).

Thus, stairs are a *hazard*. The *risk* of accidents on the stairs is reduced by providing strong handrails or anti-slip treads. A *risk assessment* could identify the risk of someone falling down the stairs. Auditing the safety of all stairs might form part of a *risk management system*.

There is a more detailed glossary at the back of this book, and the International Organization for Standardization (ISO) has a glossary, 'ISO/IEC Guide 73:2002 Risk management. Vocabulary. Guidelines for use in standards'.

For the sake of simplicity, we define risk as 'the possibility that a hazard will cause loss or damage'. But risk offers both *opportunity* and *danger*. The business that overlooks this duality may end up trying to obliterate all possible dangers. And that would prevent it from using risk as a way to create value. For example, when Chevron drills for oil in turbulent Kazakhstan, the oil company is undertaking mighty risks. But it would be wrong for the oil business to abandon exploration simply on the grounds that it poses a risk. Instead it should understand the risks of extracting that oil (whether they are political turmoil or environmental spills). Then it can try to control, share or reduce the risk. Or, if all else fails, it can avoid the risk by giving up and going home.

Risk assessment is not the same as planning for disaster. Although disaster planning is dramatic and interesting, the greatest risks to a business are much more insidious. Loss of computer data, a fire, fraud, and corporate governance are much more likely to cause a company to fail.

Which risks are important?

A study by FERMA, the Federation of European Risk Management Associations, among 289 leading European companies, showed that they saw operational, production and commercial risks as being the most important, quoted by 55 per cent of companies (see Figure 1.2). Forty-one per cent thought that legislation and regulation were also the most important, while 39 per cent were concerned about the risk of a major crisis. Thirty-seven per cent thought that data systems were among the greatest risks.

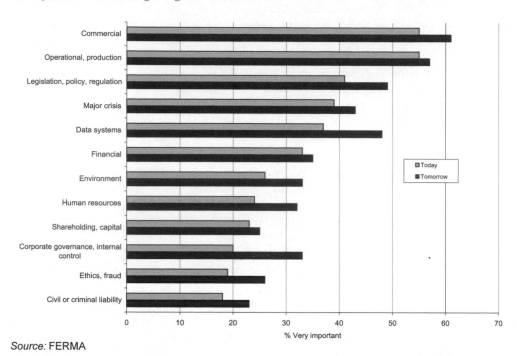

Source: FERMA

Figure 1.2   Percentage of respondents ranking a risk as very important to their company – today and tomorrow

Some risks are growing. While 37 per cent mention data systems as an important risk today, this grows to 48 per cent when companies are asked to think about tomorrow's risks. Similarly, perceived risks from environment grow from 26 per cent today to 33 per cent tomorrow, and from corporate governance rise from 20 per cent today to 33 per cent tomorrow.

In a study by FM Global, when asked what would cause the most disruption to the business, chief financial officers (CFOs) and risk managers of large firms ranked labour issues as the single most important issue (15 per cent), followed equally by production issues, supply chain matters, and fire/explosion (14 per cent). See Figure 1.3.

Despite the publicity given to terrorism, only one per cent rated sabotage and terrorism as the 'top hazard'. See also Table 16.1 for another view on the greatest threats.

However, the aggregate data conceals many differences, and the risks cited suggest that they depend on your standpoint and occupation. For example, 26 per cent of North American risk managers cited fire and explosion as the single most important threat, while only nine per cent of North American CFOs rated this the highest. And while 17 per cent of North American CFOs ranked natural disaster as the top threat, only five per cent of European CFOs agreed. Overall, the respondents ranked property-related risks as the leading threat to their main sources of income.

Moreover, when the same questions were asked of investment professionals (such as securities analysts), the answers were again completely different. The top hazard according to

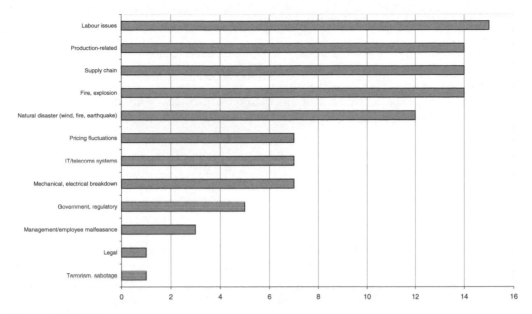

Source: FM Global

Figure 1.3   Top hazards, as rated by CFOs and risk managers, US and Europe

them was pricing fluctuations, at 39 per cent, followed by 'government and regulatory' hazards. This may indicate a lack of awareness of companies' internal hazards.

It is fair to say, therefore, that there is no easy way to rank threats. They vary according to whom you ask, which industry they work in, and the way the questions are phrased. Moreover, the importance of different risks changes over time. In the early 1990s, a survey showed the top three risks to be the environment, employee safety, and product liability.

New legislation, the economy, trends in the market and world events jostle for management's attention. In the early 1980s, the environment was not debated in the boardroom. In the late 1980s it became one of the most important items on the management agenda. By the mid-1990s, it had taken its rightful place as one of many risks that companies have to manage.

International terrorism became a major issue for many businesses after the September 11th attacks. Previously it might have been of concern only to companies operating in unsettled countries.

Moreover, after the eastern states of America suffered blackouts in August 2003, risk managers added 'power supply' to their list of worries. All of which proves that risk is dynamic – it changes over time; and some big risks are hard to forecast. Companies must regularly re-think their risks.

MISSION-CRITICAL RISKS

Which processes are essential to the survival of the business? Decide which activities are mission critical. Then decide how those activities could be interrupted. You have now defined your major risks, which is important because it is easy to get bogged down in the plethora of risks and issues.

The dangers of uncontrolled risk

A Pricewaterhouse/Bank for International Settlements survey showed that 35 per cent of firms which suffer a computer disaster lose over £250 000. As each chapter of this book shows, the costs of other risks are equally high.

Table 1.2 shows that each kind of risk results in financial loss. That makes risk an important management topic.

Table 1.2   The results of uncontrolled risk

Type of risk	Initial effect	Ultimate effect
Quality problem	Product recall; customer defection	Financial losses
Environmental pollution	Bad publicity; customer disfavour and defection; court action; fines	Financial losses
Health and safety injury	Bad publicity; worker compensation claims, workforce dissatisfaction; statutory fines	Human suffering; financial losses
Fire	Harm to humans; loss of production and assets	Human suffering; financial losses
Computer failure	Inability to take orders, process work or issue invoices; customer defection	Financial losses
Marketing risk	Revenue drops	Financial losses
Fraud	Theft of money	Financial losses
Security	Theft of money, assets or plans	Financial losses
International trading	Foreign exchange losses	Financial losses
Political risks	Foreign government appropriates assets; prevents repatriation of profits	Financial losses

Is risk management relevant to your organization?

Risk applies to all businesses, but some are more likely than others to benefit from formal risk assessment. It is particularly necessary to a business with the following criteria:

- A number of different sites
- A size that precludes any individual knowing the details of every threat
- A business with overseas operations
- A range of processes
- Many sub-contractors, suppliers or other business associates who are not under the direct control of the business
- A site that has been used for more than 30 years (old sites sometimes have buildings, equipment or work practices dating from times when lower standards were acceptable)
- Operates in a highly regulated industry such as financial services.

In short, the larger or more complex the business, the more it will benefit from risk assessment.

The benefits of managing risk

Risk management helps a company avoid cost, disruption and unhappiness. Risk analysis also helps management to decide which risks are worth pursuing, and which should be shunned. However, the benefits of risk management are not easy to quantify. It is difficult to claim that risk management has prevented, say, two major fires, a burglary and three serious accidents.

The company should collate records of losses. These are often kept by different departments and classified in ways that make comparison difficult. But a unified set of information will help the business see how much is currently being lost, and whether investment in risk management serves to reduce losses. In Table 1.3 below, we consider some advantages of managing risks.

However, companies tend to introduce risk management in response to outside factors such as scandals, legislation or regulation (for example, stock exchange reporting requirements). They are less likely to introduce risk management because it will help the corporation produce better results.

To make risk management work, the benefits may need to be explained to other managers and staff. As we have seen from Table 1.3, the corporate advantages are clear. There are also advantages to the workforce. Staff who are aware of risks can prevent them from happening, and can manage them better if they materialize. The most obvious example is fire drills. Staff who have practised a fire drill are less likely to be hurt in a fire. The same applies to other areas of risk, especially those which affect the individual – whether health and safety or kidnap and ransom.

In this book we cover the risks that are most common and most severe. That means ignoring the many smaller risks and issues that won't bring the company down or take management time.

Table 1.3   Advantages of managing risk proactively

Type of risk	Benefits of proactive management
Marketing risks	Maintain market share
Health and safety risks	Avoid worker litigation; reduce insurance premiums
Environmental risks	Avoid litigation from regulatory authorities; reduced premiums
Fire risks	Avoid loss of production, avoid going out of business; reduced premiums
Bomb threats	Avoid loss of life or destruction of a building
Computer risks	Prevent inability to invoice, lack of access to information
Theft and fraud, industrial espionage	Prevent loss of money, assets or concepts, loss of market share
Technical risks	Avoid being left behind with obsolete manufacturing methods or technologies; avoid production stoppage
Kidnap and ransom, extortion	Safeguard managers abroad or at home; prevent payment to criminals
Product contamination (accidental and criminal)	Avoid harming customers and prevent litigation

In addition, we do not focus on the risks specific to the financial services industry, such as stock market risk, hedging, or insurance risk. There are other, more specialist, books which cover those areas.

Why risk management is growing in importance

At one time, risk management meant buying insurance and having enough fire extinguishers. But several factors have conspired to make insurance and passive deterrents inadequate. Together, they make risk an important boardroom issue.

In the FERMA study quoted earlier, when asked the reasons for increased risk management activities, 69 per cent of respondents cited catastrophic events, 67 per cent mentioned legal and regulatory requirements, 57 per cent said that shareholders were requesting it, and 51 per cent mentioned a big increase in insurance costs.

Catastrophic events have always been with us, but it is only now that management is taking steps to pre-empt them. But the other factors are newer, namely legislation, shareholders, and rising insurance costs. Below we examine some of the issues that lead management to focus on risk.

- *Legislation is getting tougher:*
  - Legislation is now more extensive. In the 18 months prior to July 2004, the European Union published 276 documents concerning environmental legislation.
  - Legislation is more stringent. Company directors can be jailed for corporate offences, and fines can be high.
  - Risk assessment is growing more common in many areas of legislation. The EU now requires companies to carry out risk assessment in health and safety, product liability and finance.

- *Insurance is more expensive and more difficult to get:*
  - Insurance is no longer the cheap option it once was. Insurers are putting up premiums for many categories of risk. This follows years of major claims for environmental and product liability losses. Piper Aircraft was put out of business by product liability problems.
  - Open-ended cover is no longer widely available. For example, it is difficult to obtain insurance for environmental pollution that has developed over a period of years (for example, long-term pollution of a watercourse). Insurance companies are adding more exclusions, to the point where the insurance won't cover the business for its important areas of risk, essentially making such insurance worthless.
  - Insurance companies require their clients to actively manage their risks. More companies have to take action following an audit carried out by their insurance company.
  - Insurance may not recoup the full amount lost. A 2004 survey by the Computer Security Institute and the FBI in America found that fewer than 20 per cent of the victims of computer crime even reported security incidents to law enforcers, let alone used external insurance to recoup their losses. This may be due to exclusion clauses and the negative impact on the organization's public image.
  - Insurance pay-outs can be slow. Companies can wait over a year for a pay-out.
  - Many assets cannot be insured. Insurance cannot pay for loss of goodwill and reputation.

- Insurance is reactive. It does not prevent losses from occurring. That does not detract from the value of insurance, however, which is a valid fall-back strategy in risk management.
- Ever tried claiming on a business insurance policy? Unless the claim is small or 100 per cent robust, you may find that the insurance company is reluctant to pay out. You may receive a 'Reservation of Rights' letter from your insurer – this is a notice that even though the company is handling your claim, certain losses might not be covered by the terms of the policy. By this letter, the insurance company reserves its right not to pay out. The letter may also state that the insurance company is not obliged to pay your legal costs, which can be substantial.

- *Customer attitudes:*
  - Corporate customers want to pass legal responsibilities to their suppliers. Many companies look for evidence of risk management in their suppliers (for example, in the form of quality systems).
  - Consumers are more litigious, and less likely to accept product failure. Many examples have occurred in faulty healthcare products that have harmed consumers, who in turn have sought redress in the court. This applies to drugs which had unforeseen side effects, tampons which caused toxic shock, or breast implants which went wrong. This litigation has often been unsuccessful, but it would be rash to assume that this will continue.
  - Shareholders are more aware of risk. They are seeking more information in annual reports about the company's exposure to risk, because it will directly affect the company's future profits.

- *A more critical public:*
  - The public expects higher standards of corporate behaviour than before. It is especially critical of pollution, dangerous products and corporate fraud. This attitude encourages companies to avoid risking the public's hostility.

- *Management attitudes:*
  - Management has learnt from other firms' disasters. Highly publicized disasters, from Bhopal and Exxon Valdez to Enron, Martha Stewart, Hollinger and Parmalat, have shown management that risks are a damaging, and sometimes fatal, cost to the business.
  - Companies are becoming more professional: as companies have started to manage their environmental impacts, they have increasingly discovered that preventing catastrophe is better than trying to cure it.
  - Companies are more global: firms have had to learn how to manage their increasingly international operations. Often the solution lies in setting policies and performance standards, while leaving local management to run the business.
  - Growing private-sector involvement in national enterprises: governments are withdrawing from the management of national enterprises, such as transportation, healthcare and energy. This means that private enterprises are now running high-risk businesses, and the government will not pay the costs of a catastrophe. These companies have to take risk more seriously.

Risk management lacks maturity

Risk management has a long way to go. Many companies apply risk management only to selected areas of the business.

In the FM Global survey quoted earlier, 80 per cent of corporate respondents rated their protection measures as good or excellent, but only 51 per cent of investment professionals shared their optimism.

As Table 1.4 shows, only four in ten companies have contingency plans for losing their building or their telephone system (whether through fire, explosion or some other cause).

Many companies still rely on insurance for their protection. For example, 80 per cent of companies have computer insurance, but only 42 per cent have voluntarily adopted an IT contingency plan. Many computer recovery plans stay within the IT department, and are not discussed with other managers. Nine out of ten companies entrust the preparation of the recovery plan solely to an IT specialist, who understands IT but not the business. This indicates the flawed nature of much risk management.

Table 1.4   Incidence of contingency plans for specific risks (UK)

	%
Loss of buildings	41
Loss of key staff	24
Loss of information	36
Loss of telephones	42

Source: Loughborough University

How much risk is acceptable?

Lack of planning or precautions (as shown in Table 1.5) can ultimately lead to disaster. At the other end of the scale, excessive caution leads to missed opportunities. The middle course, involving a proper assessment of the risks, maximizes the company's profit. This demonstrates that the purpose of risk management is not to preclude entrepreneurial flair, but to ensure that it is properly guided.

This is known as 'risk appetite'. Some companies are happy to accept new ventures and risky acquisitions. Others want to run a steady course. For example, young companies with

Table 1.5   Attitudes to risk, and their implications

Entrepreneurial risk	Non-entrepreneurial risk	Result	Effect
Lack of planning	Inadequate precautions	Harm, loss	Human, financial and other losses
Proper risk assessment and management	Proper risk assessment and management	Control of risks	Maximized success
Failure to innovate	Excessive caution	Inactivity	Lost opportunities

little to lose often take big risks, while entrepreneurs who are nearing retirement might want to protect their gains.

You might decide to limit the amount of revenue from any one customer to 20 per cent. Or you might choose to set at 30 per cent the maximum proportion of the company's capital that could be put at risk in any one project. These are sometimes known as risk tolerances.

Introducing risk management can help the board to define what kinds of risks it wants to take. In some cases this has never been explicitly discussed before. Understanding their risk appetite can help board members achieve more consistent and considered decisions.

Total risk avoidance is a dangerous strategy. A freight company says: 'Our strategy is to accept more risks – calculated risk – in order to improve returns. This is being implemented by developing a portfolio of businesses, with a variety of risks and rewards, and continuing to exit from any high risk, low reward businesses.'

Primary and basic businesses, like a mine or a pulp mill, often look safe because there is little innovation. Yet these companies are affected by large swings in sales and price, in response to capacity, world demand, and raw material prices.

Comparing risk and reward

The level of acceptable risk depends on the reward. As Figure 1.4 shows, the greater the risk, the greater the reward must be to make it worthwhile.

The best business opportunity (shown with two ticks) is one where the reward is high and the risk low.

A risk greater than the reward (shown by the crosses) is not worth pursuing; while projects that carry low risk and low reward rarely make any impact on the business, and are therefore not worth pursuing.

Companies can affect the level of reward and risk. An oil company would want a greater return on investment from explorations in an unstable country. To achieve that it might negotiate tax concessions and investment subsidies to achieve that aim before starting operations there.

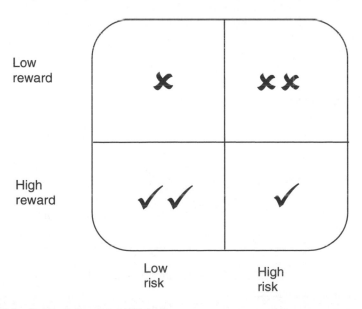

Figure 1.4 Determining acceptable risk

Likewise, a bank would want more collateral for a risky loan than for one that was risk-free. The problem comes in correctly assessing risk. The banks that lent to EuroDisney did not imagine that it would lose money, while those who lent to Eurotunnel did not think its costs would escalate and revenues would be delayed.

How much should be spent on risk management?

Companies without a risk management strategy are more likely to suffer the costs of problems and crises. There are the costs of mopping up after a pollution incident, paying to settle an industrial accident, or the cost of recalling faulty products. This is represented at the left edge of the chart in Figure 1.5.

As the company becomes aware of the need to manage corporate risk, the company starts to invest money in prevention. This includes the cost of audits, the cost of preventative maintenance, the salary of a quality manager, and so on. As the prevention costs grow, the number of incidents falls, and so do their costs. As a result, total costs also fall. The company is now at the middle of the chart.

The company can continue to invest more money in prevention, seeking to reduce ever further the likelihood of disaster. If it does so, however, the prevention costs will continue to rise.

Eventually, at the right-hand edge of the chart, the total costs are the same as they were before the company started managing its risks.

The chart suggests that there is a maximum level of investment to be made in risk management. Too great an investment will burden the company with costs and render it uncompetitive, while insufficient attention to risk will make it liable for heavy incident costs. Somewhere in the middle of the chart is the optimal position.

It is worth adding that risk management takes time, often three years. It cannot be installed overnight. The time needed to carry out risk assessments and design procedures and audits is only the starting point. Risk management then needs to be embedded into the organization, and people have to be encouraged to develop an awareness of risk.

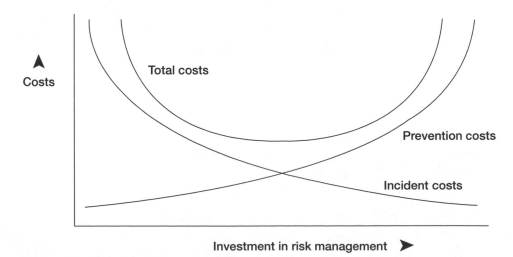

Figure 1.5   The effect on cost of managing risk

Steps to take

The process of risk management is shown in Figure 1.6. The company has to identify risks and set policies. Then it has to take action, and then monitor the risks. As the figure shows, it is a continuous process.

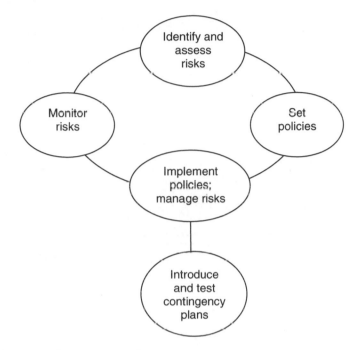

Figure 1.6   A structure for managing risk

Risk management should be done thoroughly. This applies particularly to the task of assessing risk. A company which merely identifies some minor health and safety risks is lulling itself into a false sense of security. Properly used, risk management helps a company to evaluate its strengths and weaknesses. It can help the business to re-engineer itself, and make it more competitive. Risk management is a tool that makes a company grow strong.

Useful links

Links quickly go out of date. You can find more up-to-date links at www.inst.org/risk

FERMA: Survey of European Risk Management Practices
www.ferma-asso.org/3.html

FM Global survey
www.protectingvalue.com

Institute of Risk Management
www.theirm.org

UK Business Link – business advice on many topics including risk
www.businesslink.gov.uk

2 *Defining and Assessing Risk*

In this chapter we consider the following:

- *Defining the 'revenue drivers' and 'key success factors'*
- *The four areas of risk*
- *Strategic and operational risk*
- *Operational risks classified by time and cause*
- *The four steps in assessing and managing risk*
- *Probability and severity*
- *Doing the assessment*
- *Assessing vulnerability.*

Define the 'revenue drivers'

In a recent survey, senior managers in large companies voted their production facilities, logistics and IT equipment as their top 'revenue drivers' (see Table 2.1).

The survey asked Chief Financial Officers (CFO)s, treasurers and risk managers what contributed most to corporate earnings. The objective of the survey was to find out what managers were most concerned to protect – items whose disruption would have the greatest financial impact on the business. It comes as no surprise that they listed the elements needed to get their product out of the door.

Sadly, the survey ignores some important risks. Fraud and environmental pollution are two risks not included here. And while they aren't 'top revenue drivers', such risks could bring the company down. There are also the risks of diversification or acquisition. For example, Bradford and Bingley bought the Charcol brokerage for £100 million in 2000, and sold it for only £10 million in 2004.

But the thought process behind the question is correct; and that's why we've mentioned it here. Put simply, there is no point in creating a risk strategy until you know what things are important. You need to guard against the risks that count.

Key success factors

What factors must the organization be good at? To succeed, what must we do well? These are the key success factors (KSFs). As with the 'top revenue drivers', risk management must protect these KSFs.

In Table 2.2 below, we look at the KSFs for an online business. We examine what risks could affect the KSFs, and what controls the business might put in place.

Table 2.1   Top revenue drivers

	All CFOs, treasurers and risk managers	North America			Europe		
		All	CFOs and treasurers	Risk managers	All	CFOs and treasurers	Risk managers
Manufacturing plant, equipment and process	21	20	15	25	22	17	27
Delivery, logistics	19	12	9	14	27	32	22
IT/telecoms systems	19	24	26	23	15	13	16
Personnel and customer support	19	26	33	19	12	8	16
Raw materials/ inventory	15	13	14	12	16	22	11
Intellectual property	7	5	3	7	8	8	8
Total	**100**	**100**	**100**	**100**	**100**	**100**	**100**

Since people visit the site 24 hours a day, there must be no downtime. If the internet service provider (ISP), or the company's server, keeps failing, this would damage the business. To protect itself, the company could carefully select the ISP, and monitor the server's availability. Already a risk management assessment is emerging, together with the bones of a strategy.

The four types of risk

There are four main areas of risk: strategic, operational, financial, and compliance (see Figure 2.1):

1 *Operational risks* are those relating to the organization's production or operations. They include faulty raw materials, a supplier going into receivership, or a major customer going into receivership.
2 *Strategic risks* are the big issues which require companies to think on a grand scale. These risks should be tackled at board level and require strategic planning. Operational risks require board involvement, but are successfully implemented at a lower level.
3 *Compliance risks* are increasing in importance, as government places greater requirements on reporting and risk management in public companies.
4 Internal *financial risks* include the loss of profitability, while external ones include an adverse exchange rate that reduces the company's exports.

Table 2.2   Key success factors

Key Success Factor	Risk	Control
No downtime	ISP ceases trading, or has excessive outages	Use a business-oriented ISP with track record, and service level agreement; monitor uptime
Effective website design	Amateurish design or poor usability will reduce sales	Hire a professional web designer; use a content management system to maintain quality when site content is updated; test usability
Fast fulfilment	Slow fulfilment will increase returns and cause loss of reputation	Introduce written procedures; train staff; monitor courier company; automate the stock ordering process
Effective or distinctive product range	Uncompetitive range or weak offer will reduce sales	Test new products or format; monitor competitors, both online and 'bricks and mortar'; conduct benchmarking
Profitable customer acquisition	Excessive costs will render business unprofitable	Monitor promotional costs; identify referrers
Effective customer support	Weak support will reduce sales	Train staff; use automated systems
Adequate profit margin	Wrong cost and price mix will ultimately put the company out of business	Ensure that the business has high quality management information

As the last point suggests, most risks have either an *internal* or an *external* cause. An ill-conceived acquisition is an example of an internal risk, while a change in legislation is an external one.

Many risks don't necessarily fit into one category. For example if a major customer goes bust while owing the business money, you could classify it as a financial risk (which could have been managed by better credit control), or as a strategic risk (over-reliance on a few major customers).

Strategic risks

As the names imply, *strategic* and *operational* risk have different levels of management input.

A strategic risk would be overseen by the CEO, rather than a junior manager. However, that is not to say that operational risk only has minor impacts. In some companies, for example, health and safety carries the most severe risk of all – death of employees. And if production comes to a halt because of lack of maintenance, this will have a substantial impact on the business. Thus plant maintenance requires active control by production staff and effective management attention as well. Therefore operational risk is not something that senior management can ignore.

Some strategic risks are shown in Figure 2.2. They include:

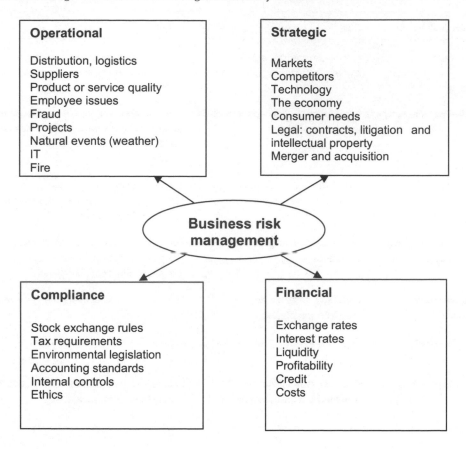

Figure 2.1   The four types of risk

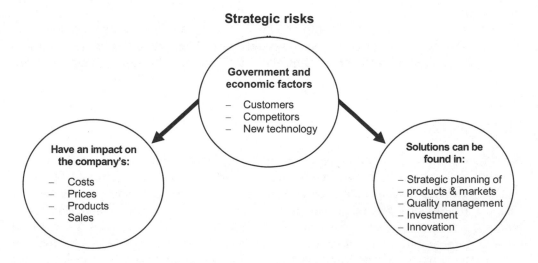

Figure 2.2   Strategic risks

- *Government* action, such as a recession or new legislation. Companies operate in an increasingly regulated world, and government plans (both at home and abroad) need to be forecast.
- *Customers* also bring strategic risk. Their changing attitudes and growing expectations make them less predictable than before.
- *Competition* is changing and becoming global. No market is immune from new competition. Any market, especially those which are profitable, will attract competition soon rather than later.
- *New technology* is bringing new threats and opportunities. If managed properly, it can make the company more competitive; if ignored, it can bring new competitors into the market.

These strategic risks all have a major impact on the company's costs, prices, products and sales. Figure 2.2 also shows some of the solutions that companies adopt. These four strategic issues are ones which management has to grasp before it can start to consider the operational risks that affect the company. Management must ensure that it isn't exposed to fundamental risks, such as being in the wrong market. Unfortunately, that isn't easy to assess.

We examine these strategic risks in subsequent chapters. In Chapter 14 we review the effects of government action, competitors and customers. And we look at new technology in Chapter 12 and throughout.

Operational risk

As Table 2.3 shows, operational risks can be categorized according to when they occur. Some take place at suppliers, others at the point of production or operations, some in the distribution chain, or when the product is consumed.

Table 2.3   Operational hazards classified by time

	Time →			
	Suppliers	Process and internal risks	Distribution	Customers
Risks	Interruption of supplies	Fire	Counterfeiting	Payment problems
	Poor quality supplies	Pollution	Tampering	Competitor activity
		Fraud		
		IT		
		Accidents		
		Labour disputes		
		Terrorism, kidnap and ransom		

The table, which also shows whether the risks affect mainly people or assets, serves to remind us that not all risks take place on the shop floor. There is often some overlap between types of risk. For example, fire often hurts people as well as consuming buildings.

WHO IS AT RISK?

As Figure 2.3 shows, the level of risk sometimes ripples outwards from the single worker towards the general population.

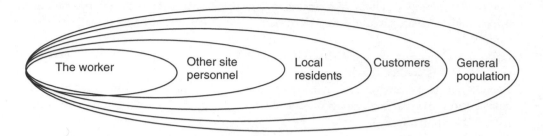

Figure 2.3   The widening effects of risk

On the front line of risk are the workers – these are exposed to the most risks: individual workers will be hurt if their clothing is caught in machinery; if sales fall, they are the first to be made redundant. Sometimes, several workers at a plant are hurt. This might be when a train ploughs into rail workers working at trackside.

Beyond the factory gates, the local population is at risk. A chemical plant might send a fireball into adjoining streets, causing damage to buildings, passers-by and local office workers. Less dramatically, dust, smoke or odour from a plant can extend over the local town.

These risks are of the 'health and safety' sort (those risks that affect the workforce), but many others are not. For example, a defective product may hurt a customer; a mass-market yoghurt could cause widespread gastro-enteritis.

At the extreme is a risk to the general population. This is not a problem facing many companies, but it is found in energy (where power stations are located whose emissions cover a wide area). The Chernobyl accident affected populations all the way from Russia to Welsh hill farmers, who were restricted from selling their sheep.

Eventually, these risks will affect the shareholder, if they cause the share price to fall.

In the case of undetected fraud, the workforce is at risk of redundancy if the fraud is substantial and layoffs take place. If the business closes, the local residents lose a source of employment, and ultimately the customers lose a service or product.

CLASSIFYING RISKS BY CAUSE

Table 2.4 shows the causes of risk, and highlights the assets they affect. This helps the company to decide what assets are vulnerable, and how they should be protected. It also reveals that all business risks ultimately affect the company's profits.

THREATS TO NON-HUMANS

This analysis has looked at threats to human health and life. But the same applies to non-humans. Water-borne pollution can quickly flow down a river, killing fish for many miles; while a major pollution incident may affect the whole continent (as the example of a nuclear accident above shows). Even when it affects only a bay (as with a damaged oil tanker), it can shock the whole nation seeing it on their television screens.

The same applies to buildings, other assets, and most other kinds of damage or harm.

Table 2.4   Classifying risks by cause

ASSETS	CAUSE OF RISK						
	Natural disaster	Govt action, economic forces	Suppliers	Customers	Production problems	Theft and fraud	Vandalism and revenge
Examples	*Fire, explosion*	*Tax changes*	*Late delivery*	*Bad debts*	*Labour dispute*	*Theft of stock*	*Computer virus*
Land	✔						
Buildings	✔						✔
Plant and eqpt	✔						
Raw materials	✔		✔			✔	
Stock	✔				✔	✔	
Vehicles	✔					✔	
Documents	✔					✔	
Computers	✔					✔	✔
Staff and visitors	✔						
Local residents	✔						
Customers							
Sales	✔			✔			
Cash	✔	✔	✔	✔	✔	✔	✔

The four steps in assessing risk

RISK AWARENESS

Risk management starts with awareness. Managers need to recognize that risks exist in business, and that these risks can and should be managed. In turn the managers need to embed risk within the culture of the company. When that has taken place, there are three further stages in risk management, which are highlighted in Figure 2.4.

ASSESS THE RISKS

The first stage is to assess the risks. Physical risks such as fire involve physical audits, while strategic risks (such as marketing ones) are more likely to involve research and analysis.

Both types of assessment require access to records. How many days have been lost through accidents? What cases of fire have been reported? These records will point to trends, and indicate management omissions or poor working practices.

Every type of risk has its own assessment format, and the figures in this book illustrate the main techniques. The company should use a standard methodology for carrying out

Figure 2.4   The four stages of risk management

assessments of each kind of risk. In other words, all fire surveys should use the same method. This ensures that the data can be compared over time, and it helps management become familiar with evaluating the risks submitted to them.

Some firms limit their risk assessment to those risks which the business can resolve. One firm decided that it could not alter some risks (attacks on staff), and therefore excluded them from the analysis. Another firm decided that it would only consider solutions which it could afford. This is a dangerous strategy: the business should avoid having preconceptions about risk. No risks should be excluded simply because of the firm's resources or because management feels the risk cannot be solved. Staff who participate in an assessment are ignoring some risks if they accept that they cannot be managed. And this prevents the business from finding solutions.

Thorough assessment includes measurement. This allows the company to analyse trends, and to make decisions based on fact, not opinion. Each chapter in this book identifies the sort of measurements that can be made.

The second stage is to set priorities. The company has to determine which risks should have the highest priority. The assessment should therefore identify which hazards carry the greatest risk.

TREAT THE RISKS

The third stage is to prevent the risks from occurring. Each chapter contains examples of best practice. Strategies include the following:

- *Avoid*: choosing not to accept the risk. A business might decide not to acquire another firm because the risks are too great. Or it might sell a high-risk division.
- *Minimize*, reduce or control: through means such as improved monitoring, changing the process, or substituting hazardous chemicals with safer ones. Defining a procedure may also reduce risk. For example, to reduce fraud a mail-order company might have two people opening the day's mail, and change the rota regularly.

- *Spread* (also known as transferring or sharing risk): by diversifying, sub-contracting, outsourcing, joint venture, hedging, or insurance.
- *Accept*: by deciding that the risk is within agreed risk tolerances.

A flow diagram for this is shown in Figure 2.5. The business also needs a business continuity plan at this stage, something that we discuss more fully in Chapter 16. This lets the company plan for the worst eventuality. If disaster happens, the company needs to be able to rescue itself and start up again. Having emergency plans will minimize the scale of the problem. The cost of the plans should be in proportion to the risk: no business can avoid risk completely.

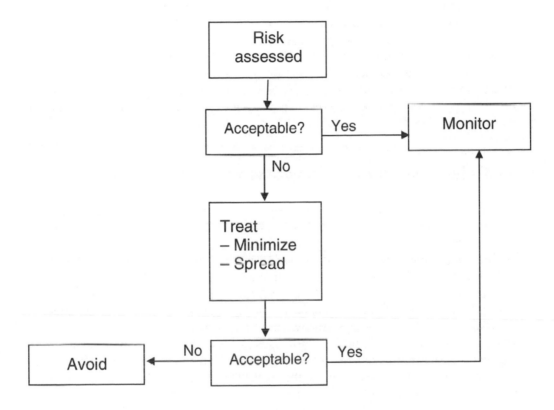

Figure 2.5   Flow diagram for risk assessment and treatment

MONITOR

The final stage is to monitor risks. This includes regularly measuring the risk (to ensure that it remains within stated tolerances), and auditing (to ensure that the procedure is being followed. The auditors should report findings to the chief executive officer (CEO) or risk manager, who in turn should discuss the findings. This review is the time to consider how the company's risk exposure could be reduced. A programme of continuous improvement will help to keep the company abreast of best practice, reduce its risks, and lower its costs.

Because there is so much information in the business, monitoring should focus on the most important risks. Managers should examine:

- trends that indicate a growing danger
- data that shows variances from the norm, or is outside pre-set limits (known as 'management by exception')
- key performance indicators
- one-off reports on new areas of risk
- information from a range of sources
- key findings from audits.

Corrective action

As part of the review process, managers need to agree on what corrective action should be taken. Some of this will already have been suggested in the internal audit reports, such as investing in new equipment, or introducing new controls in a specific area.

The options for corrective action are the same as for risk treatment as a whole (see 3 'Treat the risks', above). Management can avoid, minimize, spread or accept the risk; and there are countless ways to do each of those.

The corrective action should be minuted, and an individual made responsible for this action. At the next review meeting you should check to see that the corrective action has been carried out.

How likely is the risk? How severe would its impact be?

Probability and severity are two important factors in measuring risk (these are also known as 'likelihood' and 'impact'). Companies suffer small problems frequently, and major problems rarely. The more severe the event, the less likely it is.

Some risks are low in severity and happen frequently, such as a worker slipping in the rain. Minor accidents are common in the construction industry and, while unfortunate, they don't bring the building site to a halt. These risks are very probable but have a small impact, and are in the bottom left-hand corner of Figure 2.6. Because they are common, the company should guard against them, but they usually cause neglible loss.

Catastrophic events tend to be very improbable, such as deaths resulting from a terrorist bomb. This is a catastrophic but very improbable risk, located in the top right-hand corner of Figure 2.6. Since, for most companies, the probability is very small, there is no point in trying to manage it. If, however, the business had an office in a known terrorist area, the probability would be higher. The company might then decide to manage the risk by moving the office.

However, some catastrophic events happen frequently, such as fire. The risk of fire in a textile plant is both quite probable and catastrophic, so management should spare no effort in managing the threat.

It is worth compiling a grid similar to Figure 2.6. This will help the company to prioritize its risk management programme. Risks should be prioritized in order from the top left of the grid to the bottom right. A risk that has a high impact and is probable should be tackled urgently.

There is no point in protecting the business against risks in the bottom right-hand corner of the table. Those are risks which are unlikely to happen and will not be serious. However, if the company has many of these risks, they may add up to a serious problem. For example, the risk of fire in individual rooms A, B and C is slight. But the risk of a fire in any room is quite high.

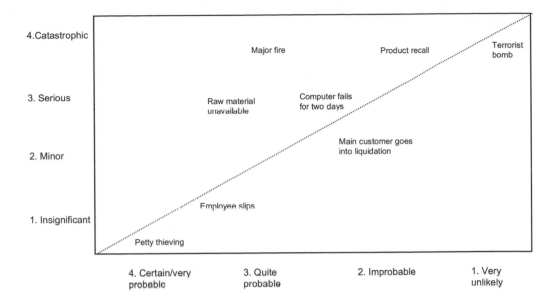

Figure 2.6 Risk severity and probability

The British government uses this kind of risk assessment to target fraud prevention. It has tried to work out where social security fraud is most likely and most serious. For example, UK citizens who claim to live in Canada but who are actually resident in the USA may be a more important target than citizens living in the Indian sub-continent.

PUTTING NUMBERS TO THE RISK

Some organizations opt for a 3 × 3 grid, as shown in Figure 2.7. The principle is the same as for Figure 2.6.

It is also useful to quantify the impact of a risk. By multiplying the probability by the severity, you can quantify the importance of the risk. To do this you need to make the analysis more sensitive, by using a 4 × 4 or a 10 × 10 grid. Thus in a 10 × 10 grid, the terrorist bomb would rate as 10 (probability 1 × severity 10). The risk of a major fire could be 54 (probability 6 × severity 9).

The 10 × 10 ranking has the added advantage of ending up as a percentage, which people readily understand.

You can make the judgement more scientific by quantifying severity. This can be done using the headings in Table 2.5, to which some examples have been added. Once a risk has been categorized, you will know where it slots into the matrix in Figure 2.7.

The analysis in Table 2.5 helps to add clarity to thinking. For example, the business might judge that damage to its local reputation will have only a minor impact. This in turn will direct attention and resources to areas that would have a serious effect.

The headings for the grid in Table 2.5 are not comprehensive; and you should add other categories that are relevant to your business. Similarly, the impacts need to be scaled up for a large business, and reduced for a small one. Under the heading of 'health and safety', a large multinational business might re-classify one death as 'serious' and multiple deaths 'catastrophic'.

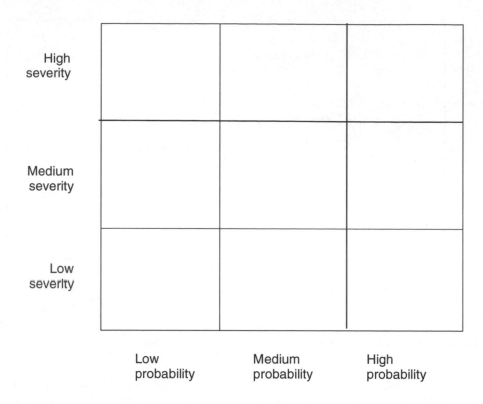

Figure 2.7   3 × 3 matrix for risk assessment

Doing the assessment

As we have seen, each kind of risk has its own assessment methodology. But there are common headings, which are shown below. In the subsequent sections, we pose the kind of questions which need to be asked.

1 What is the purpose of the assessment?
2 What is the nature of the risk? Give a description of the project, product or process.
3 What resources are involved or affected?
4 What is the scale of the impact?
5 What are the benefits of the hazard?
6 What are the mitigating factors?
7 What are the contingency plans?
8 What are the limitations of the assessment?
9 What are the conclusions and recommendations?
10 What action has been taken?

PURPOSE OF THE ASSESSMENT

Why is the assessment being undertaken? What will happen as a result of the assessment? How will it help the company?

Table 2.5   Defining the scale of impact on the business

	Catastrophic	Serious	Minor	Insignificant
Financial Impact				
Loss of revenue	*Over £10 m*	*£1–£10 m*	*£100 000–£1 m*	*Less than £100 000*
Loss of shareholder value				
Costs and penalties				
Non-financial impact				
Distribution	*De-listed by two or more major customers*	*De-listed by one major or three-four minor multiples*	*De-listed by one-two minor multiples or 50%+ of independents*	*Loss of a handful of independent accounts*
Reputation – consumer				
Reputation – local				
Environmental damage				
Quality failure				
Health and safety	*Death of employee*	*Broken limb, or hospitalization*	*Bruising, sprain, minor cut*	*Trip or slip*
Production				
Distribution				
Legal				

NATURE OF THE RISK

The project or hazard needs to be described. It then needs to be classified. It might be technical, political, financial, political, or management, customer or competitor related.

- Is the hazard a continuous or catastrophic risk? For example, inhaling carcinogenic fibres is the former, while a terrorist attack is the latter.
- Is the risk present at all times, only occasionally, or at specific times? For example, an overseas factory will only be invaded at times of extreme industrial unrest, civil disorder or war.
- Is the hazard man-made (such as an Internet denial-of-service attack) or natural (such as an earthquake)?
- How predictable is the risk? In some areas, storms and typhoons are seasonal and can be predicted.
- Is it internal (under our control) or external (beyond our control)?
- Have similar hazards resulted in loss? Are there comparable examples in other industries or countries?
- What is the attitude of interested parties (such as the local or national government, opinion formers, local residents, employees and trade unions)?
- What is the view of experts in the field? What trust does the company place on the opinion of the experts?
- What level of competence do staff have? Could they recover lost computer data?

RESOURCES

Some exercises require a separate examination of the resource. In other cases, it may be already defined in 'Purpose of the assessment' above.

The auditor should assess what resources will be affected. Some risks affect finance, while others affect people. In turn, people can be categorized as staff, customers, visitors, local residents, trade (distributors and retailers), legislators, and pressure groups.

- How would people be affected? This could be through disease, or through being injured.
- Is the whole population at risk, or just certain groups (such as maintenance staff)?
- For plant and equipment, is the resource static or mobile? For example, an oil tanker is mobile while a pipeline is static. Control and risk monitoring are more difficult for mobile risks, and they therefore need to be managed differently.
- What is the scale of the asset at risk? For example, a pipeline may extend over hundreds of miles.

SCALE OF THE IMPACT

What effect would an accident have on the company? What is the scale of the disaster – would it wipe out the business? Companies can apply an impact rating to any risk. Table 2.5 has a four-point scale (from insignificant to catastrophic).

- Would fatalities be instant or delayed? For example, some cancers take many years to develop.
- What effect would an accident have on opinion formers, pressure groups and so on? What effect would this have on the business? For example, altering the financial structure of the business might make it less attractive to investors.

- Can the risk harm future generations? This would apply in the case of radioactive materials being released.
- What effect would the hazard have even without an accident? Could its very existence harm the company's image? For example, toxic waste incinerators are often unpopular among local residents.
- What is the company's experience in this area? It may be less risky for an oil company to drill for oil in a new geographic area than to explore for gas (if it has no experience of this). New developments are inherently risky.
- How reversible would the problem be? The effects of an oil spill (such as the Prestige tanker off the coast of Spain at a cost of $42 million) on local ecosystems are now less permanent than once thought).

BENEFITS

What benefits will the topic under review (the hazard) bring to:

- the company (especially in terms of profit)
- its workers (from wages)
- the surrounding population (indirect employment).

Are there any non-financial benefits (such as the creation of amenities, or the stemming of population loss)?

MITIGATING FACTORS

Following the assessment, the business should decide how to manage the risk by avoiding, minimizing, spreading or transferring it.

- Can the risk be minimized (perhaps by engineering design)?
- What will the company do to prevent the risk from becoming a disaster? Mitigating factors might include building fire walls or installing alarms.
- What is the cost of mitigating factors? How would they affect both the scale of the risk, and the viability of the project?
- How important is the risk? What benefits does it bring? Would its absence reduce the company's ability to compete? For example, a factory might provide essential raw materials to another part of the business.
- What alternatives exist? How great are their risks?

The action should be documented – that is, written down and circulated to everyone who needs to know.

BUSINESS CONTINUITY PLANS

- What is the organization's ability to deal with an incident or accident? Are emergency procedures and equipment in place?
- Are contingency plans put to the test? When did the last test take place? What were the results?
- How long would it take to re-start the business?

LIMITATIONS

- What are the constraints of the assessment? Were some areas inaccessible?
- How much trust can be placed in the assessment of risk? How reliable are the numbers? What uncertainties exist?

CONCLUSIONS AND RECOMMENDATIONS

The final section of the assessment will include recommendations for action.

ACTION TAKEN

Added to the report should be a note of the decisions taken, and the actions ordered. This section may also include a date for a review.

Simpler assessments

Companies may prefer to undertake a simpler assessment, leaving out some of the detail discussed above. Figure 2.8 shows that each type of risk can be briefly assessed in turn. In the example, the company is examining the threat of fire.

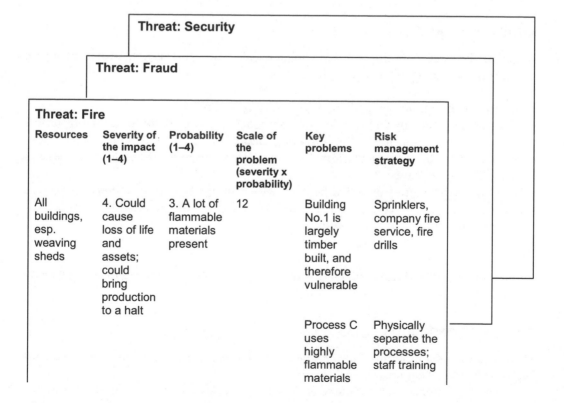

Threat: Security

Threat: Fraud

Threat: Fire

Resources	Severity of the impact (1–4)	Probability (1–4)	Scale of the problem (severity x probability)	Key problems	Risk management strategy
All buildings, esp. weaving sheds	4. Could cause loss of life and assets; could bring production to a halt	3. A lot of flammable materials present	12	Building No.1 is largely timber built, and therefore vulnerable	Sprinklers, company fire service, fire drills
				Process C uses highly flammable materials	Physically separate the processes; staff training

Figure 2.8   Risk assessment and management

The first column shows the resources that could be affected by the threat. The assessment then considers the scale of the impact. In the table, fire could cause loss of life as well as loss of assets. Next we consider the key problems. These are areas of special risk. They amplify the information contained in 'Resources'. Finally, we consider the strategy which should be adopted (or has been adopted) to prevent the risk from materializing.

This chart can be adapted to different requirements. It can look broadly at the issues involved, or it can examine a topic in detail. For example, separate charts can be drawn up for different areas of the business. A more detailed risk register is to be found at the end of this chapter (Table 2.9).

Gathering the information

Data gathering should start with published economic or industry-specific information. What are the main risks associated with the industry? What reports are available? This may provide useful data against which the company can benchmark its own records, and assess the quality of the company's risk management.

Once all relevant external data has been gathered, the company can collect internal data. Figure 2.9 is a simple questionnaire which can be given to departmental managers. Staff often have detailed knowledge about the risks that affect them, and the questionnaire involves them in the process of risk assessment.

GATHERING EXTERNAL INFORMATION

You need to gather information from as many sources as possible, and on a regular basis. Sources of information include those shown in Table 2.6. The data can be collected through informal chats, salesforce visits, market research questionnaires, staff surveys, newspapers and magazines, and many other sources.

Table 2.6 Sources of information

Suppliers, vendors	Raw materials, process improvements, technology risks and opportunities
National media	Information about risk in society
Trade media	Competitor activity
Workforce and trade unions	Operational risks
Partners	Risks in the industry, process improvements
Distributors, customers and end-users	Marketplace risks, customer needs, product quality, market opportunities
Trade body	Industry risks, legislation and regulation
Government, EU	Legislation and regulation, cross-border collaboration
Local authority, police	Crime, health and safety issues, environmental health
Shareholders	Industry, investment, corporate and governance risks
Pressure groups	Single issues that might affect the business, for example construction companies and the anti-road lobby

Risk questionnaire

Name   Department   Date

What risks exist in your department?	How should these risks be managed?

Any other comments about risks in the business?

Please return to	By (date)

What are risks? Risks can affect you or other members of staff, customers, visitors, shareholders, or the environment. Examples of risk include fire, slips or trips, chemicals, dangerous machinery, pollution, computers, fraud and theft, or unsafe products.

Figure 2.9 Risk questionnaire

The risk manager should be the central store for all the information relating to risk, and should subscribe to an online news service such as Google's.

CIRCULATING INFORMATION

Having received the information, the business needs to circulate it. The risk manager may issue an electronic newsletter that keeps relevant managers up to date on matters of risk.

Managing the information takes effort in this age of information overload. The risk information may be fed into the company's information system, and displayed on the 'dashboard' system, if the business has one. The use of red, amber and green colours (for major problem, minor problem, and no problem) quickly highlight key areas.

OTHER WAYS OF ANALYSING RISK

The company can draw flow charts or fishbone diagrams showing processes and the movement of material through the business. This may reveal points of vulnerability. To highlight major risks, you can use 'heat maps', an example of which is shown in Table 2.7. This is simply a matter of colouring high risks red, moderate risks yellow, and low risks green. This device draws the eye to the issues that need attention.

Table 2.7   Heat map

Issue	Description	Likelihood	Impact	Risk
Fleet	Driver death	Unlikely	Severe	Moderate
	Vehicle theft	Possible	Moderate	Moderate
	Theft from lorries	Almost certain	Minor	Low

You could also carry out a Pareto analysis. This is also known as the 80:20 rule. It often shows that a few issues are responsible for most of the problems. Figure 2.10 shows that ten per cent of customers account for 70 per cent of the company's debt.

TOOLS FOR ANALYSIS

Other qualitative methods that aid analysis include:

- Focus groups
- Brainstorming
- Advice from experts.

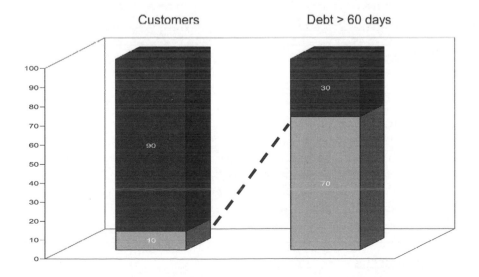

Figure 2.10   Pareto chart

Other quantitative methods include the following:

- Analysis of historical data
- Influence diagrams
- Fault tree and event tree analysis
- Life-cycle analysis
- Test marketing and market research
- Monte Carlo analysis (used to desribe processes that calculate an average by random sampling).

FURTHER ANALYSIS

The company may want to extend the analysis. For example:

- *Has the threat materialized before*? A company which has suffered a flood or industrial unrest is likely to be a victim again. A small fire is likely to be followed by a bigger one, if no action is taken. Big accidents are usually preceded by lots of smaller ones.
- *Immediacy*: how soon is the event likely to occur?
- *Ease and cost of prevention*: the risk of polluting a river may cost less (in fines) than the cost of installing expensive equipment.
- *References*: the auditor may refer to manuals, charts or consultants' reports.
- *Priority*: risks need to be prioritized since they cannot all be tackled at once.

WHAT IF…?

The risk assessment should include alternative outcomes. What if sales don't achieve their forecast levels? What if the costs of the project over-run? What if a specific chemical is banned in an important export market?

These 'what if' scenarios can alert the company to potential problems. Some risk scenarios include pessimistic, optimistic and probable forecasts. This is particularly useful for marketing or project risks. We look at scenario planning in Chapter 17.

USING A DATABASE

Using a database gives the company three advantages:

1 It lets the company quantify the data. Using the scoring system in Table 2.5, the risk manager can put a value on each impact.
2 The database can perform analyses. For example, by identifying specific buildings or work processes by number, the database can be asked:
    - Which building or which group of workers is most at risk?
    - What is the descending order of threat, by severity of risk?
3 The data can easily be updated and retrieved.

RISK REGISTER OR LOG

Irrespective of how the data is kept, the organization needs to keep a register of risks. This can be as simple as a list of the greatest risks, a note on how each is to be controlled, and who is responsible for managing it. For a more detailed register, the UK's office of government commerce suggests the following:

- Risk identification number (unique within the register)
- Risk type (where indication helps in planning responses)
- Risk owner (person responsible for risk).
- Date identified
- Date last updated
- Description
- Cost if it materializes
- Probability
- Impact
- Proximity
- Possible response actions
- Chosen action
- Target date
- Action owner/custodian (if differs from risk owner)
- Closure date
- Cross references to plans and associated risks; it may also include
- Risk status and risk action status.

A simplified risk register can be found at the end of this chapter (Table 2.9).

SITE BY SITE

Risk needs to be assessed on a site-by-site basis. Where a company owns several sites, they will vary in age, level of investment and production capability. A manufacturing site with old buildings, a large unskilled workforce and combustible raw materials is more risky than a modern office building (though no building is completely risk-free). Figure 2.11 shows that risk priorities will vary from one site to another.

HOW COMPLEX SHOULD THE ANALYSIS BE?

Academics have mathematical formulae to assess risk. This type of assessment is rarely understood in boardrooms, and still less so by shop floor supervisors. Such calculations are of little help to management (unless they can be clearly explained and have practical implications for the business).

Risk management has to be understood by those who will detect or prevent risk. So there is no point in turning it into an academic exercise. What it loses in intellectual rigour, it gains by being understood. Much risk analysis is common sense, and many hazards can be forecast. A company whose sales are declining will soon run out of money. An old product will eventually face new competitors. New legislation is preceded by years of discussion in the industry. An unguarded machine with blades is likely to hurt an operative.

The company should be aware of its threats; and the major ones are reviewed in the risk assessments at the end of each chapter in this book.

Measurements of risk can and should be taken. Most industries and most companies gather simple statistical information, such as the number of accident-free days. They identify how probable an accident is likely to be in the future. Using historical data shows management which areas of risk to prioritize.

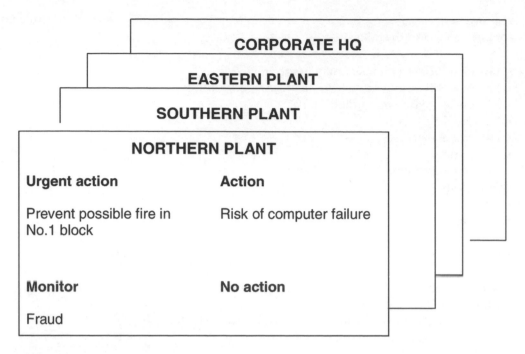

Figure 2.11   Site-by-site action plan

ASSESSING VULNERABILITY

After the data has been gathered, the company should determine which types of threat the company is vulnerable to. You can do this by using a vulnerability chart, shown in Table 2.8. This chart is particularly useful for submitting information to the board.

Taking environment as an example, the company could rank its vulnerability as low (based on the assessment in Figure 2.7), its priority as low priority and, under action, it might decide to review its water treatment facilities.

Useful links

Business Continuity Online
www.business-continuity-online.com

Office of Government Commerce
www.ogc.gov.uk/sdtoolkit/index.html

Risk Management magazine
www.rmmag.com

Risk Management Reports
www.riskreports.com

RiskWorld
www.riskworld.com

Table 2.8   Vulnerability audit

Type of hazard	Vulnerability	Priority	Action	Cost
	From 'low' to 'high'	From 'top priority' to 'low priority'	Steps to be taken to reduce vulnerability	
Quality				
Environment				
Health and Safety				
Fire				
Security				
Fraud				
Finance				
IT				
Marketing				
Buildings				
Telecoms				
Human resources				
Other				

Table 2.9   Risk register

Assessed by	Date assessed			Reviewed by	Date reviewed

No.	Risk description	Causes	Consequences	Controls	Probability	Severity	Impact (probability x severity)	Risk priority	Action needed

3 *Managing Corporate Risk*

In this chapter, we examine how to manage corporate risks by:

- *Getting corporate policies and strategy right*
- *Managing people and processes*
- *Managing the risks.*

Getting corporate strategy right

Once the company has identified its risks (as discussed in the previous chapter), it should take action to manage them. If it leaves them in place, the company and its directors may be legally liable because they knew the risks and failed to take action to prevent a disaster. In this chapter we examine the methods used to manage risk, starting by looking at corporate strategy.

As we will see in Chapter 14, the business has to be in the right markets and have the right products. This is the most basic of all threats: finding that customers no longer want the product that the company sells.

In 1999, at the height of the dot.com boom, Marconi (formerly GEC) got rid of its dull retail, defence, and food businesses, and bought exciting telecoms companies instead. Two years on, the telecoms market collapsed, and Marconi's share price fell by 54 per cent in one week. In the six months to September 2001, it lost £5.1 bn. But it's easy to be wise after the event.

Conglomerates were once seen as a way of reducing risk. If one market was doing badly, another would be performing well. Many companies diversified, only to find that they owned too many loss-making businesses that they were unable to turn around. Since then, companies have tended to return to their roots. However, some conglomerates do well. GE, Virgin and Centrica are all examples of conglomerates, the latter being into gas supply, credit cards and breakdown recovery services. Diversified companies can use their core skills in marketing, management, strategy and raising capital to direct a range of businesses. However, they tend to be short lived, and depend on one individual's management or entrepreneurial skills.

SETTING A RISK POLICY

The company needs a policy for each area of risk. Most large companies have environmental policies and health and safety policies, while fewer have a defined policy on fraud or computer failure. The policies should be as brief and simple as possible to ensure that staff read and understand them.

Defining a policy is not simply a paper exercise. The policy should be translated into strategy statements which are implemented at the lowest suitable level. For example, a quality policy should be implemented in each manufacturing plant.

Having looked at the corporate plan and policies, we next examine how the company can manage its risks.

Responsibility for risk management

Each major risk must be someone's responsibility. And that responsibility must lie with line managers and the workforce. If staff feel that risk is something managed by an 'expert', they won't take ownership of it.

Traditionally, risk management (if it was considered at all) has been the responsibility of the company secretary or the finance director, because of the importance of insurance. Fraud would be likely to be controlled by the financial director.

Some areas of risk are more likely to have a specifically appointed manager. This is especially true of the quality manager, the health and safety manager, or the environmental manager. As Figure 3.1 shows, some risks have been amalgamated, as with the SHE (safety, health and environment) manager.

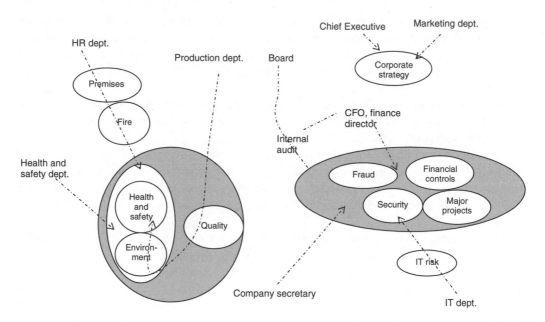

Figure 3.1   Traditional management responsibilities for risk

In other cases, the quality manager has taken over responsibility for environment, reflecting the increased importance of environmental management. At the same time, the operations manager or production manager is increasingly given responsibility for preventing the threats to the business.

Fire is often a separate responsibility, while financial risk is not often formally debated but managed by the chief financial officer. IT risk issues are managed by an IT department, while premises security would be managed by HR, the security department, or even IT.

Every organization is different, so the contents of Figure 3.1 will vary considerably. But the effect is still the same.

This separation of responsibilities is a good thing, in so far it hands responsibility to functional line management. But it prevents the business from seeing all its risks together. Only by looking at risks as a portfolio will a business be able to weigh them and judge which are the most dangerous. The alternative is to end up with a messy chart such as that shown in Figure 3.1.

THE CHIEF EXECUTIVE

Without the chief executive's enthusiasm for tackling risk, it is doomed to failure. Therefore the CEO must be committed to risk management, and be seen to be committed. The CEO must start the risk programme, if it does not already exist. He or she must appoint people to the roles described below, and be active in developing a risk strategy.

> The chief executive of a major house builder used to visit his sites, flanked by his top managers. He would stride around the sites, talking affably to the workers. But neither he nor his senior managers wore a hard hat. This contradicted the safety messages pinned up on the sites. It told employees that safety was not a major issue, and implied that short cuts could be taken.

Risk management is in part about ethics. An ethical stance is the only way to behave and, in any case, unethical behaviour will come back to haunt the business. In all the topics discussed in this book – whether finance, the environment or treatment of suppliers, there is an ethical and an unethical way to behave. And if the risk management programme is to work, the CEO must demonstrate commitment to behaving as a good corporate citizen.

In starting a risk management programme, some CEOs send a letter or email to all staff, telling them about the company's concern to manage its risk, the steps that are being taken, and how the recipients can get involved. Another necessary action is the CEO's agreement to new appointments or to revised job descriptions, whether for a risk manager or more internal auditors (both of which are discussed below).

AUDIT COMMITTEE

Some risk professionals believe that the audit committee should be given responsibility for risk management. This is because the audit committee is senior, is at least partly independent of management, and is already responsible for the external auditor and for corporate governance. It is also appropriate because the audit committee supervises internal auditors who, as we see below, are increasingly taking over the role of risk auditing.

But others see this as expanding the role of the audit committee beyond its competency or jurisdiction. It would require the committee members to take on added responsibility, training and activity.

BOARD MEMBERS

As an alternative to using the audit committee, the overview for risk can go to the board, or to a sub-committee of the board. And the board should certainly be actively involved in the strategic management of risk. In the FM Global survey of CFOs and risk managers in very large companies, 90 per cent of respondents thought that risk management should be, and is becoming, a board-level issue. For 93 per cent of the European respondents, risk is a board-level issue, compared with just 65 per cent of North American companies. This may be because of legislation in European countries requiring companies to disclose their risk management activities.

The board should discuss the big risk management issues, since that is where strategic decisions are made. Board members should:

- know the organization's attitude to risk
- be familiar with the corporate strategy
- be aware of major risk issues in the business
- receive regular reports on risk, including internal audits
- know the extent to which risk is managed in the business
- challenge management's preconceptions, cultural norms or received wisdom on issues relating to risk
- review corporate governance statements.

Management must be ready to react quickly to changing circumstances. For example, periods of boom need to be managed differently from recessionary periods.

The company must also be able to plan its future, rather than relying on its past successes and its current business formula.

The management team must also be balanced and experienced, especially in medium-sized companies. A business with a weak or non-existent finance function is unlikely to survive for long. One company in the construction industry had survived for many years without a finance director. Recognizing its vulnerability, it brought in an experienced manager. But when it quickly ran into financial difficulty, it gave him the clerical job of chasing payments from customers, rather than allowing him to examine why the company was failing. After three months of worsening performance, the company got rid of the accountant, and went into receivership a year later.

THE RISK MANAGER

Companies are increasingly allocating the management of risks to one person, the risk manager, also known as chief risk officer (CRO). First introduced at GE Capital in 1993, CROs are now found in more than 150 major corporations.

Medium-sized companies are less likely to have such a person exclusively devoted to risk management. In such cases, the task is likely to be given to the finance director, company secretary or chief compliance officer (in regulated industries such as financial services). However, if these people already have a full-time job, it is unlikely that they will be able to devote sufficient time to risk management, and so the project could flounder.

It is impractical to expect one individual to have a detailed knowledge of too many subjects. At the same time, there is a risk of duplication if similar areas are the responsibility of different people. This emphasizes the need for a risk management plan. It will ensure that everyone knows what the major risks are and who is responsible for them.

Every company is different, and size plays an important role. The large firm can have specialists in each area, while the small firm cannot afford that luxury. The risk manager has a broader understanding of corporate risks. By contrast, an environmental manager or health and safety officer may feel that their subjects are the only major risk. However, the problem with grouping risks is that managers who are expert in one of the fields often know less about the other areas, which are often thrust upon them as an added responsibility. Someone trained in health and safety rarely knows about environmental risk, let alone financial risk.

Major companies are, nevertheless, increasingly allocating the management of all their risks to one person. The risk manager does not have functional responsibility for the risks – that remains with the line manager. Otherwise, staff will not feel personally liable for the risks they might engender. Thus the risk manager could be more correctly titled 'risk advisor'. The responsibilities of this individual are:

- To embed an awareness of risk in the business
- To evaluate the risks of the business, and introduce plans to minimize them
- To advise employees how to manage risk
- To create or administer a risk management system
- To enable the directors to fulfil their statutory or regulatory responsibilities
- To keep the business up to date on changing risk issues.

Where the organization has many sites, each should be visited once a year where possible. Individual sites should have their own risk advice staff. In Chapter 17 we discuss how to implement a risk management system.

According to a survey by FERMA (Federation of Risk Management Associations), the majority of risk managers report to the President/Chief Executive or CEO (see Figure 3.2).

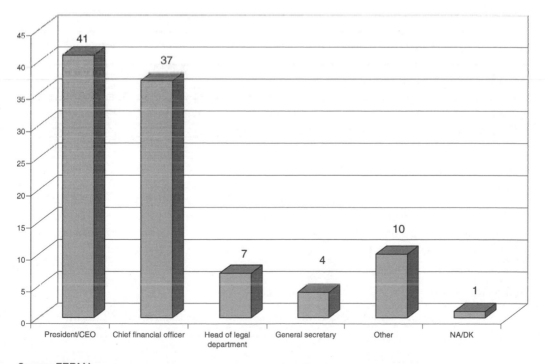

Source: FERMA

Figure 3.2   To whom does risk management report in your company?

RISK COMMITTEE

Depending on the size of the business, there may be a risk committee or risk council. This can take several forms. It can be a group of senior managers who receive the internal audit reports, or it can be representatives from each of the main departments who get together to learn from each other, and build a company-wide appreciation of risk.

Depending on its constitution and membership, the committee could:

- ensure that staff adhere to the company's risk policies
- make sure that audits are carried out
- review the findings of audits, and implement controls
- develop risk awareness among their staff
- control risks within their own departments
- make recommendations to the board for risk-related changes
- seek the support of the risk manager in facing the challenges presented by business risk.

At Aventis, the pharmaceutical business, members of the risk council are drawn from each business area (for example, science-driven research, regulatory affairs and industrial operations). The council is comprised of those people who are responsible for risk reporting in their area. Each council member provides a quarterly risk report, updating the others on the major risks in their business area. The reports are edited and presented to the audit and advisory board once a year. This format provides a unified corporate view of risk, rather than the opinion of individuals, and therefore carries more weight.

LINE MANAGERS

Line managers must have responsibility for managing the risks within their areas. Their staff must understand the kind of risks in the business, and know how to manage them.

It is easy but dangerous to over-manage line managers, by presenting them with ready-made risk management solutions, by condescending to them, or by sending in inexperienced auditors. In many cases the line managers are running multi-million pound operations. They must take control of their risks, and be given support and advice. If line managers contact the risk manager for advice, you will know the system is working.

SHOP-FLOOR EMPLOYEES

Production employees usually face the greatest level of personal risk. They are also most likely to cause environmental or operational failure, for example by emptying chemicals into a river or by allowing a fire to start. Therefore they need to thoroughly understand the nature of risk as it applies to them, and be involved in deciding how to manage it.

SUPPORT STAFF

Most of the company's staff have a role to play in risk management. They include the following:

- Company secretary or compliance officer: keeping everyone abreast of regulatory changes
- IT: helping users to understand IT risks, including the risk of downloading viruses and opening email attachments

- HR: providing training in risk awareness and risk assessment; and organizing new staffing appointments.

OTHER STAFF MEMBERS

All staff members should be involved – no matter how briefly – in considering the risks that might occur in their department, and how they can be controlled. This will help to embed risk awareness within the business. Responsibilities for risk management might be added to job descriptions, where appropriate.

Responsibility for risk assessment

In some organizations, the risk manager carries out risk assessments. However, it is better that line managers and their staff should do it. This ensures that they get involved in the process of risk management. These assessors should be trained for the job. This means they should know what risks might exist, and how to measure them. They should also know how to minimize the risk.

The assessment process should be looked upon as a learning experience for everyone involved. Through discussing the risks, the company will learn how to manage them.

Note that this is a different job from that of 'auditor'. The auditor should be someone who does not work in the department that is being audited. We discuss this work below.

Auditors

INTERNAL AUDITORS

Internal audit – and the people who carry it out – at one time an unwelcome and often ignored group, is now the means by which the directors can satisfy themselves that the business is sound. Corporate governance and risk management have been taking a larger share of management's time, not least because of growing financial regulation and because directors have become personally liable for the veracity of their annual reports. Auditors are especially important if the organization is quoted on a stock exchange, because the company will need to demonstrate that it has internal financial controls in place.

With risk becoming a strategic issue for management, internal auditors are taking on responsibility for auditing areas they might not have visited in previous years. However, many auditors are being asked to audit areas outside their traditional competency of financial controls. Management risks being lulled into believing that audits are being successfully carried out when in fact the auditors are either over-stretched and under-resourced, or insufficiently trained to understand operational risk. The word auditor means different things to different people. We can distinguish at least three types of auditor:

1 *Accountancy*. Financial auditors have traditionally carried out financial audits on corporate subsidiaries and divisions. In recent years, as corporate governance has risen up the agenda, these auditors have acquired wider responsibility for risk audits. Such individuals

are expensive, are likely to have high acumen, and are able to think and communicate clearly. Such auditors tend to be ACA (Associate Chartered Accountant), or in the USA CPA (Certified Public Accountant). Lesser accounting qualifications include the Certificate in International Auditing from ACCA (the Association of Chartered Certified Accountants).

2 *Quality*. These auditors have come from inspection and manufacturing background. From their origins in quality, supplier, and health and safety audits, they have moved into environmental issues and thence into risk management. They are especially suited to production-oriented risks, rather than risks relating to fraud or financial issues.

   Such internal auditors may need to conform to the international standard ISO/TS 16949:1999 on Internal Quality Audits – Auditor Qualification. You can also find advice on choosing auditors in ISO 19011: Guidelines for Quality and Environmental Management Systems Auditing.

3 *Internal*. It is worth distinguishing those people who have specialized in internal auditing, from accountants or production people. They may have a CIA (Certified Internal Auditor) qualification from the IIA (Institute of Internal Auditors). This requires a first degree, 24 months' internal auditing experience, an exam, and continuing professional education. They are likely to be cheaper than a qualified accountant, but less financially adept; and they may be more expensive than someone with a shop-floor quality background, but possess a wider view of risk.

Many people use auditing as a step to greater responsibility. It gives people a much wider view of the organization, as well as the opportunity to travel, and to have contact with management. Thus audit departments can include people who are in training for their accountancy exams and who are required to have a sponsoring organization.

   Internal auditors must be trained to carry out their audits, and given clear terms of reference for their audit. This must cover the objectives of the audit, audit review, and the relevant dates; and to eliminate suspicion this information must be shared with auditees. The aim of the audit should be to add value, as well as ensuring that internal controls are working. The auditors' role is to:

- conduct audits to check that the company's risk policy and controls are being followed
- evaluate whether the company is exposed to uncontrolled risks
- provide assurance to management that their risk management policies are being met
- give advice to line management and employees on how to control risk (if they have the experience or responsibility to do this).

Internal audits must be independent of the department they audit and, if the company is large enough, independent of the division. They should not be used to make policy, to manage risks, or to impose controls.

EXTERNAL AUDITORS

The company will be used to dealing with accountancy auditors. But using external auditors for risk auditing may be a new development, especially if regulations require the business not to use the firm that is hired for the financial audit.

Although the annual audit may refer to the company's risks, it is not a major part of the audit. Therefore the business may decide to conduct a separate exercise to validate its view of its risks.

There is also a different kind of external auditor, namely the type that audits quality or environmental management systems. These are more concerned with operational risks rather than (for example) fraud; but they may have more experience of shop-floor type risks than the accountant auditor.

CASE HISTORY: HOW IBM MANAGES RISK

IBM UK has a Project Assurance and Risk Assessment group which aims to increase awareness of risk among the company's project managers. The Industry Business Division provides IT solutions for medium-sized and large firms. The group uses risk management to ensure that its jobs are profitable and effective. Used in this way, risk management has become a powerful tool for gaining competitive advantage and winning more business.

In IT projects, there are many risks. They range from internal failures, such as not making a 'business case' (assessing the project's profitability), to client-based risk. For example, a project where the client thinks IT is a nuisance is more risky than one where IT is seen as useful.

The risk group works with IBM project managers, and helps them to understand the risks inherent in each contract. This lets the project manager alter the design of the project to reduce the risks. It also lets him set a price that reflects the risk.

The group does not seek to gain a detailed understanding of the risks. In fact it deliberately tries to avoid this, in order to provide independence and to encourage the project team to gain the information.

Among IBM's risk management tools is an 87-point checklist, which is broken into six categories (such as Technical and Implementation). The checklist allocates points for 'more risk' and 'less risk'. This helps the project manager see the scale of risk and where it is concentrated.

Training people to be aware of risk and to reduce error

Managers must receive training in managing those risks, and they must train their own staff. It is not enough to hand out risk management manuals to all managers. This will have no effect on the business, even though it may superficially appear that everyone has been briefed.

A more painstaking approach is needed. The risk manager should provide a training programme in risk awareness, and records should be kept. The training will not be as thorough as the auditors' training (see above); it may be segmented into the risks that affect the specific business unit, or else specific types of risk (such as environment, or health and safety).

Most problems occur through human error, especially when new methods are being introduced. The company should identify where catastrophic error could take place, and train staff to avoid it.

Training helps a company comply with its legal obligations. A major organization invites staff from its divisions to attend seminars on subjects such as waste management. By providing the training the group shows staff how to stay within the law. If staff fail to attend the training, or if they break the law, the company believes that it can reasonably plead due diligence.

Risk management qualifications

Qualifications in risk management are only now emerging. ALARM, the public-sector risk management forum, has been promoting a Registered Risk Practitioner (RRP) qualification, in conjunction with the Institute of Risk Management (IRM) and The Association of Insurance and Risk Managers (AIRMIC).

There are other qualifications that demonstrate that the individual has worked in an area relating to risk, such as NEBOSH, the health and safety qualification, or Certified/Chartered Insurance Professional (CIP).

Devolving responsibility and a culture of openness

'The devolution of responsibility is critical to making things happen. This does not happen often enough because of the desire to control risk.'

Kenwood Appliances

'If corporate value systems place too much emphasis on penalising failure than rewarding success, people will not take risks.'

Coca-Cola (UK)

Empowerment is vital. The company must let staff question existing views and criticize lax safety standards. There must be a willingness to debate issues in the business. This may require a change in corporate culture, applying total quality management (TQM).

CASE STUDY: NHS

Total legal liabilities for the National Health Service (the theoretical cost of paying all outstanding claims immediately) are estimated at an astonishing £7.88 billion. Risk management is therefore an important topic for the health service.

The Clinical Negligence Scheme for Trusts (CNST) provides a means for NHS Trusts to fund the cost of clinical negligence litigation. Membership of the scheme is voluntary for all hospital and primary care trusts in England, and there are advantages to membership: trusts get a discount off their scheme contributions where they can demonstrate they are complying with the standards.

Table 3.1, an extract from the NHS risk manual, discusses a specific requirement – that staff who operate equipment are trained to do so. This is set at Level three, which is a measure of difficulty. Trusts are assessed first at Level one, and in subsequent years will seek to achieve the more demanding Levels two and three.

The audits are carried out by an independent firm of auditors, and there is a maximum of one audit per year.

This case study highlights the merits of a scheme which:

- is voluntary and therefore has only willing participants
- has financial advantages for participants
- is graded in difficulty. (This means it is accessible to all operating units; yet higher standards can be attained over time)
- is limited in duration – with a maximum of one audit per year, and with the Level one audit taking only one day.

Table 3.1   Extract from NHS Clinical Negligence Scheme for Trusts (CNST) manual

Criterion 5.3.3	Staff who operate diagnostic or therapeutic equipment are systematically trained to do so safely and effectively.
Level	3
Source	*Code of Professional Conduct*, NMC, April 2002 *Devices in Practice: A Guide for Health and Social Care Professionals*, Medical Devices Agency, June 2001 *Equipped to Care: The Safe Use of Medical Devices in the 21st Century*, Medical Devices Agency, April 2000 *Provision and Use of Work Equipment Regulations* 1998
Guidance	This is a further development of criteria 5.1.5 and 5.2.6. All equipment that requires operator training should have been identified, and appropriate training programmes should be in place. The Trust should be able to produce evidence of all staff having received appropriate training, including Maternity Services where applicable. Frequency of training updates should be considered. The effectiveness of the system should be monitored by the Trust Board.
Verification	Training programmes. Records of attendance must cover all departments and professions, including Maternity Services where applicable.
Links	5.1.5 5.2.7
Scoring	10

Avoiding groupthink

Does everyone in your organization agree what needs to be done? Is there a strong degree of unanimity? If so, you may be a victim of 'groupthink'.

The term was coined by the psychologist Irving Janis in 1972. He noted that some individuals made decisions they felt would be acceptable to the rest of the group. Janis defined it as 'decision-making characterized by uncritical acceptance of a prevailing point of view'. Members of a group can suffer an illusion of invulnerability and morality, and construct negative stereotypes of outsiders.

A business that suffers from inadequate internal debate may stultify, leaving it exposed to danger. Innovation is an example where groupthink often holds true. For years, PC manufacturers put computers in beige boxes because 'that's how computers look'. All new models were 'safe' products of groupthink. Eventually Apple broke the mould with its colourful iMac computers, and took advantage of that sales opportunity.

One method of preventing groupthink is to use an impartial chairperson, who can lead decision-making sessions and encourage participants to 'think outside the box'. Another idea is to include a lay person in technical decision-making sessions. Alternatively, you could use an 'embedded alien', according to Cindy Barton Rabe, a strategist for Intel Corp. She suggests putting a non-expert into the team for a time to act as a catalyst for new ways of thinking. As the name suggests, this person should be foreign to the project; but also a strong innovative thinker with the capability and experience to understand the key issues at hand.

Manage the processes

Some processes and activities are more risky than others. The company should dispose of any non-core high-risk divisions unless they produce high rewards.

Within each remaining division and plant, the company should seek to replace high-risk processes with lower risks. Safer chemicals may be substituted for hazardous ones.

IMPLEMENT A MANAGEMENT SYSTEM FOR ALL MAJOR RISKS

A management system involves writing down the company's main procedures, and then ensuring all staff adopt them. ISO 9000 is used to maintain the consistency of a product or service, while ISO 14001 seeks to minimize environmental damage. The use of such systems can help to avoid crises, and we examine them further in Chapters 4 and 17.

PREPARE FOR PROBLEMS

The company should carry out emergency drills to check its preparedness. This area is examined in more detail in Chapter 16.

INTRODUCE SAFER SOLUTIONS

This may involve substituting a safe chemical for a dangerous one, abandoning a risky process, or exiting from an unstable market. You can isolate threats, by creating physical barriers for moving machinery, or building fire walls to separate one part of the building from another. You can also minimize the damage that will be caused if the threat materializes. For example, sprinklers will minimize the spread of fire, and tamper-evident containers will protect the customer.

Improved internal controls are used to prevent fraud and independent non-executive directors can restrain a board's excesses. Table 3.2 is a sample risk treatment plan.

CASE HISTORY: HOW A FASHION STORE GROUP MANAGES FASHION RISK

A fashion retailer faces two major risks, according to McKinsey, the management consultancy. The first is having unsold stock that consumers do not want to buy. The second is being out of stock in lines that consumers do want. Both these risks cost a lot of money.

One store group tackled these problems by imposing more discipline on the buying process. The company drew up a profile of the typical customer, so that all buyers knew who they were targeting. This encouraged buyers to obtain stock that had the right appeal in style and price.

The company then divided its offering into four styles, covering the spectrum from everyday wear to high fashion. It also defined how much of each type would be bought. This ensured that buyers bought the full range of goods that the customer wanted.

The change meant buying low risk (and therefore high profit) items such as jeans, not just the high-fashion (and high risk) items that the buyers preferred.

The company also determined how long each item would be in the store. Then the firm decided on its main source of supply. As a result of this process, sales are up substantially while mark-downs have fallen by a modest five per cent.

Table 3.2   Risk treatment plan

Risk Treatment			
Compiled by:	Date:	Reviewed by:	Date:

Risk no.

Risk description

Recommended action (controls, investment and so on)

Benefits of the recommended action

Resources needed (people, money)

Responsibilities

Timing

Audit/monitoring

Comments by reviewer

Spread the risk

Investment funds lessen their risk by buying the shares of many companies. Ordinary companies can do the same, by developing new technologies which could co-exist with their present ones, or by selling complementary products. For example, packaging companies which once made only metal containers have extended into plastic ones. Home Study Courses Ltd (www.inst.org) has expanded into new areas of vocational distance learning, a move that protects the business against the risk of government intervention or declining consumer demand for its older courses.

But every change creates a new risk. If the packaging company neglects its core market, or invests too heavily in new plastic packaging equipment, it could suffer more than by maintaining the status quo. Equally, if the company invests in high-risk, non-related businesses, it also increases the danger that something will go wrong.

Companies can also push responsibility upstream to their suppliers, by requiring them to be responsible for product quality and safety. This is becoming more essential as laws on product liability and pollution become more widespread and stringent.

INSURE AGAINST RISK

Insurance should not be neglected. Having put in place risk management procedures, companies should seek a reduction or stabilization of insurance premiums.

Larger companies should set up their own captive insurance companies. This keeps the cash in the business and provides insurance at reasonable rates, thereby saving the profit margin that would have gone to an outside insurance company. The risk is retained inside the company, but the business pays sufficient money into the captive to pay out in the event of claims. This assumes that the business has sufficient scale and expertise to manage its own insurance company subsidiary, though third-party businesses can provide the expertise.

Bus companies, for example, can find that insurance premiums are the largest cost after wages. London Transport for many years covered its own insurance risks. It then moved its insurance for catastrophic losses to Zurich Municipal by agreeing to pay the first £250 000 of each claim. Prior to being privatized into ten different businesses, London Transport set up its own captive insurance company to provide affordable cover. This was to ensure that the new operating companies, which had no track record in the insurance business, would be able to buy insurance at modest cost.

Other companies are now setting up their own healthcare insurance. This has the same advantage of providing insurance at modest cost. The disadvantage lies in the company's lack of core skills in what are entirely new business ventures.

Monitor the risk

MEASURE THE RISKS

The company should measure its risks. Taking measurements lets the business see where it is vulnerable, and where losses are occurring. It also ensures that action is taken. As the saying goes, 'What gets measured gets done'.

HAVE AN EARLY WARNING SYSTEM

The company should have trading information available within days of a transaction. It is no longer adequate to wait until the end of the month for information.

Senior management must be able to interpret the data and recognize the danger signals of excessive debt, falling sales, growing costs, or slow payment by debtors.

A management information system which gives the company succinct and rapid information is of major importance in risk management.

KEEP DOCUMENTATION

The risk manager (or the line manager) will need to keep a range of records. They will include:

- risk register
- procedure manuals
- insurance policies
- maintenance records
- plans of specific premises, plus maps, photographs, flow charts and other information recording location of drains, stopcock, hazards and so on.
- loss records.

AUDIT THE RISKS

An audit programme may use a checklist to ensure that risks are identified and managed. The audit may take a specific threat, such as health and safety, and check it throughout the plant. Alternatively, it can take a specific resource, usually a department or building, and carry out a comprehensive risk audit. The audit should look at all aspects of risk, or else a selected area (such as a SHE – safety, health and environment – audit).

CASE HISTORY: RISK AND THE PROFESSIONAL FIRM

For any service company, there is always the risk that an assignment might go wrong and the customer would sue the firm. A human resources consultancy knows that in recommending a new pay structure for a client, it is fundamentally affecting the client's business. A system that gives too much money to the workforce could bankrupt the client; while a miserly system could cause key workers to defect.

Before submitting a proposal, the consultancy evaluates the potential impact of an assignment on the business, and charges accordingly. Says one executive, 'It's crazy to get just £9000 for a job which exposes us to ruinous legal costs if it goes wrong.'

Setting a risk management budget

The size of the risk management budget will depend on the size of business, the complexity of its operations, and the responsibilities of the risk manager.

A survey among visitors to the continuityinsights.com website showed that the majority spent less than $500 000 on business continuity management (BCM), and we may assume that many firms spent nowhere near that amount (see Table 3.3). There is another reason for treating this with caution. A question in the same survey showed that in only eight per cent of cases were BCM funds allocated as part of a risk management budget. The greatest number, 41 per cent, said that funds were allocated on a case-by-case basis. Apart from anything else, this suggests that risk management and BCM are treated as separate issues, or that companies opt for either one or the other.

Table 3.3   The organization's annual budget for business continuity management products and services

Budget	Number of responses	%
Under $500 000	224	62
$500 000 – $999 999	60	17
$1 million – <$5 million	52	14
$5 million+	23	7
Total	359	100

Source: Continuity Insights

Some companies make the company's risk management services available free of charge to plant managers – unless the plant suffers a loss, in which case a charge is allocated to their plant. This encourages plant managers to seek advice and support rather than wait for problems to occur. Thus each plant carries a notional budgeted cost for risk. If not used, the money is allocated to the plant's profits.

Using risk management consultants

There are many kinds of consultants who could help the task of risk management. Most specialize in a specific area of risk. Some are skilled in international risks and kidnap and ransom. There are also security consultants who concentrate on building security. There are also environmental consultants who can help prevent pollution. The same applies to health and safety, and fire consultants. PR consultancies are expert at media relations, but may be less good at understanding how to introduce management systems.

The first approach should be to organizations which provide free information or help, and which have no vested interest in selling a particular solution. This includes government departments, trade bodies, and possibly the company's insurance company. There are also magazines and books on different aspects of risk. Only when these sources of information have been exhausted should the company consider hiring a consultant.

The following guidelines should be considered:

- Find a consultancy whose skills match your needs. Be cautious of a consultancy which claims to be an expert in all kinds of risk. It probably has a bias to a particular kind of risk.
- Always ask more than one consultancy to offer a proposal. This will allow you to compare prices and expertise.
- Find out how much experience the consultancy has in the company's area of concern. Which clients has it worked for? Talk to those clients, to get their opinion of the consultancy.
- Does the size of the consultancy affect the work? If, for example, the work involves many plants around the world, could the consultancy handle it?
- What will it charge for the work?
- What would be the outcome of its work? In what way would this help the company?
- Meet the consultants who would work on your business. How much experience do they have?
- Beware of a consultancy which wants to do too much of the work. Its aim should be to teach your staff how to cope with business risks. How will they ensure that your staff take ownership of the new ideas?

Useful links

Automotive Industry Action Group (AIAG)
www.aiag.org

Captive.com insurance
www.captive.com

Institute of Internal Auditors (IIA)
www.theiia.org

International Auditor and Training Certification Association (IATCA)
www.iatca.com

National Examination Board in Occupational Safety and Health (NEBOSH)
www.nebosh.org.uk

National Health Service Litigation Authority (NHSLA)
www.nhsla.com

Registrar Accreditation Board
www.rabnet.com

Treasury Green Book (chapter on risk)
http://greenbook.treasury.gov.uk

UK Government Internal Audit
www.hm-treasury.gov.uk/

Risk assessment – risk organization

This is the first of fourteen checklists which cover the main areas of risk in the business. The checklists, which are at the end of Chapters 3–16, reveal the areas in which the business is most at risk. They indicate which kinds of risk should be prioritized for action.

You can check the company's vulnerability to risk by answering the questions below. Score one point for each box ticked.

Topic	Question	
Roles and responsibilities	Is risk management the responsibility of a board member?	☐
	Has the chief executive initiated any discussion about risk in the last three months?	☐
	Has the business appointed a risk manager?	☐
Drivers	Has the business determined its top revenue drivers or key success factors?	☐
Policies	Has the company set a risk policy?	☐
Assessment	Has the company carried out a company-wide risk assessment in the last 12 months?	☐
Processes	Is risk management embedded in the company's processes and systems?	☐
Resources	Are adequate resources allocated to risk management?	☐
Information	Does the business systematically gather information about risks?	☐
Reporting	Is the business reporting on its risk to investors?	☐
Total points scored		

Score: 0–3 points: high risk. 4–7 points: moderate risk. 8–10 points: low risk.

The appendix contains a summary of all the checklists in this book. By entering the results of this one, you can compare your organization's preparedness against other, more specific, categories of risk.

4 Product and Service Problems: Operations and Production Risk

In this chapter we cover the following points:

- Product and service risks
- The consequences of mundane and catastrophic failure
- Product liability
- Service failings
- Lack of competitiveness
- How to achieve reliability and consistency
- How to use a management system to control your risks

We examine how to prevent production risk by managing people, quality, systems, technology and design. We also consider service problems, and see how they can be resolved.

Production and service problems have many causes, some of which are shown in Table 4.1 Whatever their origin, they give rise to product and service risks – whether in terms of cost, reliability, or human interaction.

When the product or service arrives at the market, the problems can become real, which result in loss of customers and other problems.

The solution, as shown in Table 4.1, is to manage all the elements of production – the people, suppliers, equipment and systems. It is the systems in particular that we emphasize in this chapter. Effective auditing and feedback should identify problems and present solutions long before they become a threat to the business.

The consequences of mundane failures

Most operational and production failure is banal – wrong products ordered, lack of stock availability, communication failures, and so on. The results are equally banal – products that have to be sent for re-work, a patient who has to be booked in again, or a customer who buys at another store.

Yet these failures matter cumulatively. For commercial companies, they can make the difference between profit and loss. For the public sector, it can mean a constant wearing down of employee morale, or a regular shortfall in the number of clients seen. In all cases, it means financial losses.

Table 4.1   Product and service risks and solutions

Manufacturing problems		Service delivery problems	
Variable supplier quality	Dated design	Weak systems	Poorly trained staff
Slow product development	Weak systems	Lack of training	
Long set-up times, downtime	High rejection rate		
Inflexible production	Under investment		

Product risks		Service risks	
Out of stocks	High costs: high inventory, write-offs and mark-downs	Lack of available staff	Poorly motivated staff
Lack of competitiveness (design, technology or price)	Variable product quality	Incorrect information, service or technique	Unsafe or risky service
Unsafe product or service	Catastrophic failure	Bad or wrong advice	High service costs

Problems in the marketplace			
Irritable customers	Legal action	High return rate	Defection of customers, and sales decline
Loss of reputation	Financial loss		

Solutions		
Manage suppliers	Manage materials	Manage design
Manage people	Manage quality	Manage technology
Manage processes		

In short, production and operational risk is all around us. Quality failures can be minimized by understanding where they might occur, and by adopting techniques that will forestall them, as will be discussed in more detail later in this chapter.

Catastrophic failure

Production and service failures that lead to recall or litigation are very expensive. Here are some examples.

- A product recall by toy-maker Lego cost them £3.5 million, even though the company had extensive procedures in place for such an occurrence.

- NEC, the mobile phone manufacturer, sub-contracted the production of phone chargers to another company. Later it was found that some of these chargers had faulty circuitry that, at worst, could cause fires. A product recall of 97 000 units cost NEC £200 000 – with £110 000 spent on advertising the recall, £80 000 spent on manning a call centre for enquiries and £10 000 on PR. These costs don't even include what the recall cost NEC's retailers or the supplier.

- Smith Kline Beecham had to recall 12 million glass bottles of Lucozade after discovering a defect that caused the neck to crack when opened. The company learned of the problem from Rockwell, its bottle supplier. Previously the company had recalled 5 million bottles of Lucozade after the Animal Liberation Front said it had contaminated some of them. The scare turned out to be a hoax, a problem we examine in Chapter 9.

- A baby car seat manufacturer estimated that a recall (due to a faulty seat-belt clasp) cost the company an entire year's profits.

But it isn't just manufacturers of consumer goods that suffer.

- A virus swept the factory of a biotechnology company that produced palm trees for Middle East plantations. It takes months to multiply and grow the crops; and this production failure lost the company much of its annual profits, as well as a loss of reputation among its worldwide export markets.

- The UK foot and mouth crisis of 2001 had massive effects on not just farming but also tourism and other rural industries. It takes years to replace the six million animals slaughtered and to reproduce the quality of the breeding stock that was lost. The outbreak is thought to have cost farmers £900 million and the rural economy as a whole close to £5 billion. In addition, the UK beef industry is still trying to recover its reputation in important export markets.

- Service companies are also prone to disaster. Computer software is often delayed reaching the market, and is notoriously and routinely faulty.

Meanwhile government services are also at risk. This is on three counts:

1 They are a huge employer and therefore there are more people who can fail.
2 Money is often in less plentiful supply, and therefore solutions cannot be achieved simply by throwing cash at them.
3 Government services deal with the big issues of life and death, children and the elderly, roads and travel, and so on. So there is more at stake.

Newspapers routinely feature scare stories of smear-test errors, social-work failures and killer nurses. And although these are statistically rare, no manager wants to make the headlines.

We cover legal issues in Chapter 13. In this chapter, we focus on how to keep products and services at a consistent standard.

Product liability in Europe

Product liability law has been standardized throughout the European Union because of the revised Directive on General Product Safety. The Directive benefits the average company by preventing it from being undercut by rogue competitors. But it also extends liability for faulty products, and any recall necessary, to everyone in the supply chain. This includes importers, component manufacturers and retailers. It also changes the burden of proof. Consumers no longer have to prove that that the supplier was negligent. Instead, everyone in the trade has to prove that they did everything to ensure the product was safe, or be liable for damages.

The legislation applies to all new or second-hand non-food products relevant to consumer health and safety that are not subject to existing European health and safety legislation (such as toys or tobacco). It does not cover capital goods, production equipment or products used exclusively in business.

The main objective of the Directive is 'to ensure that products placed on the market are safe' but this is realistically defined as being safe under normal or foreseeable conditions of use, and reflects the use to which a product is put. For example, a kitchen knife only becomes unsafe if misused.

Higher standards are required for products used by vulnerable groups, such as children. Companies may need to provide more obvious safety notices. In restaurants, for example, information sheets are now attached to children's high chairs, telling parents how to use the chair safely.

The law requires risks associated with the product to be identified on the packaging and product instructions. For instance, computer keyboard manufacturers now place warning labels on their products, urging users to avoid possible injuries and giving advice on how to avoid repetitive strain injury (RSI) – see box below.

THE RISKS OF RSI

RSI is estimated to affect 500 000 workers in the UK alone, costing employers at least £200 million a year. If keyboard manufacturers do not adequately label their products they would likely find themselves as liable as employers who do not warn their staff about RSI – one bank worker was recently awarded £250 000 damages. Microsoft and other suppliers now place warning labels on their keyboards, urging users to avoid injuries from their use.

In the US, RSI is the leading form of job-related injury. Some believe that it affects five million US workers. The American Academy of Orthopaedic Surgeons estimates that such injuries cost $27 bn (£17.4 bn) a year in medical costs and lost income.

FORESTALLING PRODUCT LIABILITY THROUGH RISK ASSESSMENT AND CONTROL

A producer (as the Directive terms it) should be aware of the risks that their products might present, be able to identify unsafe products, and to withdraw them from the market if necessary. This can mean:

- carrying out supplier assessment
- doing inspections during manufacture
- investigating complaints
- using batch numbers so that faulty products can be identified
- keeping distributors informed of the results of monitoring.

There are no set rules: companies have to decide what measures to adopt in the light of their particular circumstances. This avoids bureaucratic rigidity which might require companies to undertake excessive monitoring.

A producer also has to provide consumers with information that lets them evaluate the risks of the product. This applies only to the risks that are not obvious without warnings.

Distributors have to monitor the safety of products they sell. They should pass on information about product risks to producers and consumers, and cooperate in taking action to avoid those risks. This can mean helping a producer to recall faulty goods. After a television report linking baby mattresses to cot deaths, Boots, one of Britain's leading high-street chains, withdrew all its baby mattresses from sale. Bavistock, a manufacturer of baby mattresses, also withdrew 35 000 mattresses.

PENALTIES FOR BREAKING THE LAW

In the UK, the Weights and Measures authorities can issue warning notices, and notices telling the company to stop selling the product. Failure to comply with a notice can lead to a custodial sentence and/or a fine. The fine is likely to be modest compared with the unlimited fines and longer prison sentences that other laws impose. However, a court of law might decide to impose higher penalties using different legislation.

Companies can escape prosecution by demonstrating 'due diligence'. In other words, they can prove that they took reasonable steps to avoid contravening the regulations. For example, they might show that they printed safety warnings on the label, or provided childproof closures. Nevertheless, the authorities might decide that the product was 'unsafe', and order it to be withdrawn.

Other industries where liability is a constant threat are the pharmaceutical firms (where drugs such as Gammagard have been the subject of recent claims). Other high-risk companies are those which operate in hostile environments or with dangerous products (such as oil companies, whose catastrophes have included the Prestige tanker spillage in 2002).

In Chapter 7 we examine ways in which companies can minimize the likelihood of damaging the environment. It is reiterated here because many companies do not realize they are causing pollution until the government inspector arrives. One of the UK's biggest claims for environmental damages was against not a chemical company but a tannery whose fluids had seeped into the local watercourse for many years.

Service failings

This chapter has so far examined the problem of product failure. But 24 million out of 30 million jobs in the UK are service based. They include:

- public administration, education and health
- retail, hotels and restaurants
- transport and communication
- finance and business services.

SERVICE ORGANIZATIONS ALSO USE PRODUCTS

Service operations often contain a mix of products and services, as can be seen in Table 4.2. Organizations should 'map' their processes to see exactly what goes on. Until this is done, people often have only a hazy idea of the component parts of the system, let alone how the system fits together.

Table 4.2   Types of services found in service organizations

Examples of services that involve products	Sample operational risk
• Restaurants and catering – food needs to be supplied and served	Food poisoning
• Tyre and exhaust fitting: this is more product-oriented, with physical removal of the old tyre and fitting the new one	Wheel nuts come loose
• Physical distribution requires the movement of goods around the country, vehicle management, as well as route planning and warehouse management	Vehicle accidents
• Housing management requires the construction and maintenance of buildings, as well as the processing of applicants, financial control, and record keeping	Repairs backlog
Active services	
• Education: activities, events and trips involve increased risks	Physical accidents
• Retail: in addition to the checkout activities, the store has to organize products to a warehouse, thence to the store, and then on to the shelves	Out-of-stock problems
• Surgery involves physical activity of meeting patients, diagnosing them, moving them, the surgical procedure, and post-operative care	Anaesthetic error

Continued

Table 4.2 *Concluded*

Examples of services that involve products	Sample operational risk
Service only	
• Insurance services require visits to clients, information gathering, credit-risk analysis and proposal writing, and paperwork for compliance	Faulty decisions
• Banking processes involve activities such as data processing, paper transactions and credit-risk assessment	Data-entry errors
• Software writing is predominantly a desk-based activity (this does not mean to say it is risk-free: software project failure is common)	Project failure

As Table 4.2 shows, many service organizations engage in activities that have physical end-products. Such organizations need to be able to manage both the product and the service. Where the service organization has a product, it will also have all the paraphernalia of suppliers, raw materials, and production units. Some managers may be less familiar with how to control such elements, and in such cases greater risk accrues.

Other organizations have an active service component which, if not provided correctly, will lead to customer dissatisfaction. Purely service businesses have their own risks, which are no less hazardous.

LACK OF COMPETITIVENESS, OR FAILURE TO ADAPT

We have seen that companies need to avoid operational disaster or crisis. A more insidious problem occurs when the company's service or products do not match the customer's expectations. Customers rarely complain: instead they buy from a different supplier. And the not-for-profit organization eventually gets a bad grading or banner headlines.

It is important to know what measures your customer use. For example, customer satisfaction can mean speed of delivery, design quality or value for money. Sometimes organizations don't assess themselves on the same scales that the users choose.

A survey by YouGov found that most people agree that their schooling left them ill-prepared for the problems of everyday life and work. Most blamed this on traditional textbook learning and inadequate careers advice. Eight out of ten felt their school, college or university could have given them more help in identifying their strengths so they could find a career that would suit them. Inevitably, organizations never ask the same kinds of fundamental questions (for example, is this the right business to be in?), because it never occurs to them to do so.

As we examine how to control the variations in product and service quality, remember that this will also serve to boost competitiveness.

Good practice blends many issues: technology, people and systems. On their own these topics do little. But when combined, they can revolutionize the organization. For example, excessive costs can drag down the organization. They can be caused by many factors: lack of technology, lack of process control, failure to control suppliers, and demotivated staff. Some of the solutions in this chapter help to remedy these.

Financial risk for government bodies

One of the biggest risks for local authorities and municipalities is a shortage of money. With much of their annual budget coming from central government, and with many areas of cost, such as pay awards, being outside their control, local authorities risk sudden deficits.

Other risks for local authorities and government bodies include:

- disaster (such as flooding)
- failure to perform – for example, in fostering, environmental health, tendering or in managing housing
- litigation – by employees, tenants or citizens
- legionella
- occupational road risks
- school trip risks
- health and safety risks
- workplace risks
- risks to reputation
- environmental issues
- security
- risk financing alternatives
- other operational and business risk.

How to achieve reliability and consistency

The basic tool for managing reliability and consistency is the management system, of which the best known is ISO 9000. As we see below ('Using a management system to control your risks'), ISO 9000 is based on sound ideas of inspection, control of important documents, and written procedures. Companies which have implemented ISO 9000 often go on to adopt total quality management, or (especially in manufacturing) statistical process control. These are all ways of reducing risk.

As Figure 4.1 shows, there are three ways of approaching quality. The most risky is the *failure* area where complaints and recalls take place. This is rarely very dramatic, because often the customer simply decides to buy from another supplier in future. The failure mode does, however, include the dramatic product recalls described earlier.

Somewhat more successful is the *inspection* mode. This was the way many goods were produced in the past. In inspection mode, quality is the responsibility of inspectors, and their job is to 'inspect out' faults. This makes it easy for ordinary production staff to ignore the quality of the product, because it is not their responsibility. Likewise, production managers come into conflict with the quality department, whose staff are seen as meddlers.

The least risky area involves the *prevention* mode. In this strategy, quality is 'designed in' to the product or service. A system is in place to cover all areas where quality can go wrong.

A management system such as ISO 9000 encourages the organization to identify a fault or hazard through audits and checks. It prompts people to investigate the root cause, to correct the fault, and to prevent it from happening again. Applying the standard will help to prevent a catastrophe because it aims to catch problems before they turn into a crisis. For example, ensuring staff check their own work before it leaves the plant will reduce the chance of a consumer finding foreign bodies in a food product.

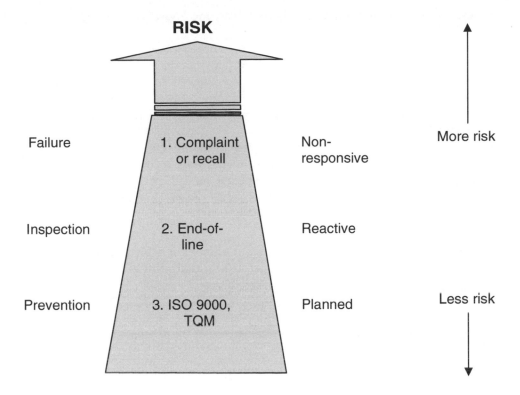

Figure 4.1 The three production modes

Mapping the company's processes often yields valuable and surprising information. BhS, the chain store, analysed its supply chain and found that there were 63 unconnected parts to the supply chain process, many of them operating in parallel and duplicating each other. In some cases it was taking three months to agree a sample because it went to and from the supplier several times. Now the company has four parts rather than 63: create, make, move and sell.

FORESTALLING PROBLEMS IN A MATERNITY HOSPITAL

Alarmed at a spate of baby snatching from maternity hospitals, St Mary's Hospital in Manchester now straps a tagging device to the wrists of the 4000 babies born there each year. The tag, which cannot be removed with conventional scissors, sounds an alarm if the baby is taken from the ward by an unauthorized person.

The tag, which looks like a teddy bear, was developed to guard prisoners in the first Gulf War. It now helps to minimize one of the hospital's 'production' risks.

Using a management system to control your risks

There are several elements to a quality management system, which are now summarized:

- *Understand your main processes* – unless you can see how transactions occur, you can't begin to improve them or manage them.

- *Have an organizational structure* – so that everyone knows who is responsible for each area.
- *Have written procedures* – so that everyone knows how a job should be carried out.
- *Keep records* – so that, if anything goes wrong, faulty products can be traced.
- *Do regular checks* – so that faulty goods are not allowed into the market, and to keep the whole system running smoothly.
- *Identify faults and correct them* – so that the company learns from mistakes and does not keep making them.
- *Seek continuous improvements* – so your product or service is regularly enhanced.
- *Communicate well* – The design department must talk to manufacturing; and everyone must have the information they need to do their job.
- *Allow an external organization to regularly assess the system* – so that you get an independent view on its effectiveness.

The well-organized firm does all these things as a matter of habit; but ISO 9000 ensures that they are formally adopted. Without a proper structure and without inspection by an outside firm, parts of the system may quickly lapse into disuse.

VARIANTS OF ISO 9000

ISO 9000 has many offshoots for different industries. And even where ISO 9000 does not exist in your industry, there will be a similar system.

- Automotive industry: ISO TS 16949, VDA 6
- Telecoms industry: TL 9000
- Laboratories: ISO 17025
- Food: ISO 9001 HACCP (ISO 22000)
- Medical devices: ISO 13485
- Aerospace and Aviation: AS9100
- Information security management: ISO 17799.

Part two of ISO 9004 concentrates on guidelines for services. It includes the following:

- level of service to be provided
- the service organization's image and reputation for quality
- objectives for service quality
- approach to be adopted in pursuit of quality objectives
- role of the personnel responsible for implementing the quality policy.

Management needs to do the following:

- define customers' needs, with appropriate quality measures
- design preventive actions to avoid customer dissatisfaction
- minimize quality-related costs to achieve the required performance
- create a collective commitment to quality within the service organization

- undertake regular reviews of service requirements and achievements in order to identify opportunities for service quality improvement
- prevent adverse effects by the service organization.

People, technology and design

Operational and production risk involves people, technology and design. In the final section of this chapter, we look at each in turn.

MANAGING PEOPLE

The at-risk company has staff who don't care about their product, or have restrictive practices. But even a company with motivated staff will fail if it does not harness their skills. *Multi-function teams* are common where a problem stretches across functional boundaries. To find new solutions, companies bring together people from purchasing, production, engineering and quality.

Cell manufacturing is a similar theme. It reduces alienation, and gives people control over the final product. In many instances, the cell acts as a complete profit centre and has its own chief executive. More flexible manufacturing allows units to be quickly reconfigured to cope with shorter product life cycles. Self-managing teams increase quality and employee motivation.

Reward systems are another area where employees can share the rewards of the business. Employee share ownership programmes (ESOPs) help staff to acquire a long-term stake in the business, while performance-related pay (PRP) provides bonuses related to the level of profit. Reward systems which build a better team will entail a common payment system for the whole of the workforce, payment which reflects the output of perfect goods, and which rewards skill, flexibility and commitment.

Flatter organization structures help to get rid of inertia and overheads, improve morale, decentralize decision making, and help the company respond more quickly to change.

MANAGING TECHNOLOGY

Companies which lag in technology are disadvantaged through reduced flexibility, speed, information and quality. To achieve world-class manufacturing requires the introduction of computer-aided design (CAD) and computer-integrated manufacturing (CIM). Using barcodes, a company can track its work-in-progress in real time, and use computers to produce smaller batches which meet customers' individual requirements. The introduction of robots and automated picking and handling systems can also boost efficiency.

For example, in the high-tech Laufen sanitary ware plant in Austria, toilet bowls are moved on an automated assembly line through robotic spraying booths. In some UK plants in the Potteries, by contrast, workers laboriously apply the glaze by hand. In certain cases, hand finishing is an essential element of a luxury product; while in other cases, it represents lack of investment.

In the Rehrig Pacific plastics plant, automatic guided vehicles (AGVs) move silently around the plant, transporting the company's returnable plastic pallets from the manufacturing area to storage or to a staging area for shipping. When the bumper sensors detect an obstruction, such as a person, the AGV slows or stops until the obstruction has gone. Bumps, crashes, injury and damage normally associated with transport of materials are virtually eliminated. And when not in use the AGV drives to an in-floor charge shoe and recharges itself.

Yet, in other businesses, such as roof-tile manufacture, workers still trundle wooden wagons laden with scrap through dusty Dickensian passages.

There may be cases where manual handling does not affect profitability; but the payback from investment should always be investigated.

Companies which intend to stay at the forefront also investigate *new materials*, such as fibre optics, ceramics, carbon fibre and adhesive technology.

MANAGING DESIGN AND DEVELOPMENT

The length of time taken to bring new products to market is crucial in a world when time is being compressed. One computer company reduced its product development time for a new mainframe computer from six years to three. The secret is *concurrent engineering*, which combines the previously separate disciplines of design and production. At the heart of the system is an integrated information system which allows design data to be used in manufacturing. This overlapping of design and production acceleratess new product introduction.

But speeding up new product development is only one aspect of managing design. It is also a question of understanding the market's needs. *Benchmarking* has a role to play here. The company should identify what is important to the customer, whether ease of use, economy in use, lighter weight products or better service. Benchmarking can also provide quantified information on production efficiency, whether product cost, inventory costs, or type of equipment used.

CASE HISTORY: HOW ONE HOUSE BUILDER STAYS OUT OF TROUBLE

Not every company manufactures a standard product, nor do its problems take place on a shop floor. A case in point is the house builder, who faces many areas of risk. Paying too much for land, and allowing part exchange to get out of control, are two major risks. One house builder, a £200 million business, has systems designed to prevent the company from being exposed to excessive risk.

PAYING TOO MUCH FOR LAND

House builders need land; and they sometimes pay a premium for a plot, based on rising house prices. When the houses are built in 18 months' time, houses may be selling for 10 per cent more than they are today.

On the other hand, in a recessionary period UK house builders can buy expensive land, only to find that house prices fall. They are then stuck with land on which they can't make a profit.

The house builder in this example only allows itself to buy land priced at today's house prices plus the cost of one year's expected inflation for building materials. This means it has to work harder to find land; but it makes it less likely to own unsaleable sites.

THE PART-EXCHANGE RISK

'Part-exchange' deals are another hazard for house builders. Today, more customers trade-in their old house when buying a new one, just as they would their car.

Some house builders pay too much for second-hand property, and are then unable to sell the old houses at the price they had paid, becoming stuck with unsaleable houses. The builder minimizes this risk by

Continued

obtaining three independent estimates of the house's value.

These procedures reduce the likelihood of the company buying land and second-hand houses on which it cannot make a profit.

REDUCING THE SCALE OF THE IMPACT

Another construction and quarrying company found that 40 per cent of its capital was invested in new house building. Since the housing market suffers from peaks and troughs, this made the group's profits volatile. In one year, profits leapt from £2.5 million to £23 million. To solve the problem, the company has taken a policy decision not to invest more than 25 per cent of its capital in housing. The two companies' different approaches demonstrate that there is more than one way of tackling the same risk.

Useful links

ALARM – risk management in the public sector
www.alarm-uk.com

Department of Trade and Industry (DTI) consumer recall guide
www.dti.gov.uk/ccp/topics1/pdf1/consumer.pdf

HM Treasury risk portal
www.hm-treasury.gov.uk

ISO (for ISO 9000)
www.iso.org

Risk assessment – operations and production

You can assess your vulnerability to operational and production problems by answering the questions below. Score one point for each box ticked

Topic	Question	
Liability	Are the products or services potentially unsafe? Could they result in legal action?	☐
Quality	Does the organization lack a quality management system (such as ISO 9000)?	☐
Supplies	Is the organization heavily dependent on few or distant suppliers?	☐
Technology	Has the business failed to invest in up-to-date production technology or other assets?	☐
	Has the organization failed to fully investigate new materials?	☐
Services	Does the organization lack effective controls over its services?	☐
Staff	Are staff inflexible, lacking in skills or paid for piecework?	☐
Design	Are development lead times slower than the average in the industry?	☐
	Are designs worse than the average in the industry?	☐
Costs	Are costs higher than others in the industry?	☐

Total points scored

Score: 0–3 points: low risk. 4–6 points: moderate risk. 7–10 points: high risk.

The appendix contains a summary of all the checklists in this book. By entering the results of this one, you can compare operations and production risk against other categories of risk.

5 *Purchasing Problems*

In purchasing, the major issues of risk relate to quality, integrity and availability, as well as conflicts of interest. In this chapter we look at those topics under the following headings:

- *Single source or not; oligopolies; reverse auctions versus partnership sourcing*
- *Outsourcing, and sourcing from abroad*
- *Reputation issues*
- *Supplier unreliability*
- *Just in time versus overstocking*
- *Conflicts of interest; corruption risks*
- *Controlling price hikes*
- *Supplier assessment*
- *Vertical integration*
- *E-business.*

Supplies risk

Components and raw materials, whether plastic parts or janitorial supplies typically account for 35 per cent of a company's costs, according to Benchmarking Partners Inc.

Moreover, the threat of lost production – with customers fuming and orders lost – weighs heavy on the minds of purchasing managers. This puts purchasing at the heart of risk management. Procurement risk divides into two categories:

- risk from suppliers (unreliable or slow supplier, supplier goes bankrupt, disruption from natural event)
- risk from the company's procurement policies (purchasing from far away, single sourcing).

It can be hard to disentangle these two issues. If a supplier becomes insolvent, supplies cease and the plant stops producing goods, that could be attributed to a bad supplier, or to management's decision to rely on a single, distant supplier about whom too little was known.

However, for the purposes of simplicity, we'll examine supplies risk under the following headings:

- single sourcing of supplies
- oligopolies
- reverse auctions
- partnership sourcing and supplier development
- outsourcing, and sourcing from abroad
- reputation issues

- supplier unreliability
- JIT
- overstocking
- conflicts of interest
- corruption risks
- controlling price hikes.

At that point we look at some ways to reduce procurement risk, notably:

- supplier assessment
- vertical integration
- e-business.

SINGLE SOURCING OF SUPPLIERS

There is a growing tendency to source raw materials from fewer suppliers. Many companies aim to have only one supplier for each product they buy. Others have found that reducing the number of suppliers saves time and money, avoids duplication, and gives them greater control and an improved relationship with suppliers. But single sourcing can also make companies more vulnerable to an interruption of supplies.

According to the Procurement Strategy Council (PSC), which is comprised of large businesses, 40 per cent rely on a single supplier, with the rest using several. Those who use several suppliers are likely to have between two and five (see Figure 5.1). The choice is driven largely by the size of the spend in that category, and the importance of the component or category. Each of these dictates the scale of risk to the business.

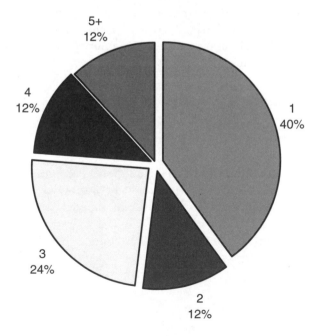

Source: Procurement Strategy Council

Figure 5.1   Number of suppliers used by large companies per item

With single sourcing, the company no longer sees bids from competitors, so there is a risk of higher prices. Some companies use target pricing, where the supplier is asked to supply a product at a price determined by the customer. At the very least, the supplier may be asked to quote a firm price for 12 months.

So, while modern management techniques may preach the benefits of restricting the number of suppliers, or of sourcing goods from cheap and distant lands, the risk-aware manager should seek to avoid over-reliance on one or a small number of suppliers.

It is especially wise to keep more than one supplier for those products with a fluctuating price, such as products made from commodities. Companies which buy, for example, copper, will buy on the futures market of the London Metal Exchange or a similar financial institution.

Some other companies are now moving away from single sourcing. At Kodak, managers have their bonuses tied to their performance in meeting supplier diversity targets. These targets are set by region and by commodity, according to PSC.

According to Ralph Szygenda, Chief Information Officer of General Motors, it is important to be able to change suppliers quickly. 'You should, when they fail to deliver the right service, be able to move to another company quickly.' This means ensuring they don't set up proprietary systems that lock you in. 'And you never give it all to one company,' he says.

OLIGOPOLIES

An oligopoly is a market with few suppliers, which presents a risk to downstream businesses. An example of an oliogopoly is the electronics industry, where, if there is a worldwide shortage of a certain chip it has to adjust computer prices and specifications accordingly. In the first four months of 2004, DRAM (dynamic RAM) prices rose by around 40 per cent. This particular increase was due to the larger producers struggling with upgraded technology in their production methods.

This issue presents the same problem as we saw before in single sourcing.

REVERSE AUCTIONS

Reverse auctions are a completely different model to single sourcing. Here, suppliers are bidding the lowest price for a commodity or component.

According to *Purchasing* magazine, some requests for quote (RFQ) from Welch's, the food business, have received 250 bids for a particular ingredient. 'The risk associated with reverse e-auctions is that you can make more supplier changes than in the past. And making supplier changes can result in disruptions to your plant operations,' according to Welch's. But incumbent suppliers often retain the business, not least because they know more about the client, and are able to offer a cogent case. However, this is unlikely to be the case in bids based purely on price.

Supplier quality is another issue. An unknown supplier has an unproven track record.

PARTNERSHIP SOURCING AND SUPPLIER DEVELOPMENT

At the opposite end of the 'arms-length' purchasing model is partnership sourcing, where suppliers are more deeply involved in the client's business. It entails giving more information to suppliers, involving them at an early stage in development projects, and giving them advance notice of production plans.

Using supplier expertise also helps to boost the quality of the final product. Kodak uses an online database where suppliers can submit cost-reduction ideas and feedback, and then easily check the implementation status of their suggestions.

Partnership Sourcing Ltd (PSL) is a not-for-profit organization set up in 1990 by the Confederation of British Industry (CBI) and the Department of Trade and Industry (DTI) that helps UK businesses to achieve better links with one another, thereby improving price, quality and innovation.

According to the Department of Trade and Industry, 76 per cent of companies that engage in partnership sourcing report significant reductions in cost. Seventy-three per cent have reduced their inventories, and 70 per cent have increased their quality of supply. Overall, 90 per cent of companies considered partnering practices to be a succcess.

Working closely with a supplier can reduce risk, because the supplier better understands your needs. In addition, there is the opportunity to harness the supplier's skills to improve your product or service. However, there are attendant risks. The supplier can use the knowledge acquired to win contracts with competitors; but this kind of risk can be reduced by the wording of contracts, non-disclosure agreements or a non-compete agreement (a contract that restricts participation in a certain market by a company or individual under specific circumstances).

A worked-out plan can focus attention on important issues such as how to add value through collaboration, how to share that value, and what exit strategy should be agreed. Partnership sourcing is a good example of how to use risk as an opportunity, rather than simply treating it as a threat.

In Table 5.1, supplies are graded into three categories, with different purchasing strategies and managers allocated to each.

Table 5.1   Grading suppliers

Level	Items	Level of procurement staff
A	High-value items valued above $5 million dollars Includes critical mass items such as raw materials	Commodity teams with strategic skills handle A suppliers
B	Middle-range items valued between $1 million to $5 million dollars Includes supplies such as specific packaging items	Commodity teams with mid-level strategic skills handle B suppliers
C	Low-value items valued under $1 million dollars Includes Maintenance, repairs and operations (MRO) items	Commodity teams with transactional and tactical skills handle C suppliers

Source: PRC

OUTSOURCING AND SOURCING FROM ABROAD

Sourcing more materials from other companies, and sourcing them from overseas carries advantages, such as lower costs and greater flexibility. But it also carries risks.

Sourcing from low-cost countries such as India or China gives you a competitive advantage – but only until your competitors do the same. At that point, sourcing from abroad becomes the norm in your industry.

Sourcing from abroad also carries a higher risk. Apart from foreign exchange risks (discussed in Chapter 11), suppliers often require bigger orders, and the lead times can be longer. Therefore, for niche markets, and for those companies which need to be able to respond quickly to changes in the market, manufacturing in your local market may be an advantage.

As well as distance and time, there can also be political and cultural risks. When the EU imposed quotas on goods from China, teddy-bear companies found that they could not acquire stock. One firm that normally imported £2 m worth of bears found it could get only £300 000 worth.

In electronics, an industry that operates on a global scale, products can take a mere four days to get from a Belgium warehouse to a UK customer. But sometimes supplies come from the opposite side of the world, and this can cause long delays.

A major audiovisual products manufacturer told a customer that it would take 18 days to get a part from Japan. When he offered to fly to Japan and collect the part himself, he was told that orders were only accepted from the official UK distributor. He was also informed that the Japanese manufacturer could not simply take items from its warehouse without proper paperwork.

A different sort of problem can occur because of heightened security threats. Companies that source supplies from abroad should consider the supply problems that can occur as a result of terrorism, banditry or even from pirates. In 2003 there were 445 reported pirate attacks. Half of these were in the Malacca Straits, close to Indonesia, through which half of the world's crude oil supplies pass, according to ft.com.

One solution is to seek alternative suppliers closer to home. This is likely to be more expensive, so you would have to make a trade-off decision between speed of logistics and cost.

REPUTATION ISSUES

Leading apparel companies such as Nike and Gap have been targeted in the past by activists protesting about the companies' suppliers. Employment practices, notably child labour, indentured labour (using indentured or slave labourers), and conditions of work have been the main complaints. This can lead to adverse headlines in the press, consumer boycotts, and ultimately a loss of reputation, especially among important long-term consumer groups such as students.

Auditing your suppliers is one solution. But this can be hard to adequately achieve, particularly if your suppliers are in distant locations or if they use sub-contractors. Moreover, a company's internal audits are rarely credible to non-governmental organizations (NGOs) or protest groups. Moreover self-declarations or statements such as the following are unlikely to carry much weight in the eyes of critics:

We ask all suppliers to sign an agreement stating that they understand HP's expectations and that they agree to work with us towards conformity with our Supplier Code of Conduct. (www.hp.com)

CHILD LABOUR

Around the world, 120 million children aged under 14 work full time, especially in Honduras, Guatemala, Haiti, Bangladesh and India. Employers use child labour because it is cheap – the children will work long hours for low pay and without overtime. Often their parents hand them over to work as indentured labour to pay off debts. Human Rights Watch reckons that 15 million children in India work as bonded labourers, and are often cheated by fraudulent accounting. As a result of cramped repetitive work in dusty conditions (especially in weaving carpets), the children suffer spinal deformities and breathing problems.

The use of such labour is controversial – as well as being unethical – and could damage your reputation if a pressure group decides to target your business. The way to avoid this is to ensure that suppliers (and their suppliers) are independently audited, and by ensuring that the (adult) workforce is paid a fair wage.

Another option is to use an independent audit body such as the Fair Labor Association (FLA, www.fairlabor.org). The FLA is a non-profit organization that promotes adherence to international labour standards and improves working conditions worldwide. Participating companies adopt the FLA code of conduct, and implement a compliance programme throughout their supply chain. The FLA then uses accredited monitors to monitor each company's high-risk facilities, works with companies to resolve problems identified in their facilities, and independently verifies internal compliance programmes.

The FLA is most visible in US university campus shops. But though in 2004 it audited 3000 factories in 80 countries, with sales totalling $30 billion, the FLA worked with only 15 companies, and these were almost exclusively in the clothing industry.

A similar scheme is SAFE, which is run by the US National Food Processors Association (NFPA). It audits the suppliers of 30 major food companies including Nestle, Pillsbury, and General Mills.

The 'Link-up' and 'Proof' schemes involve the independent auditing by Achilles (www.achilles.com) of 1000 suppliers and contractors. The 'Proof' scheme is used by 80 rail organizations in the UK, Norway and Sweden.

Call centres are another issue. Companies are becoming aware of the risk to their reputation by employing overseas call centre staff to deal with customers. A survey by ContactBabel revealed that one in seven of those Britons who have knowingly come into contact with an overseas call centre responded by taking their business elsewhere. Three out of four people have a negative view of companies who route their enquiries abroad.

Environmental issues also impinge Sainsbury's superstores, which have faced public demonstrations against their milk. Although the company claims to have a no GM products policy, it was found that some of its milk was supplied by cows fed on GM modified fodder. We discuss environmental issues in Chapter 7.

SUPPLIER UNRELIABILITY

Suppliers can be unreliable for various reasons, notably financial problems and quality control/internal control issues.

Major difficulties arise if a supplier succumbs to financial problems and goes insolvent, especially if it is a key supplier. The sudden cut in supply can cripple production and will, ultimately, affect the purchasing company's bottom line. Remember, too, that a recession can have a major effect on smaller or undercapitalised suppliers.

The best ways to avoid the problem of unreliability are to not become too dependent on a supplier and to institute a warning system. Gap, the international clothing retailer, uses a scorecard that tracks delivery failures and is a leading indicator of viability concern. In this way, a delivery failure automatically triggers the exploration to find alternative suppliers.

Two developments are helping companies to reduce the amount of risk from quality failure by suppliers:

1 Companies are asking their suppliers to agree targets for quality (in some cases targets are as strict as 20 defective parts in a million).
2 Others are asking suppliers to accept responsibility (and the costs) for warranty work which can be attributed to their parts.

JIT

The principles of just in time (JIT) when it comes to reducing warehouse inventories and avoiding dated stock. However, like any good idea it can be taken to extremes, and many companies are now reducing the scale of their JIT activity because it increases supplier risk. There are four main problems:

1 In Japan, where the idea originated, a traffic hold-up on the motorway can bring a factory to a halt. Some businesses now have only two days' parts in stock, and receive daily supplies from the supplier. This makes them vulnerable to having their plant activities halted if suppliers fail to deliver the goods. An earthquake in Kobe virtually ceased operations of some motor manufacturers.
2 The extra pollution is undesirable.
3 Suppliers are increasingly unhappy about providing a high level of flexibility (and the costs that go with it) unless they are paid for it. For many sub-contractors, JIT is simply a means to shift cost to the small company.
4 Dominance by a major customer can lead to major problems for the supplier if orders are reduced.

OVERSTOCKING

At the opposite end of the spectrum from JIT is overstocking. For smaller businesses, stock kept in inventories will represent the largest asset on the balance sheet. This is especially true for retailers, where not having products in stock translates instantly into lost sales. However, inventories can easily grow to an unacceptable size and this will often result in heavy mark-downs, driven by a desire to generate cash flow.

A good example of this was the collapse of Sinclair computers. Their 1983 development, the 'QL', was a good, reasonably priced microcomputer. They soon received 13 000 orders. However, problems emerged as customers complained about slow delivery times and poor build quality. Demand collapsed but Sinclair continued to accumulate stock. At the beginning of 1985, Sinclair was forced to slash prices to generate cash. In the end, the company was forced to sell its entire stock to Dixons for a tiny proportion of its value.

The solution to these stocking dilemmas is somewhere between the potentially risky JIT principles and wasteful overstocking. While it is impossible to forecast demand exactly, managers should be able to estimate future sales. This might be done using the sophisticated software that is available, or a simple spreadsheet that shows historical sales data, depending on month, events or other important factors. According to Ted Hurlbut, merchandising expert, companies should also avoid making inventory purchases too far in advance. Generally, the goal is to be flexible enough to respond to most changes in demand, while not being wasteful.

Some retailers have adopted scan-based trading (SBT). Even though they are on a retailer's shelves, the goods are owned by the manufacturer, and the retailer is not invoiced until the goods are scanned at the checkout. But the trade-off is that the retailer pays the supplier faster than when traditional methods are used.

CONFLICTS OF INTEREST

Eliot Spitzer, the New York Attorney General, accused Marsh & McLennan, a leading insurance business, of stifling competition and cheating customers by paying 'contingent commissions', also known as placement service agreements (PSA). These are additional payments made by lenders on the basis of business volume and profitability. The action against the company led to its share price falling 45 per cent in just a week.

Such discounts are common practice in industry – they reward middlemen for loyalty and encourage more business. But while this is a taint-free issue in food retailing, it has ethical implications in financial services, where the broker is supposed to obtain the best value or lowest price for their client. PSAs encourage the broker to place their business with a specific underwriter, and therefore represent a conflict of interest.

According to Spitzer, Marsh made $845 m (£460 m) from contingent payments in 2003, equating to 28 per cent of its annual profit. Other markets attacked by Spitzer include the music industry for payments (payola) via promoters who induce stations to play their records.

Judging by precedent, if such payments are banned in one jurisdiction, legislation follows in others. Therefore, companies should check to see whether they could face allegations of conflict of interest. This is most likely to occur in the financial services industry, but could apply in any case where a firm is recommended to a supplier based on discounts or other inducements. For example, there have been regular rumblings about doctors being taken on lavish conferences by drug companies. Wherever an organization is paid by a supplier rather than the customer, the company's ability to service the client dispassionately must be in doubt.

In a similar case, The European Court of First Instance upheld a fine on British Airways of €6.8m, which had been imposed by the European Commission for operating an anti-competitive scheme. BA had given higher commissions to travel agents who sold more tickets. Virgin Atlantic argued that this encouraged travel agents to sell BA flights rather than those of its competitors. BA subsequently changed its system and later appealed.

Where large sums of money are involved, companies need a written undertaking from its suppliers that they are not receiving payment from a third party to place the business with them. In other cases, the company may decide it has sufficient in-house expertise, or the sums of money are sufficiently large to merit bringing the task in-house. Thus some businesses can place their own insurance or else self-insure.

CORRUPTION RISKS

With suppliers desperate to get orders, the buyer is vulnerable to corruption. Aware of this, many companies have stringent codes of conduct about accepting gifts and inducements from suppliers. Sometimes the inducements are subtle, and take the form of company events and hospitality. The insurance industry, for example, entertains brokers or big company clients with golf days, outings to motor racing circuits, and industry awards ceremonies. The drug companies also do this with doctors, though on not such a grand scale.

Apart from publicizing the company's buying or anti-corruption policy, the business can avoid corruption risks by:

- routinely switching buyers to different purchasing categories
- installing a purchasing system that makes collusion difficult, such as the use of competitive tendering
- undertaking audits to check for abuse
- implementing a continuous improvement programme
- formally warning suppliers that they will lose the business and be reported to the police if corruption is discovered.

CONTROLLING PRICE HIKES

Some industries, such as construction and engineering, are heavily exposed to raw material price changes and, when prices rise, their profitability is threatened. StoraEnso is an example of a company that is weighing its risks, as shown below. The solutions that companies can adopt include:

- Negotiating with suppliers to keep their prices down. Some buyers require a price drop of two per cent a year, rather than the more usual increase. These have to be found through productivity rises at the supplier.
- Shopping around for different suppliers – not everyone puts their prices up at the same time.
- Hedging – buying futures in their selected raw material.
- Adding a clause to your contract with customers, allowing you to add rising costs to your price. This isn't possible for every customer, especially where they are powerful or unbending – as in the case of some government contracts.
- Choosing substitute raw materials. For example, the cement industry uses limestone, clay, shale, sand and iron ore, as well as fuels such as coal. Many of these raw materials can be changed. For example, you can add fly add to the limestone, reducing the amount of limestone needed.
- Building alliances and joining buying groups. The French car maker Renault cut three per cent of its parts' costs from its Modus people carrier by sharing half of the components with Nissan. The resulting savings are expected to double the company's profit margin on this class of vehicle.

SUPPLY AND DEMAND RISK: EXCERPTS FROM STORAENSO'S ANNUAL REPORT 2003

- Product prices, raw material and energy costs are cyclical and therefore a period of low product prices or high raw material costs affects profitability.
- Reliance on imported wood may oblige the Group to pay higher prices for key raw materials or change manufacturing operations.
- Reliance on outside suppliers for the majority of energy needs leaves the Group susceptible to changes in energy prices as well as shortage of supply.
- Changes in consumer preferences may have an effect on demand for certain products and thus on profitability.
- Exchange-rate fluctuations may have a significant impact on financial results.

SUPPLIER ASSESSMENT

Supplier assessment often starts with a form completed by a prospective supplier. This requires references, history, and evidence of quality control procedures such as ISO 9000.

Subsequently, the client visits the supplier from time to time to audit their premises and processes. Finally, receiving inspection takes place at the client's premises when goods arrive.

Figure 5.2 is a one of several forms used by Cow & Gate to monitor the quality of its suppliers. One set of forms is sent as a questionnaire to its suppliers; staff use a variant as a checklist when visiting the supplier and auditing it. This helps the company to assess the suitability of a new supplier. It also provides regular factual reviews of the supplier's delivery reliability, its management's ability and flexibility, and the quality of its products. This is the minimum requirement for any major supplier. It ensures that the customer checks the supplier in a methodical way. Beyond that lies greater involvement with the supplier and partnership sourcing, which was discussed earlier.

VERTICAL INTEGRATION

Some companies minimize the risk to their supplies by buying their suppliers. For example, Kentucky Fried Chicken bought chicken farms. Other companies extend downstream. Oil companies own petrol stations, while an egg producer started making egg products, including the liquid egg that caterers use to produce omelettes.

However, this also contains risks. In order to provide a complete service to clients, advertising agencies have often added direct response or PR departments. But these offshoots have been hard to manage; and if the client is dissatisfied with the direct mail business, for example, this can sour the relationship with the core – and more valuable – advertising account.

Vertical integration can also have unexpected results. Banks have found that their online payment service, such as NatWest's Worldpay, are open to competition from competitors such as Barclays PDQ. While business clients have historically been reluctant to move their bank accounts, they might get used to dealing with a different bank for their online payment system, which could in turn prompt them to move their bank account. However, this would require marketing cooperation between different banking business units, which is not easy to achieve.

E-BUSINESS

E-business, also known as electronic data interchange (EDI), has been around for many years. It issues orders to suppliers via a computer network; orders are often triggered by the customer's warehouse computer or production planning system. Sophisticated EDI systems can then initiate production at the supplier's plant, without the need for human involvement. By speeding the information between customer and supplier, and by avoiding the dangers of lost paperwork, the customer reduces its risks. Suppliers can also use EDI proactively as a business tool to embed themselves more firmly into the customer's system.

Wells   # Quality Assurance

Subject	Date	Nr.
PURCHASING PROCEDURES	16.09.03	PUR/06.22
	Page	Modification Nr.
SUPPLIER AUDIT CHECKLIST	9 of 11	1

5.	MANUFACTURING PROCESS CONTROL	COMMENTS
5.1	Processing Equipment – condition cleanliness	
5.2	Equipment Checks – documents frequency	
5.3	Process Documents – document checklist	
5.4	Process Systems – GMP HACCP	
5.5	Process Records – temperature dwell times	
5.6	Non Conforming Products – area documentation	
5.7	Weighers – area checks	

5.8	Packaging Handling – area
	                            checks
	                            frequency	

5.9	Personnel Training – equipment documentation	
5.10	Train Review – scope frequency	
5.11	Maintenance logs used?	
COMMENTS		

Drawn Up:	Approved	Q A Verification

PUR/06.22.8

Figure 5.2   Supplier assessment at Cow & Gate

E-BUSINESS IN CONSTRUCTION

Because chip-making plants are big and expensive, Intel is now using e-business to improve its construction projects. Its e-business programme links building owners, suppliers and construction managers. It facilitates cost tracking, requests for information (RFI), document management, collaborated design reviews, procurement and forecasting.

Intel says e-business is helping the company to build more capacity with tighter schedules, and it also eases the labour shortage problem in the construction industry. E-business lets the company speed up the design, construction and maintenance of its facilities. By integrating Intel's systems with its suppliers, the company can reduce the time required for designing, reviewing, approving, ordering and invoicing. And by allowing the company's computers to 'talk' to each other, e-business can improve the exactness of information that is travelling between Intel and suppliers, and eventually reduce the project life cycle and total cost.

BUSINESS CONTINUITY

According to a survey by Ernst and Young, of 50 leading retail and consumer products, nearly all backed up supply chain data to world-class or adequate standards, though less than 25 per cent tested themselves for business continuity and recovery. The firm believes that most effort is put into ensuring IT continuity, and that operational issues are often overlooked.

DISTRIBUTORS AND OTHER PARTNERS

It is not just suppliers who can put the business at risk. Other partners, such as distributors, retailers and agencies can also create problems. The issues discussed in this chapter, from single sourcing to e-business will help the company manage its business partners.

Useful links

Institute of Purchasing and Supply
www.cips.org

Office of Government Commerce – Procurement
www.ogc.gov.uk

Partnership Sourcing
www.pslcbi.com

Procurement Strategy Council
www.psc.executiveboard.com

Risk assessment – purchasing

You can assess your vulnerability to purchasing risks by answering the questions below. Score one point for each box ticked.

Topic	Question	
Suppliers	Are you dependent on supplies from distant countries?	☐
	Do you rely on a single supplier for major supplies?	☐
	Could negative PR from your suppliers affect your reputation, for example, the use of child labour?	☐
JIT	Do you rely on 'just in time' supplies?	☐
Conflicts of interest	Does the business face a possible conflict of interest between suppliers and customers?	☐
Raw material prices	Do raw material prices have a big impact on the company's profits?	☐
Supplier assessment	Has the company failed to formally assess its suppliers?	☐
IT	Does the business lack an e-business system?	☐
Partnership sourcing	Have you failed to introduce partnership sourcing or supplier development?	☐
Business continuity	Have you failed to test your ability to recover operationally from a supply chain failure?	☐

Total points scored

Score: 0–3 points: low risk. 4–6 points: moderate risk. 7–10 points: high risk.

The appendix contains a summary of all the checklists in this book. By entering the results of this one, you can compare your supplies risk against other categories of risk.

6 *Managing Health and Safety*

In this chapter we examine the risks caused by:

- *Dangerous machinery and equipment, noise and vibration*
- *Electrical dangers*
- *Substances which harm lungs, eyes or skin*
- *Confined spaces*
- *Lifting and handling; repetitive strain injury*
- *Slips, trips, and falls; falling materials*
- *Injury caused by vehicles, driving.*

We demonstrate how to carry out a health and safety risk assessment, and how to reduce the number of occupational accidents.

The real cost of accidents

Occupational injuries and ill health cost seven million working days in 2002, according to the UK's Health and Safety Executive (HSE). The Trades Union Congress (TUC) estimates that just one category – slipping at work – costs UK businesses £1.1 bn.

The Self-reported Work-related Illness household survey of 2001/2002 estimates that 2.3 million individuals in Great Britain were suffering from an illness in the last 12 months which they believed was caused or made worse by their current or past work.

An HSE survey examined five firms with lower than average safety records. Over a 13-week survey period, all lost large amounts of money due to accidents which caused injury, damage or disruption. This included a transport firm which lost 37 per cent of its profits, an oil platform which lost 14 per cent of its output, and a construction company which lost 8 per cent of its tender price on a project. Below we look at these cases in more detail.

- The transport firm suffered 296 accidents, costing £48 000. One bill, for £2000, was the result of damage done by lorries manoeuvring in tight spaces.

- The building contractor (part of an international civil engineering company) suffered 3626 preventable site accidents over the 13-week period. This cost the firm £245 000. Accidents included the collapse of a five-storey column, 20 cases of vehicles or cranes hitting property, and six accidents when fork-lift trucks dropped their loads.

- A creamery lost £3000 when food-handling equipment was bacterially contaminated. A further £1800 damage was caused when a tanker drove away while still connected to the factory pipe. During the 13 weeks, there were 926 accidents, and the bill was £243 000.

- The North Sea oil firm lost £940 000 because of 299 accidents. They included a £2000 health bill after a worker hit his head with a 7 lb hammer. Fire-fighting foam was also accidentally set off. This caused workers to assemble at fire stations, and the launch of a standby vessel.

Only a small proportion of these costs were covered by insurance. During the survey period, no accidents involved death or large-scale loss through fire or explosion. In other words, large losses occurred from everyday accidents.

ADVANTAGES OF MANAGING HEALTH AND SAFETY

- Improved staff morale and lower staff turnover
- Improved standing in the local community
- Better working conditions
- Less absenteeism
- Increased productivity.

DISADVANTAGES OF NOT MANAGING HEALTH AND SAFETY

- Injury or death of employees
- Damaged machinery
- Lost output
- Poor industrial relations.

Risk is strongly associated with health and safety because of the EC's Directives on health and safety which require a risk assessment to be undertaken. Health and safety is an important area because the risks are high. Unless the company takes precautions, an employee will trip over a wire or hurt themselves using a machine. In some companies, inattention to health and safety causes death.

Corporate risks in health and safety

The health and safety risks to a company include:

- Being sued by an employee or his or her family for causing death, injury, loss of hearing, cancer or loss of limb. These are insurable, but preventing accidents is better than dealing with the problems they cause. For example, the number of court actions over RSI (repetitive strain injury) is set to grow around the world.

- Being prosecuted by a regulatory authority (in the UK, by the Health and Safety Executive), or being ordered to cease production.

- Loss of output caused by loss of a key worker. 'Key person' insurance is growing in the US as a way of offsetting financial losses.

Risk assessment in health and safety

Traditional views of health and safety try to ensure a healthy and safe place of work. Risk management adopts the same attitude, but takes it a stage further. It asks what are the real dangers of the site, and aims to tackle them. This is not to overlook the other less hazardous aspects of health and safety. Risk management expects that the highest standards of health and safety will be met, but concentrates on prioritizing the danger areas.

Carrying out a risk assessment is better than preventing a recurrence after the event. The risk assessment should be written down, and should be available to health and safety inspectors. It need only be a simple document: simplicity aids understanding. The risk assessment should include the following elements:

IDENTIFY THE DANGERS

To identify the dangers, companies can:

1 Ask staff about health and safety risks. They often know what hazards exist (though they still manage to suffer accidents).
2 Review all purchases. Check suppliers' data sheets, especially for toxic substances. The sheets are not always very helpful, often being vague about the danger while also suggesting excessive precautions, probably to avoid legal liability.
3 Audit the workplace for dangerous processes. Hardwood dust can cause nasal cancer, making it as deadly as any chemical, and staff in buildings with cooling towers may be exposed to legionella.
4 Check a government list of dangerous substances (in the UK, available from HMSO). Any substance listed as 'irritant', 'harmful' or 'corrosive' is hazardous to health.
5 Read trade publications or information published by trade associations.

ASSESSING THE HAZARD

As we saw in Chapter 2, the organization should consider how grave the accident could be, how probable it is, and who might be affected by it. This analysis will help the business to concentrate on the biggest risks. In most firms there is a small number of obvious dangers. In a metalworking plant, workers are at risk from flying metal; while in a board processing plant they may be at risk from glue fumes. Most accidents can be forecast and are avoidable. They happen to staff who open bags with a knife, who lift heavy weights, or who walk over floors covered in granules. There are also ancillary processes which can harm workers. Workers can be hurt by fork-lift trucks, and by poorly stacked finished goods.

However, some hazards are not immediately obvious, and many are specific to an industry. Cabin crew are likely to suffer viruses and bacterial infections from germs being re-circulated. Crews are seeking an increase in the amount of fresh air pumped into the plane. And keyboard operators can suffer from carpal tunnel syndrome, an affliction of the nerves in the wrist.

Table 6.1 categorizes the main hazards into groups. Not every hazard can be listed here. You can add other risks at the bottom of the chart.

Table 6.1   Risk assessment chart

Auditor	Specify the danger	Who might be harmed?	Date: Controls and precautions	Further action needed
Dangerous machinery				
Pressure systems				
Noise and vibration				
Electrical safety				
Hazardous substances (fumes. dust, toxic chemicals)				
Lifting and handling				
Slips, trips and falls				
Computer screens				
Radiation				
Vehicles				
Fire				
Other risks				

This chart can be adapted to meet the specific needs of the organizations.

DECIDE WHO MIGHT BE HARMED

It is easy to omit people from the assessment, so you should include everyone who might be affected. Apart from staff, this comprises visitors, members of the public, cleaners, contractors, or other companies which share the workplace.

LIST CONTROLS AND PRECAUTIONS

The company should show how the hazard is managed. What systems exist? Are there written procedures, permits to work, or training? If procedures are listed in a safety manual, the chart should state where the manual is located. We consider relevant precautions below when looking at the main types of hazard.

Anyone included in the previous section (Who might be harmed?) needs to be made aware of the risk. That is why many firms give visitors brief health and safety booklets. It will help visitors stay safe, and it may mitigate the company's liability if a visitor is hurt.

ASSESS WHAT FURTHER ACTION IS NEEDED

The auditor should now assess whether the controls are adequate. In the course of the assessment you may discover some unforeseen problems, perhaps relating to a new machine.

In Table 6.1, the column 'Further action needed' is an action list. It shows what needs to be added to the 'Controls and precautions' list. The action list may include ways of making the hazard less risky, such as fitting extra guards, upgrading machinery, or installing monitors or alarms.

ACT ON THE FINDINGS

There is no value in doing an assessment and not acting on it. The real purpose of the assessment is to make sure that the company rectifies any problems that are unearthed. The ideal solution is to get rid of a hazard completely, but this is often not possible. However, many improvements are inexpensive or even without cost, such as putting a non-slip coating on a slippery surface, or marking separate lanes for pedestrians and vehicles.

REVIEW THE ASSESSMENT PERIODICALLY

Assessments should be done at least annually. This will ensure that safeguards are still in place and are being used. Each assessment also serves to update the assessment chart (Table 6.1). Each new piece of equipment or change to a process makes the old assessment increasingly out of date. The updated assessment will ensure that the safety system remains current and relevant.

Minimizing the risks

As Table 6.2 shows, some solutions are better than others. In a noisy environment, it is easy to give ear protectors (personal protective clothing) to staff – but they may not use them. A better solution is to substitute or alter the process, or improve the design. A commonly used phrase is 'Re-design the job, not the person'. We look at each of these strategies next.

Table 6.2   Strategies for minimizing risk

	Control staff and exposure	Control the hazard	Remove the hazard	
Less effective	Personal protective clothing	Audit regularly	Change the activity to remove or minimize the risk	More effective
	Train staff	Good housekeeping		
	Use work methods that minimize the chances of spill or escape	Adapt; use in a safer form		
		Isolate and enclose; ventilate		

REMOVE THE HAZARD

Getting rid of the hazard is the only sure way to prevent accidents. Often this is not possible, but sometimes processes can be changed or even discontinued.

Companies should *substitute* safer processes for hazardous ones. This might mean using less dangerous chemicals, or substituting mechanical handling devices for manual lifting.

CONTROLLING THE HAZARD

Regular audits help to prevent accidents from happening. If devolved, they encourage the workforce to become aware of dangers. Audits should be professionally planned and executed. This means making sure that all areas are audited during the course of a year, and that staff do not audit areas for which they are responsible. The results should be written down and acted upon.

Good housekeeping is essential. Companies that have wet floors, flammable materials all around, and obstructed exits are more likely to have a poor health and safety record. There should be nothing on the floor which might trip a worker, and adequate space for movement.

Modifying a process or making it safer is one of the more common solutions, which includes fitting guards. Isolating and enclosing a process, or ventilating the area, are similar examples. *Improving* a process might involve reducing machine vibration, a subject which is discussed further below.

CONTROLLING STAFF AND EXPOSURE

'Sticking plaster' solutions leave the process as it is, and adapt workers or their conditions. In the case of the noisy machine above, the 'sticking plaster' solution would be to hand out ear plugs.

Training workers and making them aware of the dangers is a continuing process. As processes change, and new staff are hired, it is important to prevent standards from slipping. Staff should sign their training records to show that they have been trained and have understood what they have been told. This will emphasize to staff the importance of safety, and it may reduce the employer's liability in the event of an accident.

Dangerous work should be controlled by using '*Permit to work*' documents which state how the work is to be carried out and what the dangers are. The permit is signed by the worker, though liability stays with the company.

Isolating and enclosing equipment helps to minimize its effect on other staff.

Ventilation can be either general (to reduce the likelihood of fumes building up), or local exhaust ventilation (to take dust away from a specific process).

Minimizing exposure can be implemented by using devices which switch off a computer for ten minutes an hour, to ensure that a worker takes a break. In a conventional factory, there may be a written procedure stating the maximum length of time to which a worker may be exposed to a process.

Personal protective equipment can be as simple as providing overalls to ensure that employees do not have clothing which could catch in moving equipment. Personal equipment also covers ear, toe and head protection.

Workplace hazards

DANGEROUS MACHINES

Any machine which could cut a worker or catch clothing is hazardous, and should have safeguards. Workers should be trained to be aware of the hazard, and know how to use it properly. They should also have the right to stop a dangerous machine. Fail-safe devices should be used: for example, a guillotine should not operate unless the guard is in position. Emergency cut-off buttons should be prominent and in easy reach. Regular auditing should be carried out, using a written checklist.

Many accidents occur during cleaning and maintenance. Only trained staff should be allowed to clean or service machinery. They should wear proper protective clothing (including glasses or footwear), and the machine should be disconnected. Workers sometimes ignore safety procedures or override switches to make the cleaning job simpler. Some machines are easier to clean (if a lot more hazardous) when in motion. If workers are found to be taking short cuts, you should find ways to make cleaning simpler.

PRESSURE SYSTEMS

Steam boilers can scald workers, and compressed air can damage eyesight. All kinds of pressurized containers can explode, maiming or killing those nearby. Consequently, it is better to avoid the use of pressured systems where possible. If they are essential, they must be properly maintained, and properly used.

NOISE AND VIBRATION

Noise can be measured in metres, and there are laws governing noise levels. If you can't clearly hear someone talking two metres away, you need to take action.

Noise can often be reduced by improved maintenance (including lubrication), running the machine at a slower speed, fitting exhausts, by surrounding machines with sound-deadening panels, and separating noisy machines from the rest of the plant.

New machines should be evaluated for the noise they produce. Giving workers ear protection should be the last solution. It tackles the symptoms not the causes, and is often put aside by workers because it is uncomfortable.

Vibration from continued use of hand-held tools can lead to 'white finger', caused by a reduced flow of blood to the fingers. Vibration can be reduced by better installation and maintenance, and by using better quality equipment.

Noise also affects local residents, and the company should seek to stay on good terms with its neighbours. This may necessitate sound-deadening doors, earthworks and trees to reduce the volume. The company should also avoid revving lorries early in the morning or late at night, or letting vans roar through residential streets when people are asleep. Failure to be a good neighbour can make a company the loser if local residents gang up against it.

ELECTRICAL SAFETY

According to the Health and Safety Executive (HSE) in the UK, 12 people died from electrocution at work in 2002 and 124 suffered major injuries (50 of which were in service industries). Electrical faults also caused many fires, resulting in more injuries and death.

Electrical safety starts with proper planning of installations, with maintenance and alterations being carried out by qualified electricians, and with the use of an electrical audit.

Some installations are more dangerous than others. Outdoor use, where cables and workers can come into contact with water, is most dangerous. Overhead electric lines are responsible for many deaths. Even when there is no direct contact, electricity can arc across to a nearby ladder, scaffolding or crane.

The use of circuit breakers, correctly rated fuses, and adequately sheathed cables is essential. In construction work, care should be taken against cutting through electrical cables.

HAZARDOUS SUBSTANCES (DANGER TO LUNGS OR SKIN)

Hazardous substances include those which can be swallowed, which can harm or burn the skin, or whose vapours can be inhaled. The substances can be in the form of liquids, gases, powders, solids or dusts. Hazardous substances can be produced while being poured or mixed, during processing, as waste, or when disposed of. They occur not just during the process, but also in research, cleaning, repair work and maintenance. Hazardous substances are found everywhere, in factories, farms, swimming pools and offices.

The importance of these hazards cannot be underestimated. In the UK at least 50 people are dying every week from long-term occupational cancer. Mesothelioma, a cancer that can be caused by asbestos, has a latency period of 20–40 years. By the year 2025 it is likely to have killed 50 000 people; and people who carry out improvements to old office buildings are still contracting the disease when they disturb long-dormant fire insulation material.

Table 6.3 shows how to assess hazardous substances, and incorporates an action plan. It asks the assessor to state the basic information (such as the name of the product and its known effect). It also asks who will be affected, and to what extent. This leads the assessor to provide an assessment of the risk. This is then followed by a plan of action. It will include work procedures, precautions to be taken, training, and emergency action.

At the famous Guinness brewery in Dublin, staff who cleaned the empty vats had a rope tied around their waist. When the cleaners started singing, staff knew that the beer fumes had reached them, and it was time to haul them out. That was long ago. Today the company has more contemporary methods of cleaning.

SMOKING

It is in the company's interest to minimize the extent of smoking, since second-hand smoking (known as passive smoking in the UK) is thought by most authorities to make up a significant proportion of all smoking-related illness. Moreover, smoking is a fire risk and workers can seek compensation for the effect that smoking has on them while in the workplace.

Karen Whitehead from Plymouth won £17 000 in compensation in an action brought under the Disability Discrimination Act, after she was sacked from her job as an administrator in a community centre. The passive smoke she inhaled there antagonized her asthma, causing her to miss 16 days' work out of 45.

Smoking should be prohibited except in designated smoking rooms, and these should not be rest rooms or canteens. The same applies to office workers, since the legal, health and safety risks are the same.

Table 6.3   Hazardous substances assessment

Assessment	Name of substance
	Toxic or irritant effect
	Process involved
	Staff involved
	Level of staff exposure
	Extent of risk to health
Action plan	Method of safe working, and controls to be applied (for example, measurement, protective clothing)
	Training and information needs
	Action in the event of an emergency

CONFINED SPACES

Fifteen UK workers die each year when working in confined spaces, and many more are injured. Confined spaces are common in all kinds of industry, from vats and silos to sewers. Workers can be overcome by fumes or lack of oxygen, drowned in liquid or asphyxiated in grain. Others die in fire or explosions, and others die trying to help them.

This kind of dangerous work needs to be more stringently controlled, using a permit to work system. The dangers should be carefully forecast, and safety measures put in place. Checks should be made for gas or fumes, and fresh air must be kept flowing into the confined space.

In construction, similar problems occur with trenches, which are prone to collapse. Care should be taken not to drill through electricity or gas cables, and service plans should be consulted before work starts.

LIFTING AND HANDLING

More than a third of major injuries reported to the HSE each year arise from manual handling – the moving of loads by hand or bodily force, as Figure 6.1 shows. In 2001/2002, according to the HSE, over 3500 major injuries arose from handling, lifting or carrying. Back pain is now the most common cause of work-related ill-health and costs the UK 5.7 million working days a year.

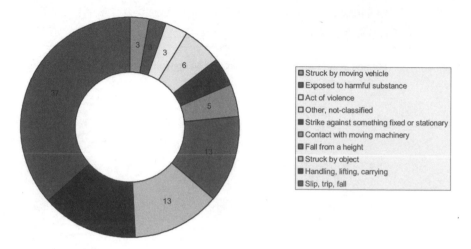

Source: HSE

Figure 6.1   Non-fatal major injuries to employees, 2004

Back injuries are just one of the problems that arise from moving goods around. Back trouble accounts for many days lost; and even allowing for malingerers, the problem is all too common.

Where possible, lifting aids should be used, ranging from trolleys and forklift trucks to conveyor systems. Apart from any other consideration, they should reduce the amount of damaged goods. Another strategy is to make the load lighter: one manufacturer found that sales were suffering because their products were packed in 20s compared with the competitors' boxes which were packed in 10s. The trade disliked handling the heavier boxes.

Using mechanical handling devices adds further hazards, because they can fall or break loose. Loads must be balanced and securely packed, and hooks firmly attached. With hindsight, most people can predict an accident: the aim of the risk assessment is to predict it before it happens.

REPETITIVE STRAIN INJURY (RSI) AND WORKING WITH COMPUTERS

Legal claims are likely to increase from workers who have suffered from carrying out a repetitive job. The most common complaint has come from journalists or secretaries who have typed for extended periods, and with a keyboard now on every desk the claims are set to mount. But anyone who carries out a repetitive movement of the arm, wrist or neck, or whose occupation involves awkward movements, is at risk.

Repetitive strain injury (RSI) can be avoided by altering the job, or broadening it, by allowing rest periods, and by varying the work. Improving the workstation, so that the worker does not have to bend or twist, can also help.

In financial services and many other service industries, computer terminals are the basis of many employees' work. RSI has become a real threat. Anyone is likely to suffer complaints if they spend eight hours a day hunched over a screen, tapping data non-stop into a terminal whose screen reflects glare from lights, and with harsh sunlight streaming through the windows.

EU legislation covers people who work with computers, and employers should check that there is no glare or flicker from the screen, that the chair supports the small of the back and is at the right height, and that both legs are on the floor. The screen should be moveable, and breaks should be allowed (10 minutes in every 60). Table 6.4 below shows the effects of other forms of radiation.

Table 6.4   Radiations: causes and effects

Hazard	Emitted from	Possible effects
Microwaves and radio frequency	Plastics welding, some communication, catering, drying and heating equipment	Excessive heating of parts of the body; headaches, eye pain
Infra-red	Any glowing source, for example glass production, and some lasers	Reddening of skin, burns, cataracts
Visible radiation	All high-intensity visible light sources. High-intensity beams, such as from some lasers, can be especially damaging	Heating and destruction of eye or skin tissue
Ultraviolet (UV)	Welding, some lasers, mercury vapour lamps, carbon arcs, the sun	Conjunctivitis, arc eye, skin cancer
Ionizing radiations (x-rays, gamma rays and particulate radiation)	Radiation generators, some high-voltage equipment, radiography containers, gauges, other radioactive substances, including radon gas	Burns, dermatitis, cancer, cell damage or blood changes, cataracts

Each type of radiation has its own method of safe working: the company should get advice from the equipment supplier. All hazards should be clearly marked, equipment should be carefully maintained, and workers should be informed about the risks.

SLIPS, TRIPS, AND FALLS

Floors should be kept dry, free of grease, and without obstructions, especially cables and pipes. Floors should be smooth and level, and stairs should have handrails. Good lighting is important, especially on stairs. There should be vision panels in doors, and there should be no unprotected floor openings such as inspection pits. People working on upper floors should be protected from falling by the use of railings or scaffolding. Great care needs to be taken when working on ladders, scaffolding or roofs. Ladders should be anchored and at the right angle (one length out for four lengths high, about 75 degrees). People should not remain on mobile tower scaffolding when it is being moved.

The business should prevent materials from falling by enclosing scaffolding with sheeting, and by having solid floors without holes. Mobile tower scaffolds should be fitted with guard rails and toe boards.

INJURY CAUSED BY VEHICLES

In the UK 32 people a year die and over 2500 are injured at work in accidents involving transport. Workers are crushed by moving, reversing or runaway vehicles, including Heavy goods vehicles (HGVs) and fork-lift trucks.

Good practice includes separating people and vehicles, by marking separate routes, and building ramps to reduce the speed of a vehicle. The company can provide mirrors, audible alarms and visible clothing. Vehicles may also require an escort when reversing. The company should make sure other companies' vehicles adopt its safety procedures when on company premises.

DRIVING

Employers have a responsibility for the health and safety of their employees such as van drivers, lorry drivers and sales people, when they are driving in the course of their work.

In many cases, the employee is 'out of sight, and out of mind', but the statistics show that driving is a dangerous activity. More than 1000 employees are killed each year in work-related motor accidents – far more than the 249 deaths reported annually to the HSE. Employees driving more than 25 000 miles as part of their job have the same risk of being killed as a construction worker. And there are 77 000 injuries to employees every year because of 'at work' road accidents.

Employers should carry out an assessment of the driver's behaviour, and implement training. This can include induction training, and on-the-job training, especially for drivers with high accident rates. An inexpensive solution is to use desktop or web-based e-learning.

RISKS FOR SERVICE BUSINESSES

Health and safety risks relate to service companies just as much as manufacturers. The HSE made a 13-week study of the health and safety costs sustained by a cheque-clearing company. The workplace was an ordinary office environment where the majority of work was clerical. In the 13-week period, nine injuries were sustained and there were four work-related ill-health absences. These incidents cost £23 000, including equipment replacement or repair, lost working hours and reduced output. Insurance paid out £5000, leaving over £17 000 worth of costs that the company had to pay.

HUMAN FACTORS

As we have seen above, people often override corporate systems. At a busy theatre, staff are told to wear hard hats when lighting is being rigged, in case equipment should fall, but are never used; instead, the hard hats are neatly hung on a rack in full view of staff. Staff think that an accident could never happen to them. Unless management decides to ensure that staff obey the rules, there is a heightened risk of accidents. This shows that senior management must get involved in risk management.

Safe systems of work

All accidents should be investigated. A report should be written and action taken. Many companies post a notice showing the number of days that have passed without an accident. This encourages people to be aware of the possibility of injury.

In Chapter 4 we looked at how a management system can improve quality. The same process applies to health and safety. The management system is particularly relevant to tasks that are dangerous. Written procedures are the basis for staff training, because they represent best practice. They should never be handed to staff in the form of a thick manual. Staff should receive only the procedures which relate to them; these should be read aloud and demonstrated.

Useful links

European Agency for Safety and Health at Work
http://europe.osha.eu.int

Health and Safety Executive (UK)
www.hse.gov.uk

Occupational Health and Safety Administration (USA)
www.osha.gov

National Institute for Occupational Health and Safety (NIOSH)
www.cdc.gov/niosh

Risk assessment – health and safety

You can check the company's vulnerability to health and safety risk by answering the questions below. Score one point for each box ticked.

Topic	Question	
Machinery	Do staff work with dangerous machinery or pressurized systems?	☐
Hazardous substances	Do employees work with hazardous substances?	☐
Electrical safety	Do staff work with electrical tools or equipment?	☐
Slips, trips and falls	Is the work environment ever wet? Do employees work at heights? Can staff trip over wires or other obstructions?	☐
Lifting and handling	Does the business store a lot of stock? Does anyone manually lift goods?	☐
Computers	Do any staff spend long periods working at computer monitors?	☐
RSI	Do employees carry out repetitive tasks?	☐
Noise and vibration	Is the work place noisy? Is vibrating equipment in use?	☐
Confined spaces	Does anyone work in confined spaces?	☐
Vehicles	Does the work involve vans, lorries or forklift trucks?	☐

Total points scored

Score: 0–3 points: low risk. 4–6 points: moderate risk. 7–10 points: high risk.

The appendix contains a summary of all the checklists in this book. By entering the results of this one, you can compare your health and safety risks against those in other categories.

7 *Preventing Environmental Damage*

In this chapter, we explore the threats posed by environmental damage. They include solid and liquid waste, toxic materials, and air pollution. We consider the problems associated with environmental hazards, and the costs involved in environmental protection. We then examine strategies for reducing environmental risk.

The seven penalties of environmental damage

Society regards pollution as harmful. To make firms reduce their emissions and discharges, society has placed burdens on the polluting business. As a result, pollution now carries a variety of burdens, some financial, others social. There are seven types of penalty, which we consider below.

1 *Costs of compliance.* In the USA, European Union and other parts of the world, companies have to buy consents for pollution. In some places pollution is still free, but this is unlikely to continue for very long. In China, for example, city managers in Beijing intend to 'punish' factories that create air pollution. For a company with many polluting processes, consents can prove costly.

2 *The costs of breaking the law.* Companies which exceed their consent or which cause a pollution incident are increasingly prosecuted. Penalties vary around the world. In New Zealand, it is punishable with up to two years in jail. In the US, executives have been jailed, and large fines are common. For example, Hoegh Fleet Services A/S, a Norwegian shipping company, was ordered to pay $3.5 million for intentionally dumping waste oil into the ocean.

3 *The polluting company is more vulnerable to changes in environmental legislation.* A government decision to tax energy, to ban landfill or to outlaw a polluting product could have a major effect on companies which produce carbon emissions or other waste, or make hazardous products.

4 *Polluters will increasingly find it difficult to get finance and insurance.* Banks are less keen to provide loans to companies which could make them liable for cleaning up after a pollution incident. In the US, for example, banks and insurance companies may be liable for pollution clean-up. Sustained criticism from pressure groups can lead to some financial institutions selling the company's stock, and other shareholders being less likely to support the board. In such cases, the company will find it less easy to raise money.

5 *The polluting firm will find it harder to attract and retain good staff.* Staff prefer not to work for a polluting firm. This is particularly prevalent among younger graduate staff. A survey carried out by the National Union of Students found that three-quarters of student job hunters would not work for a company with a poor ethical record and half those surveyed would take less pay to work for a company with a good history.

6 *A company that damages the environment can be attacked as being anti-social and uncaring.* Many companies have gained a bad image because of constant media reports about the environmental problems they caused. Pressure groups and journalists combine to attack the firm, which can result in consumers buying from competitors.

7 *The polluting company can find itself left behind by competitors which adopt greener products and processes.* Even without the pressures mentioned above, the polluting firm can lose out if it fails to develop a more environmentally sound approach. Companies like 3M are always looking for ways of gaining a competitive edge using environmentally superior technology. However, many companies still find it cheaper to produce emissions and (in the case of solid waste) dump it rather than invest in pollution control. Companies that adopt this strategy need to be alert to changes in legislation, taxation or other economic factors that would change the equation.

Equally, there are many advantages of improved environmental performance:

- lower costs – from less tax, less waste, less packaging, less energy use
- less risk: from bad pr or environmental catastrophe
- less likely to be targeted by environmentalists
- increased sales from improved reputation
- easier to recruit and retain staff.

Eight ways to pollute

There are eight ways that a company can cause environmental damage:

1 Emissions to air
2 Discharges to water
3 Solid waste
4 Owning (or acquiring) environmental damaging assets, especially contaminated land (some experts see this as merely the purchase of existing pollution, rather than a separate cause; but it is convenient to discuss it here as a separate issue)
5 Producing or using toxic or hazardous materials
6 Consuming fossil fuels or energy derived from them (that is, non-renewable energy sources)
7 Consuming scarce or non-renewable resources
8 Damage to nature (for example, by building projects), through destruction of natural habitats or amenity space.

In the following section we examine each in more detail.

EMISSIONS TO AIR

Air pollution comes from combustion - through industrial chimneys, cars, lorries and buses, and other engines. It also comes from the fumes in petrol stations, dry-cleaners, paints, and household products such as varnishes. Any plant that emits air pollution is at risk; for if a process goes wrong extra amounts of pollution can be emitted. This in turn may lead to prosecution and bad PR.

In recent years, major companies have substantially reduced their discharges to air. In the USA, according to the Climate Group (an environmental group), General Motors has reduced its greenhouse gas emissions by 72 per cent in 13 years. Dupont has cut its emissions by 69 per cent, and IBM has reduced its emissions by 65 per cent for the same period.

Ways to reduce air pollution and atmospheric emissions include the following:

- Switch to more fuel-efficient engines.
- Use renewable energies, such as bio fuels or solar power.
- Use less polluting fossil fuels, such as low-sulphur or methanol.
- Maintain engines and boilers better; improve route planning of fleets.
- Use thermostatic heating controls.
- Apply filters and scrubbers to clean emissions.
- Insulate buildings and pipes.
- Use vapour recovery systems.
- Use low volatile organic compound (VOC) paints and coatings.

DISCHARGES TO WATER

Forty years ago, residents of the city of Durham could tell by the colour of the river Wear what flavour the local toffee factory was producing. At that time, water pollution was accepted; today it is regarded as socially deplorable. Most companies have now substantially reduced their water pollution. River water downstream of a Volkswagen factory is actually cleaner than the water upstream. The factory returns waste water to the river in a cleaner condition than when it was extracted.

Society values clean waterways, and dead fish or a river foaming with chemicals is an affront. Companies which pollute water courses will find increasing restrictions placed upon them in the future. A typical case was when thousands of fish died when caustic soda was spilt into the unspoilt river Ellen in Britain's Lake District. Experts reckoned that the polluted water, which could blister the skin, would damage kingfishers, otters and other important wildlife. Investigators linked the incident to a Dairy Crest creamery, where the chemical is used to clean milk vats. For the firm, embarrassing nationwide publicity could be merely the start of its problems.

Here are some ways to reduce water pollution:

- Limit the use of cleaning materials and pesticides.
- Use less chemical fertilizer in landscape maintenance.
- Filter and treat effluent before it reaches the drains or watercourses.
- Adopt cleaner processes.
- Use biodegradable and less toxic cleaning fluids. For example, instead of using a commercial drain cleaning fluid, you can use a plunger, followed by a mix of half a cup of baking soda, half a cup of vinegar, and eight cups of boiling water.

- Introduce spill control measures, including bunding (watertight surrounds for oil tanks) and above-ground oil storage (that enable visual inspection of leaks and corrosion).
- Use of overflow alarms for storage tanks.
- Replace solvent cleaners with aqueous ones.

Reducing water usage is not strictly speaking a business risk issue, though it is good practice in areas of water shortage. You can reduce water use by means of the following:

- Use percussion taps that turn themselves off (a tap that's left running wastes 10 litres of water per minute, or 14 400 litres a day).
- Repair leaks.
- Use high-pressure, low-volume cleaners.
- Reduce the water pressure in taps.
- Reduce the amount of water used in processing.

SOLID WASTE

The cost of solid waste disposal is likely to grow. Politicians are agreed that solid waste is a bad thing, particularly as its disposal to landfill can lead to explosive gas being created. It is therefore likely that the production of solid waste will be restricted by taxing it, or by passing laws which reduce the company's flexibility in waste disposal.

Companies with a substantial amount of waste will therefore find that the cost of their products will rise. The sensible business will find ways of reducing waste, either through substitution of raw materials, better housekeeping, or recycling.

TACKLE THE MAJOR ISSUES

Business should distinguish between relevant environmental activities, and those that are 'greenwash'. Recycling plastic cups in a major corporation will not reduce the company's pollution. In some cases, the energy and monetary cost of collecting, cleaning and recycling used material is higher than making the product from new. However, many valuable commodities can be recycled including glass, most metals, batteries, tyres and plastics.

CONTAMINATED LAND

The UK's Environment Agency estimates that there are between 5000 and 20 000 contaminated sites in England and Wales. Many of these sites may require decontamination in future years as the government looks to eliminate the risks they pose and also reach its target of 60 per cent of new housing built on brownfield sites. Therefore businesses that purchase land must remain vigilant.

When property developer Mountleigh bought a development site, it had no idea of the problems that would ensue. Various potential purchasers carried out site surveys and discovered that the land was contaminated. All decided against going ahead. The land value was finally reckoned to be worth £35 million less than Mountleigh had estimated, and the company went into liquidation.

Even government bodies are not free from risk. The Ministry of Defence is one of the UK's biggest landowners. Over the years various processes have taken place on its land, ranging from weapons testing to vehicle maintenance. Partly because of the scale of its ownership, the Ministry lacks a complete record of the contamination. Like any landowner, the Ministry wants to know the extent of contamination so that it can carry out remedial works, especially as government regulations on contaminated land are likely to become progressively more stringent. In other words, remedial works are likely to become more costly.

The business can undertake the following measures:

* Conduct a site assessment.
* Establish the scale of contamination, if any.
* Implement a plan to reduce the contamination and improve the ecological value of the land.

USE OF TOXIC MATERIALS

Unless handled carefully, toxic materials will not only endanger the workforce but could also escape into the drains and rivers where they kill fish and get into the food chain. Regulatory authorities are increasingly hostile to companies that create such problems. The most dangerous materials are shown in Table 7.1. EU nation states have to stop discharging these substances, and other nations have similar lists.

Table 7.1   EU list 1 dangerous substances

Cadmium	Mercury	Lindane (hexachlorocyclohexane)
Pentachlorophenol	DDT	Carbon tetrachloride
Chloroform	Hexachlorobenzene	Hexachlorobutadiene
Dieldrin	Aldrin	Isodrin
Endrin	1,2-dichloroethane	Trichloroethylene
Perchloroethylene	Trichlorobenzene	

Where the business sells toxic materials to the consumer there is an added risk of product liability. Some harmful substances have been found to be carcinogens in the long term, and this can have a devastating or even terminal effect on the company's profitability.

> A defence contractor found nuclear radiation in the grounds of one of its manufacturing sites. It discovered that the radiation came from World War Two aircraft dials lying just under the grass. The company's staff had painted luminous dials by hand on aircraft instruments, and had thrown faulty dials out of the window (quality control being less scientific than it is now). As a result, the site was still emitting nuclear radiation. This is an example of unforeseen hazards which leave the company with a liability.

Useful actions include the following:

* Substitute less powerful substances wherever possible.
* Modify or eliminate environmentally damaging raw materials, processes and products.
* Use more recycled and recyclable raw materials.

If none of these solutions work, consider exiting from such markets. The loss of short-term profits will be softened by the lack of corporate blame in the longer term. If the product is not part of the company's core business, you could cease producing the product, or sell the assets to another firm. If the product is central to the company, the problem is less easy to solve.

CONSUMPTION OF ENERGY

Smoking power stations and factory chimneys are visible targets for protesters, but for the ordinary company the use of energy is not particularly visible. Apart from major energy users such as foundries, the cost savings can sometimes be slight. However, as energy costs rise, companies need to see where they can cut energy consumption. Solutions include the following:

- Improve insulation and draught-proofing.
- Using energy-efficient lighting and equipment, including timed switches and motion sensors.
- Improve boiler efficiency.
- Reduce excessive use of air conditioning.
- Increase the use of energy management systems.
- Conduct an energy audit, with the aim of cutting energy use.
- Turn down space heating and hot water thermostats.

USE OF SCARCE OR NON-RENEWABLE RESOURCES

The extraction of rainforest timber and even quarried stone have become major environmental issues. Conservationists can easily brand a company which uses scarce materials as a corporate vandal. There are often substitutes which the company can use, and such substitutes pre-empt the company from law suits and protesters at its gates. This kind of threat emphasizes the need for companies to ensure that they have proper *systems for protecting the environment*. These systems need to be documented, to ensure that they are implemented and as insurance against future litigation.

Between 1964 and 1992, Texaco sought oil in eastern Ecuador, during which time 17 million gallons of oil escaped into local water supplies. In comparison, the Exxon Valdez disaster involved 11 million gallons. The native peoples of the region brought a billion-dollar suit against Texaco but lack of support from their own government meant that only $5–10 million was offered in compensation.

Ensuring that the local population gets benefits from the activity will substantially reduce opposition. The UK's Sellafield nuclear plant, while controversial nationally, is locally supported because of the massive employment it creates. Local support does not, however, mitigate the risks.

The business should adopt the following measures:

- Audit its use of scarce or non-renewable materials.
- Substitute with materials that have less environmental impact.
- Reduce overall use of materials (for example, through lightweighting or waste reduction).

DAMAGE TO NATURE

Mining and quarrying companies, developers, construction companies, and even super-market chains are likely to build on greenfield sites. The same applies to petrochemical companies as they explore for and then extract oil and gas. The destruction of natural beauty is an obvious and easy target for conservationists, and some companies have been paraded on television news for several years as they battle to develop a site.

In order to minimize damage to nature, the environmentally aware company will take the following steps:

- Work on brownfield (urban, developed and possibly run-down) land.
- Carry out an environmental impact assessment (EIA).
- Introduce mitigating environmental measures (such as maintaining habitats).
- Engage in a full consultation process with stakeholders.

However, customers often prefer not to live or shop in brownfield sites, which is one of the inherent conflicts in planning land use.

Eight changes that will create environmental risk for some businesses – and opportunities for others

What will the future be like? In this section we examine the changes that are likely to happen.

INCREASED ENERGY COSTS

Several factors are likely to push up the cost of energy. Governments and the EU are likely to seek reduced energy usage in order to reduce airborne pollution and global warming. Governments will also see it as a legitimate way of taxing less efficient companies. Oil will also have to be extracted in less favourable locations. The net result will be a rising cost of energy.

WASTE DISPOSAL

Landfill will be much reduced. European governments will require firms to recycle, incinerate or microwave its waste. Incineration is a more expensive process than tipping, especially as greater controls will be placed on incinerators to ensure that they do not produce atmospheric pollution.

PHYSICAL DISTRIBUTION

As car ownership increases, city centres will increasingly become polluted and gridlocked. As a result, city centres will become increasingly less efficient and pleasant places to work. Physical communications will become more costly and difficult, and deliveries will take longer.

Municipal authorities will take action against cars in order to make the air cleaner and to keep their cities moving. This will include curbs on vehicle access to city centres, as has happened in cities such as London, Athens and Hamburg. Companies will have to make choices about the location of their premises and the way they distribute their products.

LITIGATION AGAINST CORPORATE POLLUTERS

Regulatory authorities will have increasingly sophisticated monitoring devices in place (for example, in rivers), which will detect whether a company is causing pollution. Legal action will become an automatic response, especially if governments see this as a legitimate source of revenue. Few taxpayers will complain if the government prosecutes polluters. Fines and jail sentences will become heavier and more frequent, as pollution becomes less socially acceptable. Directors will be held liable.

SUPPLIERS' ENVIRONMENTAL PROBITY

Corporate customers will want to avoid liability for environment damage. As a result, they will demand evidence of good environmental practice from their suppliers. Customers will increasingly issue questionnaires which will be used to determine the choice of suppliers. They will also undertake audits of the supplier, and will demand evidence of management systems such as BS 7750 and EMAS (the EU's environmental management and audit system).

TOXIC OR HAZARDOUS RAW MATERIALS

Legislators will ban dangerous products. Assessment of product safety will be more public than in the past, so research methods and findings will be available to the public and to pressure groups. Some products now in common use will be no longer available for sale.

ECO-LABELLING

In future, consumers will have more comparative information about the products they buy. This will apply to a varied range of products. Companies will no longer be able to hide behind witty but spurious advertising; and businesses with environmentally superior products will have an advantage.

PRESSURE GROUPS

Pressure groups have become adept at blocking outflow pipes, hoisting protest banners from tall chimneys, and immobilizing contractors' vehicles. Companies will find that pressure groups such as Greenpeace will adopt more sophisticated tactics, such as hacking into corporate files, infiltrating companies by seeking employment, and using the annual meeting to publicize their case. Companies that don't relish a fight will aim to avoid controversial products and processes.

BALANCING IMPACT AND BENEFITS

Though brominated fire retardants are thought to accumulate in the body and pose a risk to health, Greenpeace and the chemical industry have agreed to join cause and support their continued use. Both the protest group and the Chemical Industry Association agree that their use on furniture and clothing prevents fire and thus saves lives. And thus their usefulness outweighs the risk they pose. Greenpeace believes that some hazardous substances should remain on the market while the industry researches safer alternatives. This suggests that dialogue can lead to common-sense solutions, and that risk must be weighed against usefulness.

Does being green give a company an advantage?

Green issues are now established headline issues across the western world. A DEFRA survey in 2001 found that when asked whether 'prices and jobs are more important than protecting the environment for the future', 55 per cent disagreed and only 30 per cent agreed. It was also found that 20 per cent of people regularly buy organic foods, despite the higher costs.

In short, consumers continue to be concerned about the environment. But do these attitudes really affect purchase behaviour? Will the consumer (or the corporate buyer) prefer to buy from a green supplier? Some markets are more environmentally sensitive than others. Some consumers buy toilet paper made from recycled fibres out of concern for the environment. But others do so because the product is cheaper than luxury non-recycled toilet tissue. So the price and performance of products that claim environmental superiority should at least match that of traditional products.

Consumers will become hostile to companies which are revealed to disregard the environment. This could have a long-lasting effect on the corporate brand image and therefore sales.

Strategies for reducing environmental risk

There are ways to avoid these risks. This involves the action shown in Figure 7.1.

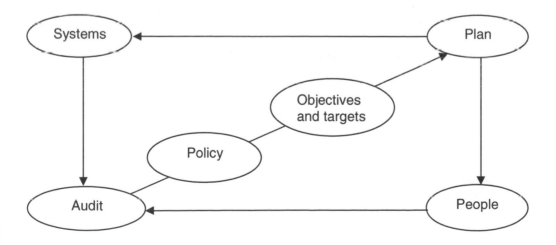

Figure 7.1   Action to prevent environmental risk

CARRY OUT AN ENVIRONMENTAL AUDIT

The environmental audit is a tool for finding out the extent of the company's impacts (sometimes called 'environmental aspects'). It should bring together all relevant information about the way the company affects the environment. By carrying out an environmental audit, companies can assess the environmental risks associated with each of its divisions. It lets the corporation determine whether any division is likely to cause an environmental problem.

Someone who is independent of the activity being audited should conduct the audit. In other words, production managers should not audit their own factories.

Measuring impacts

Companies keep lots of financial and production information, but many have little environmental data. This is because in the past the environment was not seen to affect the business, and nor was it a cost. Things have changed; and companies need to start collecting environmental data. But it isn't easy. RTZ, the mining company, found that all over the world its mines used different measures, and had different production methods. Trying to harmonize the data was not easy. But recognizing the problem and identifying the goal is a good starting point.

It is also important to standardize the measurements. The amount of pollution will grow if production rises, so the company should adopt a measure such as 'kilowatts of energy per tonne of output'.

DEFINE A POLICY ON ENVIRONMENT ISSUES

Once management has information, it can make informed decisions about its impacts. The company can decide to become an environmental Leader (a company against which others measure their progress), or a Conformer (a company which simply obeys all statutory obligations). See Figure 7.2.

It should avoid being a Laggard (a company which falls below the environmental standards set by the rest of its industry), or Punished (that is, a Laggard which continues to take no action, and eventually loses customers to other businesses or is taken to court by regulatory authorities).

To communicate its environmental stance, the business should produce a policy outlining its attitude towards green issues.

The Co-operative Bank's ethical policy includes its policy on ecological impact, animal welfare, genetic modification and other topics. The bank declares that it will not invest in any business whose core activity contributes to:

- global climate change, through the extraction or production of fossil fuels
- the manufacture of chemicals which are persistent in the environment and linked to long-term health concerns
- the unsustainable harvest of natural resources, including timber and fish.

And it will seek to support businesses involved in:

- recycling and sustainable waste management
- renewable energy and energy efficiency

- sustainable natural products and services, including timber and organic produce
- the pursuit of ecological sustainability.

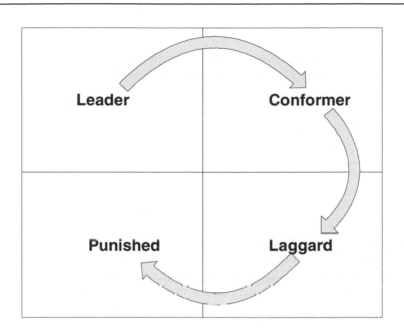

A Leader is committed to being foremost in its field. A Conformer aims to obey the law, but doesn't seek environmental excellence.

Leaders that rest on their laurels become Conformers, as the rest of industry catches up. Similarly, Conformers can slip into the Laggard category, and Laggards can easily become Punished.

The reverse is also true. Punished companies can become Leaders in response to an environmental crisis. One such example is Shell, which changed course following criticism over its plan to sink the Brent Spar platform in the Atlantic, and criticism over its damage to Ogoni lands in Nigeria.

Figure 7.2   The green grid

SET OBJECTIVES AND TARGETS

Next, the company needs to quantify its policy statement. It can do this by producing an annual target for reducing its solid waste or for reducing the biochemical oxygen demand (BOD) level of its waste water. Setting targets allows the business to determine whether it is achieving change.

PRODUCE A MANAGEMENT PLAN WHICH WILL MEET THE TARGETS

Targets do not in themselves produce results. So the company needs a plan. This might include investing in a water treatment plant or undertaking a study to reduce the company's solid waste.

It is important to select the right action to take. Some companies cherry pick their environmental actions. One UK electricity company boasted that it had given £200 to a wildlife charity, and had sponsored a children's painting competition. Meanwhile it was bulldozing areas of outstanding natural beauty, evicting wildlife and disfiguring the countryside with its pylons. Such behaviour is risky because its acts of charity may be seen as mere window-dressing.

Businesses should take action on the most important impacts. An agricultural business found that water pollution was its major impact, and installed a water treatment plant. Other, less rigorous, firms might have chosen instead a less significant problem, such as recycling old packaging.

INTRODUCE AN ENVIRONMENTAL MANAGEMENT SYSTEM

An environmental management system (EMS) includes the topics mentioned throughout this section. It also includes writing procedures for all processes that impact on the environment. Providing these procedures are followed, there is less chance of environmental damage.

ISO 14000 is the best-known environmental management system. It helps to ensure that the business understands and controls its environmental impacts in a systematic and comprehensive way. The standard was developed from BS 7750 (the original British environmental management standard), which in turn was developed from BS 5750, the quality standard. They all share a common style. This means that any company which has ISO 9000 is already half way towards getting ISO 14000.

ISO 14000 requires a company to produce a register of significant environmental 'aspects'. These are activities, products or services that interact with the environment. An aspect might cause an environmental impact. A sample blank register is shown as Table 7.2. The chart summarizes the company's environmental impacts in a simple way. This aids clarity of thought, and helps the business focus on the major effects. It also serves as an environmental risk analysis. Where the business does not have one of the effects listed here, the auditor can state in the relevant box that it is 'not applicable'.

The European Union's eco-management and audit system (EMAS) is similar to ISO 14000. Since it began in 1995, 3073 companies have registered with EMAS, 54 per cent of them in Germany.

For businesses that are reluctant to implement a complete EMS, there is another option: BS 8555. This standard is aimed largely at small and medium-sized enterprises (SMEs) but is applicable to organizations of any size, and all types of business activity. It lets the business develop its EMS over time in six separate stages, and demonstrates to interested parties that the company is making progress on its environmental impacts. BS 8555 can be useful in demonstrating the company's environmental probity to large customers.

INVOLVE PEOPLE

The company must ensure that all its staff are motivated to manage the company's environmental impacts. This means undertaking a period of consultation, and delegating action to the lowest appropriate level.

The company also has to manage its external communications. Corporate customers are increasingly asking their suppliers to show how they are managing their environmental impacts. The media, pressure groups and local residents are also keenly interested in a company's environmental activity. To respond to these questions, you will need:

Table 7.2 Register of significant aspects

	Current activities			Future planned activities	Past activities
	Normal operating conditions	Abnormal operating conditions*	Incidents, accidents, and emergencies		
Emissions to air					
Discharges to water					
Solid waste					
Toxic materials					
Energy use					
Scarce or non-renewable material					
Damage to nature (incl. contaminated land)					
Noise					
Odour					
Dust					
Visual impact					
Other impacts (list)					

*Including start-up and shut-down activities

- environmental policy
- printed information about the company's successes
- environmental plan (this should show the steps you are taking to manage the environment).

Supplier assessment

Life-cycle analysis is an important concept in environmental management. It means being aware of all your product's impacts, from cradle to grave. For example, an environmental consultancy gives a plaque to clients that gain the quality standard ISO 14000. It discovered that the plaque caused several environmental problems. The engraving process used polluting acids, and the plaque was mounted on a tropical hardwood base. The company switched to a pine plaque which was not only better for the environment but was also a lot less expensive.

The starting point for any life-cycle analysis is a supplier questionnaire. This asks suppliers to state the ingredients or composition of the raw material, and the nature of environmental impacts involved. Most suppliers will respond positively to this request for information. A few suppliers will not; and they may need to be replaced. B&Q, the DIY chain, has de-listed many suppliers who failed to enter a dialogue about the environment.

Choosing environmentally sound suppliers is important because environmentally aware suppliers are likely to be low-risk suppliers. A supplier that responds positively to the environmental challenge is likely to be concerned about its other challenges, including quality, health and safety, and customer service.

Companies should categorize their supplies into high, medium and low risk. They should then seek to substitute their high-risk purchases. This may involve working with other departments, especially production.

Many companies report difficulty in finding out where responsibility rests. A product has often been processed by several companies in turn. For example, a food processor that buys a puree has a supplier chain which stretches from a farmer who sprays the fruit with pesticide, to a local processor which pulps the fruit, before it reaches a third company which mixes it with other ingredients.

Is environmental conformance a threat?

Some businesses fear that the cost of environmental protection is excessive and therefore threatening. Such companies can take a hard-nosed approach to environmental protection by adopting the following steps:

1 Gather information about the company's environmental impacts, and quantify them.
2 Assess the environmental gains against the cost savings.
3 Rank the most profitable measures.
4 Implement low-cost and no-cost measures. They will bring an immediate return.
5 Plan for higher-cost measures in the longer term (for example, replacing a boiler with a more efficient system).
6 Seek innovative solutions which replace environmental hazards with cheap and safe solutions.
7 Pass the costs of pollution control on to the customer.

Animal rights

Animal cruelty will continue to be a topic for protesters. The issue occurs in many different markets, especially agriculture, food processing, cosmetics and toiletries, and drug development. The two main issues are

1 The use of animals in research.
2 The treatment of animals raised for food or for their skin.

Many toiletries companies use cruelty-free products as a selling point.

ANIMAL RIGHTS – SOLUTIONS

Companies should pre-empt the threat of animal cruelty by *avoiding animal testing* where possible. In many markets where animal testing was thought to be essential, alternative methods have been found. Where the use of animals is central to the product (such as chicken farming), the company needs to ensure *good husbandry*. Cage sizes for battery hens are now thought by many academic researchers to be too small, and even a modest increase would result in improved conditions. The company should have an animal welfare policy, backed up by effective documentation and procedures.

Good communications are also essential. Some companies become the focus of protest because they come to symbolize all that is wrong with animal treatment. To prevent this, the company should maintain a visible local presence. A dialogue with local environmental groups may help to reduce the threat.

In the USA, the FBI regards ecological and animal-rights extremists as the country's leading domestic terror threat, and it believes the pharmaceutical and biotech industry is at risk from increasingly violent activists. Yet those industries have not handled this as a strategic issue, says Phil Celestini, FBI special agent supervising operations against animal and ecological extremists. 'There is a certain amount of denial going on. But until the issue is addressed, it won't go away.'

In addition to harassing and intimidating employees and directors of these businesses, activists now target businesses that have business or financial relationships with the primary target. This means that the most mundane office-cleaning business is at risk.

Useful links

BS 8555
www.bsi-global.com/environmental

Business in the Community – Environmental index
www.bitc.org.uk/environment

CIS
www.cis.co.uk

EMAS
http://europa.eu.int/comm/environment/

Global Environmental Management Initiative
www.gemi.org

ISO 14000
www.iso.org

SustainAbility
www.sustainability.com

World Resources Institute
www.wri.org

Risk assessment – environment

Use this chart to determine the scale of your environmental risk. Tick any boxes which apply to your business.

Topic	Question	
Resources	Does the business consume scarce or non-renewable resources (such as rainforest timber)?	☐
Hazardous materials	Does the company make or use hazardous or toxic materials?	☐
Solid waste	Does the business produce substantial solid waste?	☐
Air pollution	Does the company produce substantial air pollution?	☐
Water pollution	Does the business discharge polluted waste water?	☐
Energy	Does the company consume large amounts of energy?	☐
Land use	Does the business damage nature (for example, through construction projects)?	☐
	Is the company acquiring, or does it own, contaminated land?	☐
Policy	Does the business lack an environmental policy?	☐
Corporate image	Has the company been criticized by environmentalists in the last 12 months?	☐

Total points scored

Score: 0–3 points: low risk. 4–6 points: moderate risk. 7–10 points: high risk.

The appendix contains a summary of all the checklists in this book. By entering the results of this one, you can compare the scale of environmental risk against other categories.

8 *Protecting Against Fire*

In this chapter we examine how to develop a fire risk strategy. We consider the risk from:

- *Electrical fires*
- *Hot work*
- *Machinery*
- *Smoking*
- *Flammable liquids*
- *Bad housekeeping*
- *Arson.*

We then look at how these risks can be minimized.

Fire as a commercial risk

Fire is one of the most common commercial risks. Most companies think they are well protected, and most believe that fire could never happen to them. Yet 70 per cent of businesses involved in a major fire either do not reopen or fail within three years of the fire. Moreover, fires occur not just in chemical plants, but in ordinary places such as textile factories as well.

Fire is a major problem in the workplace. According to the Association of British Insurers, fire claims represent nearly 60 per cent of commercial insurance claims. In 2001, businesses claimed £679 million for fire damage.

According to Chubb, the majority of workplace fires that are put out by a fire extinguisher start accidentally (see Table 8.1). However, data from the fire service shows arson to be a much bigger source of fires, causing around half of all non-domestic fires. That is because the fire service attends bigger fires, many of which are at night, and of which arson is more likely to be the cause.

By contrast, commercial fires that are put out by an extinguisher are more likely to occur by accident, happen during the day, be spotted more quickly, and therefore be smaller.

Designing a fire risk strategy

As Figure 8.1 shows, a fire risk strategy starts with a fire survey, which should be carried out at regular intervals. This will identify the most likely causes of fire, and indicate how to prevent them. The audit should cover all areas of the building, including production facilities, offices, storage areas, basements and roof spaces. Fires often start in unlikely places because those are the areas where fire safety has been overlooked.

Table 8.1   Causes of fires put out by fire extinguisher

Fires by industry	% of total fires	% started accidentally	% unknown cause	% due to arson
Hospitality and leisure	25	79	15	6
Manufacturing	18	83	17	–
Retail	15	83	14	3
Transport/ distribution	13	80	20	–

Source: Chubb

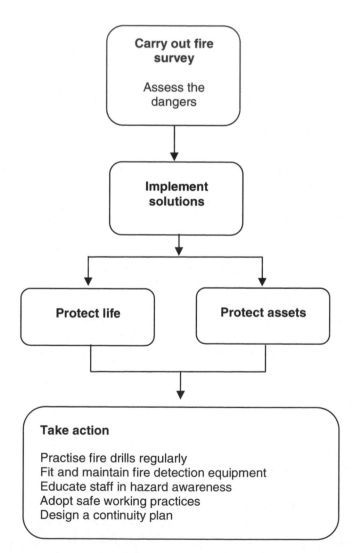

Figure 8.1   Fire risk strategy

In assessing the risks of fire, the auditor should look for examples of the main causes of fire, such as electrical hazards, hot work, smoking, flammable liquids, and the threat of arson.

ELECTRICAL HAZARDS

As many as one in three electrical fires take place in the office. Overloaded circuits are an increasing problem as companies buy additional printers and computers. Electrical fires can also start when circuits overheat, having been wired wrongly or overloaded. Wiring is usually installed properly, but may then be modified by a self-taught amateur. Over a period, a factory's wiring may become full of spurs, transformers become overburdened, and inadequately sized wiring is introduced. A lack of socket outlets often results in the use of adapters, which can overheat and cause a fire.

Good practice involves using qualified electricians, and planning electrical installations properly. It is also useful to conduct an electrical audit, to check for unsafe and overburdened wiring.

HOT WORK

Fires caused by hot work often come from unexpected sources. The painter who burns old paint from a door, and the plumber who tries to thaw a frozen pipe, are just as likely to cause a fire as a welding or cutting operation. Staff may take short cuts when doing a job, and procedures may not be followed.

Good housekeeping is essential for hot work. The work should be supervised, and the area should be checked for four hours afterwards. The company should avoid using radiant and portable heaters if possible. Hot pipes or lamps should not come into contact with combustible material such as paper or fabric.

MACHINERY

Machinery should be regularly serviced, and kept properly lubricated. Vents should be kept clear to prevent overheating. Oil leaks and drips should be absorbed using mineral absorbents, not sawdust; drip trays should be used where necessary and emptied regularly.

Hot equipment such as pressing or soldering irons should be switched off immediately after work, and placed on rests – not on the work surface.

SMOKING

Most UK companies have now banned smoking, not just from factories but from offices as well. Health risks were the prime motive among many but the reduced fire risk is a benefit - the Home Office estimates that 12 per cent of accidental workplace fires are caused by smoking.

At the very least, smoking should be banned from any area where combustible materials are present, for example in storage areas where fire can quickly take hold and rapidly spread.

FLAMMABLE LIQUIDS

Solvents are a major hazard, causing nearly half of all fires started by flammable liquid. The flammability of solvents is not always recognized, and cleaning fluids are often kept in opened drums which are moved around the plant.

Flammable liquids should be stored in enclosed metal containers, and drip trays should be used. A stringent 'no naked lights' policy should be placed in their vicinity.

Liquefied petroleum gas (LPG) cylinders are a fire hazard, and should be stored safely, as should other compressed gases such as propane and butane. They should be kept outdoors in a fenced container, with prominent notices prohibiting smoking and naked lights.

BAD HOUSEKEEPING

Rubbish should not be allowed to accumulate, especially in boiler rooms, under stairs, basements or store rooms. Fire exits should not be obstructed. In offices, piles of computer printouts and sheaves of paper tend to litter executives' desks after they have gone home for the night: a clear desk policy can reduce the risks.

Combustible waste should be kept to a minimum, and it should be caged: old pallets are often targeted by vandals. Ensure good work practices.

There should be a procedure for *closing down the premises when work finishes*. All non-essential electrical equipment should be unplugged, including computers and heaters. Fire doors should be closed.

ARSON

In the UK, arson is responsible for 45 per cent of fires in commercial buildings costing an estimated £300 million. In the USA it represents 25 per cent of fire losses by value, and in Europe the level of arson is growing.

Much arson is either an attempt to conceal a crime, or stems from a personnel dispute. A company with a labour dispute, layoffs or poor industrial relations is more likely to suffer arson. Other likely targets are empty buildings, and political targets (such as oil companies).

Companies can beat arson by ensuring that fire protection systems (including sprinklers and alarms) are tested regularly. Improved security is also important. Staff should not be allowed to wander around sensitive parts of the site, and perimeter security should be enforced (see Chapter 9).

FIRE PRECAUTIONS

The most important part of fire precautions is to *protect life*. The emphasis should be on evacuating the building. Companies should ensure that staff know the emergency procedure. Fire drills should be held regularly, and fire officers appointed. The firm should make sure that the building can be quickly evacuated and personnel accounted for. Staff must be trained to be aware of fire risks, such as overloaded electrical circuits.

The next task is to *minimize the threat to the building*, plant, equipment and materials. Fire detection equipment, such as alarms and sprinklers, should be installed as well as extinguishers. *Automatic fire detection* (AFD), which uses sprinklers, is the preferred choice in buildings where many people work or live. Sprinklers must be maintained, while smoke detectors are essential in buildings which do not have AFD.

GETTING OUT SAFELY

Emergency signs (showing the way to the fire exit) should be clear and consistent. In an emergency, misleading signs could lead to death.

Fire exits should be free from obstructions, such as potted plants, furniture or storage. If fire starts, people need to be able to escape easily. Fire doors should not be propped open – this will speed the path of a fire. People wedge doors open to stop them slamming; yet the noise can be reduced by altering the closure and latch. In other cases, doors are propped open to improve air circulation; but proper ventilation will improve the atmosphere.

To delay the spread of fire, the company can introduce *fire-rated construction materials*. For example, some wall panels give an hour's protection against fire. Separating office and production workers from warehousing is one example. Escape routes should be constructed from non-flammable materials.

CASE HISTORY: WHO ATTACKED RIVERSIDE OFFICE SUPPLIES?

According to police forensic experts, the fire that destroyed the premises of Riverside Office Supplies had been started deliberately. Someone had cut a neat hole in a window, having first applied sticky plastic to prevent noise. Then they had poured petrol into a waste bin and dropped a match into it. They had even tinkered with the engine of a van parked inside the loading bay, to make it look as though an electrical fault had started the fire.

Riverside Office Supplies was not the obvious target of an arson attack, yet someone wanted to stop the five-month-old company before it became too big.

An office supplies company stocks a lot of paper, so the blaze was all-engulfing and completely destroyed the premises. Apart from the stock, the fire also destroyed the computers and all the company's records.

Just one thing saved Riverside Office Supplies. June Rathmell, the Managing Director, had made a back-up copy of her computer records and taken it home with her that night. She could find out who had ordered goods, and who owed the company

money. Without this single fragile disc, the company would never have continued trading.

'At 7pm on the Friday night, I was pretty tired,' said June. 'I wasn't going to bother with the back-up. But I told myself not to break the habit of a lifetime, and it was lucky I didn't. Many firms take back-ups, but they leave them in the same premises. You have to take the back-up with you.'

Many companies which suffer fire never trade again. Despite June's precautions, Riverside Office Supplies found it difficult to get started again. On the following Monday, June began to trade again from her living room, but sales fell dramatically. Customers believed that the company had stopped trading because its premises had gone.

The insurance took ten months to pay out, largely due to hold-ups with the neighbouring firm's insurance company.

This case history demonstrates the importance of backing-up computer information, and keeping it off the premises, as a precaution against fire.

Minimizing the effects of fire

The company should decide what it needs to keep the business operational. It may be computer records, certain equipment, or specific raw materials. The firm should then take steps to safeguard them. It might need to take back-up copies of computer data, and store them in fire-proof safes. Certain products may need to be stored in more than one warehouse. Some equipment might have to be protected by sprinklers. The company should also check whether it could sub-contract work to a competitor, or another part of the group, while the business gets operational again.

Liaising with the fire service is always beneficial. Plans showing the location of emergency exits, sprinkler system control valves and gas lines should be provided for the fire service, and be kept away from the main building.

AFTER A FIRE

Around 60 per cent of every insurance premium goes to cover the cost of rectifying water damage. Thousands of gallons of fire fighting water are used to bring a commercial fire under control, leaving the insurers and the occupiers with a big problem. The sooner that dryers can be brought into a building, the more likely it is that capital equipment on site can be saved and the fabric of the building preserved. Storing goods away from the floor also helps to minimise water damage. In Chapter 16 we look at the steps to take after a crisis like a fire.

Useful links

Chubb
www.chubb.co.uk/fire

Fire Protection Association (UK)
www.thefpa.co.uk

National Fire Protection Association (USA)
www.nfpa.org

Risk assessment – fire

You can assess your vulnerability to fire by answering the questions below. Score one point for each box ticked.

Topic	Question	
Type of work	Does the company use combustible materials?	☐
	Does the company carry out flammable work?	☐
Track record	Has the company suffered from arson in the last two years?	☐
Fire alarms	Does the company lack an automatic fire detection and alarm system?	☐
Sprinklers	Does the company lack sprinklers?	☐
Escape routes	Are escape routes combustible?	☐
Age of occupants	Are occupants aged under 5 or over 70?	☐
Experience	Have some occupants not participated in a recent fire drill?	☐
Familiarity	Are occupants unfamiliar with the building (for example, hotel guests)?	☐
Alertness of occupants	Are occupants asleep or not alert (for example, watching television)?	☐
Total points scored		

Score: 0–3 points: low risk. 4–6 points: moderate risk. 7–10 points: high risk.

The appendix contains a summary of all the checklists in this book. By entering the results of this one, you can compare the risk of fire against other categories of risk.

9 *Maintaining Security*

In this chapter, we consider the precautions needed to:

- *Safeguard buildings and stock*
- *Prevent unauthorized people from seeing paperwork and computer information*
- *Thwart industrial espionage*
- *Avoid tampering, kidnap, ransom and terrorist attack, and how to respond if it happens*
- *Deal with extortion.*

What are security risks and what damage can they cause?

For all kinds of companies, security is a complex issue. The assets to be protected now include computer data and intellectual property. A company's buildings, stock, staff and assets are all at risk from thieves, vandals or even extortionists. Some organizations can easily achieve tight security. But others, such as hospitals, have to be accessible to the public, and are often regarded as free supermarkets by thieves who routinely walk away with handbags and computers.

For companies with a high profile or overseas operations, security can be a life and death matter, with kidnap and ransom being a real possibility.

Conducting a security review

The security process starts with a security review. This entails checking the current security arrangements, and assessing the areas of vulnerability. This will take into account the issues shown in Table 9.1 (which are discussed further in this chapter):

DEVISING A SECURITY STRATEGY

Once you have completed the security review, you can devise a security strategy. Every set of premises is different, so each company needs an individual strategy. The strategy should operate at several levels, as shown in Figure 9.1.

1 The outermost level is the perimeter, together with the entrances to it.
2 Within that is the clear zone, the area between fence and buildings.
3 The third area is the windows and doors of the building.
4 Once inside the building, you may want high security exclusion zones.
5 Within these zones, you may need to secure individual items of equipment, material or information.

Table 9.1   Security review

In a security review, include all relevant information under the following headings:

- Past incidents; history of break-ins and losses
- Building location, type of perimeter, type of premises, attractiveness to criminals, and likely method of theft
- External and internal security
- Assets which could be stolen or damaged
- Control of access for employees, visitors and unauthorized people; parking
- Guards, radio contact and internal communications
- Alarms, closed-circuit TV
- Fire and emergency planning
- Management systems and procedures
- Recruitment processes
- Business partners: suppliers, agents and customers
- Company structure and personnel.

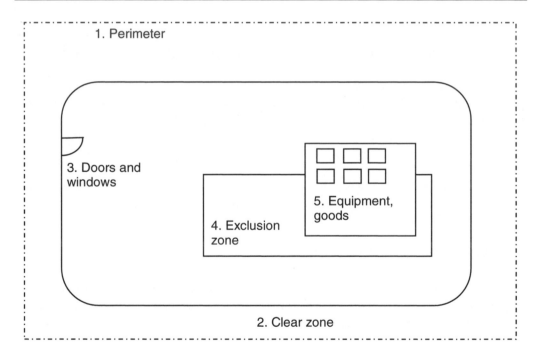

Figure 9.1   The five security zones

MATCHING SECURITY TO THE THREAT

The extent of security must reflect the degree of risk. A company which stocks large amounts of desirable merchandise, or which has a commercially sensitive R&D laboratory, needs tighter security than an office which simply processes information. However, even offices have large numbers of computers which are attractive to thieves; and the loss of their data could cause a major disaster.

The techniques for protecting your premises and goods involve an ascending order of action, each representing an additional barrier to be overcome. As Figure 9.2 shows, they are as follows:

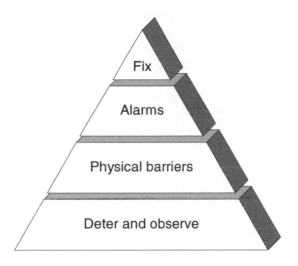

Figure 9.2 The four elements of a security strategy

1 Dissuade people from illegally entering the premises, by notices and presence of cameras and security staff.
2 Make it physically difficult to enter, by means of fences and locks. This element of the strategy can be applied all the way from the bolt on the perimeter fence to the lock on a filing cabinet.
3 Announce illegal entry by alarms or lights.
4 Make it difficult to remove items by physically securing them.

Not all four elements are always needed. Each represents an additional obstacle for the criminal.

SECURING THE PERIMETER

The first security zone is the business perimeter. The premises may be surrounded by lawn, vegetation or trees, or they may be restricted to the building itself.

The company will have to balance security risks against the needs of employees and suppliers to enter the building. People need to get in and out of your premises without undue difficulty, and without employees feeling that they are under undue observation.

The perimeter should be protected by a fence. This should be high enough to prevent casual burglars from getting over it. A chain link fence is better than a masonry wall, which gives cover to intruders. Companies gain extra security by adding razor wire or barbed wire, angled outwards at the top. A masonry wall can be embedded with broken glass. However, these additions make the business look like a prison.

One organization in special need of security is MI6, the British secret service. It moved to new buildings in the centre of London, where the arrival and departure of staff and visitors can now be observed by passers-by. Its building is also overlooked by other office blocks.

MANAGING THE PERIMETER OPENINGS

There should be as few openings as possible, and the fence should be lit at night. It can also be alarmed so that an attempt to cut the fence will be noticed. 'Keep out' signs should be posted, with possible additional warning about guard dogs or security patrols. Your aim should be to discourage people from even attempting to get inside the property.

Factories or warehouses which receive and despatch lorries loaded with valuable goods require barriers with security guards to monitor and check vehicles. Service companies have a lower level of security need: some firms issue staff with magnetic cards which will raise the barrier. Visitors and suppliers can call reception on an entryphone system. Reception should be able to see the vehicle, if only by video camera.

CREATING CLEAR ZONES

A clear zone should be kept all around the fence. Low vegetation and a limited number of sparse trees can be planted to prevent a desert-like appearance. Closed-circuit cameras should be mounted in a way that allows the whole area to be seen. Attention should be paid to fuel storage tanks, skips or waste paper bins which could be of use to a criminal.

SECURITY OF THE BUILDING

The success of some firms, such as retailers, depends on having many visitors during the day. In such cases, security will be moved to the building itself. The same applies to a company that is based in a business park or in a terrace of buildings.

The vulnerable areas are doors and windows. There should be as few openings as possible. Even department-store retailers like to make customers enter and exit through a restricted number of doors. Doors should be illuminated at night, and windows should be secured. Burglars can easily open old sash and casement windows unless they have been reinforced. Sliding doors and windows can be secured with a wooden pole in the bottom track, while window frames should be lockable to the window frame. Without such precautions, a burglar can easily jemmy open most windows and doors.

Doors should be solidly made, and fitted with security locks and hinges. Only one door should be openable from outside. The others should be replaced with fire doors openable only from inside. This will give the intruder only one method of entry. Each fire door should be alarmed, so as to sound a warning when it is opened.

INSIDE THE BUILDING

Many firms now have coded door locks. These are effective against intruders, but they need to be regularly changed. One Newcastle city centre hotel has codes for each floor, and these remain the same whenever guests stay there. At another company, it is obvious from the dirt marks around the door lock that only two numbers are being used: 9 and 4. It would not take a criminal long to discover that the code is 9494. A final problem with door codes is that a criminal can watch staff hand movements to ascertain the number.

Similarly, photocopiers at one management consultancy can now only be operated by entering a departmental password. Consultants now do their illegal and personal copying using other departments' passwords. Since the amount of illegal copying is only a small percentage of the legitimate work, the problems created outweigh the benefits. Targeting the heavy users of illegal copying would be more effective.

Sometimes security can rebound to the company's disadvantage. Dunkin' Donuts was embarrassed to discover that a member of staff had spied on diners, using its video and audio security system, and had then gossiped about what he had learnt.

SECURING THE INTERIOR

The interior of the premises can be secured by circuit-breaker alarms on doors and windows. Other kinds of protection include pressure pads, ultrasonic movement detectors, and photoelectric beams which sound an alarm when broken. These devices can be wired to sound an alarm or make a telephone call. They are, however, known to fail or sound a false alarm. Care must be taken to choose a system that will not be set off by passing traffic. Low-cost motion-detection cameras can be linked to the computer network, and can transmit an image of the scene to a distant location, whether reception or (during out-of-office hours) to someone's home PC.

EXCLUSION ZONES

Departments categorized as security zones will include:

- research and development offices
- cashier's office
- finance offices
- mainframe computer; servers.

The boardroom and directors' offices should be swept for bugs if commercially sensitive information is likely to be discussed. Ideally, the room should not be overlooked by other buildings where long-distance microphones could be used, nor where information shown on flipcharts could be seen through a telephoto lens. Paper shredders will destroy sensitive information.

SECURITY OFFICERS

People should not be freely able to enter the building without being questioned and without providing identification.

Large premises will need to be patrolled by a security officer at night, at predetermined frequencies but at irregular intervals, possibly accompanied by a dog. Dogs act as a strong deterrent to criminals.

Security staff are not always well trained. At the BBC in London, members of a pressure group arrived at the studios and asked the way to the newsroom. The security guard courteously directed them to the right place, where they briefly got on air.

Security patrols have been found to be effective in reducing crime on large estates; in business premises they may similarly deter criminals, and spot security problems. However, mobile guards also add more cost.

END OF DAY AND NIGHT TIME

The company needs an end-of-day routine, with one named individual responsible for securing the building. This person should check that:

- all doors and windows are secure
- no combustible material is left lying around, and flammable liquids are locked away
- no unauthorized people are on the premises

- alarms are on
- outside lights are on.

Night is a vulnerable time for many companies. The periods when cleaners are working are a time when a thief could enter. At one company, a deranged person wielding a knife got into the building late at night, when few staff were around. Security failed to answer the telephone, so the staff had to disarm the man themselves.

Natural threats to buildings

Fire is the greatest natural threat to a building, and is examined in detail in Chapter 8. *Water* is an often underestimated risk. A dripping tap or a blocked drain can flood a basement, and if it happens over a long weekend, it could be four days before the problem is discovered. Mainframe computers, lift equipment and power supplies are often located in basements, and are therefore at risk from water, whether from flooding or from a burst pipe.

Public events

Conferences and exhibitions are sometimes targets for attack by pressure groups or terrorists, for a number of reasons: prominent VIPs or the media will be present; disrupting the event can cause havoc in the city; disruption will harm the government's standing.

It is important to create an exclusion zone before the event starts, with the area being swept for bombs or incendiary devices. Thereafter, everyone entering the area should be registered and badged. Security should be particularly stringent before the event when stands are being erected or dressed by technicians or sales people. During the event, security guards should constantly check for suspicious packages. Arrangements must also be made to protect VIPs. Protesters should be treated courteously and should be escorted off the premises as quickly as possible but without undue force.

Retail security

Average shrinkage (stock loss from crime or wastage) suffered by stores throughout Western Europe is around 1.3 per cent of turnover. While this may sound small, it equates to €31 million or €71 per head of the population. Table 9.2 shows the causes of shrinkage, as perceived by retailers, while the most popular items are shown in Table 9.3.

Table 9.2   Percentage losses caused by shrinkage

	%
Crime related	
Customer thieves	48
Employees	29
Suppliers	7
Non crime related	
Internal error, process failures and pricing mistakes	16
Total	100

Table 9.3   List of products and items most likely to be stolen

Bed linen/textiles	Leather wallets
CDs	Locks and security devices
Cellular phone cards	L'Oreal perfume
Children's clothes	Major designer-brand clothing
Chocolate	Mobile/cellular phones
Contraceptives	Olay skincare
Cosmetics	Other fine fragrances/perfume
Costume jewellery and earrings	Ready-made curtains
Designer accessories	Skincare
Designer handbags	Sony Playstation, computer games
Duracell batteries	Spare parts for electrical items and power drill
DVDs	bits
Electrical power tools (well-known makes such as	Spirits, mainly whisky, vodka, and so on
Bosch)	Sportswear
Electrical skin care and toothbrushes, for	Sunglasses
example Braun and Gillette	Tea and coffee
Female lingerie	Trainers, sports footwear
Kodak films	Videos
Leather belts	Vitamins
Leather jackets and other leather garments	Wrist watches

Source: European Retail Theft Barometer

STAFF PILFERING

Staff can either take goods and cash themselves or by collusion with suppliers or customers. Supermarkets are the worst affected, losing around 2–3 per cent of turnover. The two main problem areas are the cash tills and the stock room.

There are many methods of stealing at the tills: staff can fail to ring up purchases, or they can short change customers and pocket the difference (this affects not the company's profit but customer attitudes). In the stock room, goods are piled high, and the room is often empty, making a tempting target for the thief.

Electronic point of sale (EPOS) equipment reduces the prevalence of theft, as does the use of mystery shoppers to check staff honesty. Tills should be regularly changed and checked. Staff coats and bags should not be allowed near the tills.

In the stock room, expensive stock should be locked, while cheaper stock should be delivered shrink-wrapped. Procedures for deliveries should be properly managed, and any goods entrance should be supervised, or locked if possible, to prevent goods being removed.

SHOPLIFTING BY THE PUBLIC

Making goods easily accessible encourages the shopper to buy them, but it also makes it easier for them to be stolen. Asymmetrical store layouts lead the consumer around the store but reduce lines of sight and make shoplifting easier.

Electronic tags prevent high-value items from being stolen, while closed-circuit television can deter thieves, and store detectives can identify culprits.

Loop alarms can protect small electrical goods, while some clothes stores operate a tag system to prevent shoppers from taking several garments into a changing room.

Easily pocketable items such as electric shavers may be displayed under glass counters, while small items such as batteries can be blister-packed.

PROTECTING THE STORE AT NIGHT

The shop should remain lit at night to discourage theft, and cash should not be kept overnight on the premises. Shop windows should be made of resistant glass, capable of withstanding attack for a sustained period. Security grills are useful for higher-value items, and grill alarms can be set. Even toughened glass is vulnerable to 'ram raiders' who attack a window using a stolen car. Bollards or a low metal bar extending the length of the window may be the only way to deter this kind of problem.

THE HOLD-UP

Most robberies are over very quickly: robbers rightly fear being apprehended if they stay too long. For this reason, they rarely get to the safe, preferring instead to grab what cash they can from the nearest till. The store (or bank) should therefore keep only as much cash in each as is needed for the business. Staff should be dissuaded from heroic action: safety is more important than the petty cash.

Where the business takes cash to or from a bank, the timing and route should vary, and two people should make the journey together. The money bag should be unobtrusive.

Vandalism

Vandalism is usually associated with run-down inner-city locations, and carried out by bored youths. While this is true of vandalism to bus shelters and telephone boxes, many city centre buildings are secured against the problem.

Good community relations can also play a part. When race riots erupted in London's inner city area of Brixton, the Marks and Spencer store was unscathed. It is thought that the company's investment in inner-city renewal was responsible for its escape.

Vandalism is also prevalent among companies whose property cannot be observed all the time, such as bus and train companies. Vandalism usually comes from a small number of areas, for example where poor housing estates back on to railway tracks. Targeting these areas with observation, video cameras, and good lighting can reduce the problem.

Sometimes vandalism is carried out by staff. A sailor poured sugar into the fuel tanks of his destroyer in order to prevent the boat from leaving port. He had formed an emotional attachment to a woman, and was reluctant to leave her. But more usually, the member of staff has a grudge against the company. Ensuring that door entry codes are regularly changed, that the individual surrenders his or her security pass, and that dismissals are well managed, will minimize the problem.

Espionage

Espionage can involve the theft or sale of information, whether records or formulae. Typically, this involves confidential research data being sold to a competitor. It is cheaper for an unscrupulous company to buy competitors' secrets for a few thousand pounds than spend millions in R&D. Industries such as computing, telecommunications and aerospace are particularly vulnerable.

Tender information or product plans are also worth money. Detergent companies routinely try to spoil a competitor's launch by rushing out a similar product a few weeks earlier. The success or failure of a launch can have a huge impact on market share and profits.

Active espionage, where one company bugs another's boardroom, is rare. Usually, the perpetrators are disgruntled employees, and information is usually freely available to them. Sometimes, the employee has a friend, relative or spouse who works for a competitor. Many precautions can be taken, and these are included in the following section.

SECURITY OF INFORMATION

It is easy for an employee to take confidential information, whether by taking photocopies of documents, by taking drafts of tender documents, or by copying the contents of a computer on to a CD-Rom or memory stick. Often, the company never knows that the theft has taken place.

The company should make an assessment of:

- What information is sensitive?
- How could it be used or taken?
- How can the theft be prevented?

Paperwork security

Important documents should be shredded, not binned. All departments should have shredders, since even apparently innocuous documents can be risky or have economic value. Sensitive data should be locked away at the end of the day, not left lying on desks. Staff should have lockable filing cabinets if they need them, especially in the HR department. Plans should be restricted to those who need them.

Computer security

In Chapter 12, we look at the problems of computer theft, viruses, unauthorized access and other problems leading to a loss of data. See also 'Natural threats to buildings', earlier in this chapter.

Staff relations

Companies should seek to ensure that staff do not have cause for resentment, thereby pre-empting the idea of espionage. This includes treating staff fairly and having transparent and honest procedures for promotion. Companies should also try to resolve complaints and personal problems, so that staff do not grow disaffected.

INFORMATION LOSS

If information has been taken, you should assess:

- What information has been taken?
- How was it taken?
- What can be done to stop a recurrence?
- What legal or disciplinary action should be taken?

Before taking action, it is worth checking that the information has really been stolen, rather than misfiled or simply buried in an in-tray.

TELEPHONES

Telephone conversations can be transmitted to a listening post. Computerized telephones contain diagnostic tools which can check for this. However, cellular telephones are particularly vulnerable, as proved by well-publicized cases involving transcripts of the UK royal family's private telephone conversations. Some telephones transmit signals which can easily be picked up, though security is improving over time.

Sometimes employees are simply nosy. In some cases, anyone who wanted to eavesdrop on board meetings could set a boardroom phone to auto answer, and mute the ring. Then they can dial it, and listen in to the conversation.

HUMANS AT WORK

Staff can ignore or break the most stringent security controls if there is a conflict with workplace needs. A typical example is the emergency door which gets propped open, despite the warning notices. This may be because the building otherwise becomes hot and airless, and staff enjoy the breeze. Or it may be a short-cut from the building to the car park.

Recruitment

It is important to have comprehensive application forms for potential recruits. References should always be followed up, preferably by telephone (which, being a more informal and instant method of communication, will be more revealing). Checks may be made on the applicant's current address, former employment, academic background, credit rating (to identify the larcenous or dishonest recruit), and personal references. All information should comply with current legislation.

Safeguarding intellectual property

Inventions, designs, trade marks and brand names are worth money, especially if a competitor copies them, or if they can be licensed to other companies. Therefore, it is essential to establish the company's rights to all intellectual property. The company secretary or a firm of patent agents should be used to secure these rights. This work needs to be continuous, because the infringement of corporate designs is a continuous threat. We discuss this further in Chapter 13 along with identity theft in Chapter 10.

Tampering

The company should assess who might want to tamper with its products. What benefit might they get from doing this? Companies at high risk are those:
- with a well-known brand name
- whose products are eaten or drunk (and where contamination or poisoning of the contents would damage the company's reputation)
- in a controversial market (such as testing cosmetics on animals).

This makes branded grocery products and supermarkets especially vulnerable.

Tampering can take place at any point along the route from production plant to retail shelves. There are three main types of people who tamper with a product:

1 Current or former employee with a grudge.
2 Pressure group (especially animal welfare groups, political groups or environmentalists).
3 An extortionist who demands money.

The threat of tampering can be minimized by using tamper-evident packaging. With the help of the packaging industry, most industries have developed their own solutions with the help of the packaging industry, such as paper seals, vacuumed lids, or transparent collars, all of which demonstrate to the customer that the package has not been opened.

However, none of this prevents tampering in the factory. Security control, vetting of employees, supervision and good management will help to prevent tampering in the workplace.

Extortion

Internet extortionists have threatened to ruin the reputation of Blue Square, an online betting firm by saying they would send out emails containing child pornography in the company's name. This follows previous blackmail attempts on the company where the gang bombarded its website with thousands of bogus emails, in a denial-of-service attack. This made the site unavailable to customers for five hours. The extortionists then emailed a demand for €7000 (£4680) to prevent further attacks. Attacks on other betting firms, including William Hill, have sometimes been timed to coincide with an important period for the business, such as the Cheltenham Gold Cup Festival.

To combat this type of crime, the UK police's High Tech Crime Unit has liaised with their counterparts in Russia, where they have carried out raids on suspected extortionists.

Extortion demands should be immediately reported to the police, and you might decide to call in specialist consultants.

Terrorism

Large offices and companies in city centres often receive terrorist threats. Fewer suffer a bombing, though bombs at airports, railway stations and city centres do happen. For example, Ferrylink postponed plans to export British livestock after receiving a bomb threat presumed to have come from animal rights activists. On a trial run from Sheerness in Kent to the Dutch port of Vlissingen, an anonymous caller rang to say that a bomb was on board. This caused the ferry to be held up by six hours outside Vlissingen harbour while Dutch port officials searched the boat.

Threats which contain a recognized code are regarded as more serious than those that don't, but it can be difficult to distinguish between a hoax call and a terrorist call, particularly as terrorists are known to use hoax calls as a weapon.

BOMB THREAT SOLUTIONS

It is important to have procedures in place to cope with telephone calls announcing a bomb.

The greatest requirement is the ability to move fast. The company should be able to evacuate all staff within the time frame given by the caller. Organizations liable to bomb attack, such as government departments, use a colour to denote the scale of the security alert. This allows security to be scaled up and down to meet the perceived threat, and helps staff and visitors to respond accordingly. A graded scale is better than requiring staff to be on a constant 'red alert'.

HARDENING THE BUSINESS

Any terrorist or criminal will select the easier of two similar targets. Therefore companies should harden their premises. This can mean making it more difficult to get past reception, or adding bollards outside the building to stop a vehicle driving into the building. And since the post room is an easy target for letter bombs or anthrax attacks, experts suggest moving it off-site, so that the main building is protected.

PROBABILITY VERSUS ABILITY TO RECOVER

Yossi Sheffi, head of Massachusetts Institute of Technology (MIT) Centre for Transportation Studies, says terrorist risk assessment can be viewed on a two-by-two matrix, with the probability of an attack on the vertical axis and the company's ability to recover on the horizontal axis (see Figure 9.3).

US airlines would be on the high end of both axes of the chart. 'They are at a high probability of being attacked and if the airplane goes down due to, say, a missile, my guess is that the company goes out of business,' says Prof Sheffi, quoted in the *Financial Times*.

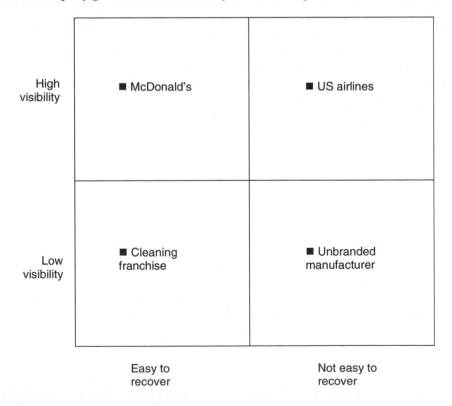

Figure 9.3   Visibility and recovery

McDonald's has a high probability of attack, he says, because of the visibility of its brand. But because it has thousands of outlets worldwide, attacks on individual restaurants would not put the company out of business.

An unbranded manufacturer of fashion goods might have a low probability of attack, but if it has a single distribution centre, an attack on that facility might disrupt business permanently or for a long time.

At the low end of both axes would be a cleaning franchise business. No one would want to attack it, it has many outlets, and they are all locally operated.

Kidnap and ransom

There are 15 000 kidnappings a year, mostly taking place in developing countries, particularly Colombia. Recently, a senior banker was kidnapped in Mexico by armed extortionists, and two British MPs were kidnapped in Somalia. Tourists have been held in northern India and a British restaurateur was snatched by Khmer Rouge guerrillas in Cambodia. Unicef paid a six-figure ransom for an employee abducted in Kabul.

Companies can take out an insurance policy that will reimburse the costs of releasing the victim. This includes payment of the ransom, consultancy fees, medical costs, travel and accommodation. Business is brisk in oil, engineering and construction companies where executives frequently travel to high-risk locations.

Seventy per cent of all kidnappings are resolved by a ransom payment, according to Aon, and 95 per cent of victims survive their ordeal. Most of those who die, do so because of a medical condition, shock, or a failed escape or rescue attempt.

In Europe, kidnap and ransom is relatively rare, though taking hostages prior to a robbery is more common. Normally, hostages are only held until the robbery has been carried out. But even in Europe, terrorists may seize employees, particularly in areas where political terrorism exists, such as Sicily.

Companies subject to kidnap risk need a *corporate policy*. This should cover:

- Attitude towards concessions to kidnappers
- Negotiation strategy, including police and government involvement, and use of specialist consultancy
- Handling the family of the kidnap victim
- Handling the media.

Such companies also need a *contingency plan* for kidnapping. This will set out the responsibilities of a management team and a local team. It should define the procedures for immediate action (including the notifying of responsible bodies). It should identify the policies to be followed. It should enable the company to handle a future kidnap situation. The plan should ensure that local managers know how to protect themselves when in high-risk countries.

A company which could be subject to kidnap should also carry out an *exercise*, simulating a kidnap event. This should be played over a suitable period, and will serve to familiarize corporate executives with the possible course of events.

In the event of a kidnap, the company should seek to gain as much information as possible. It should evaluate the effects of different courses of action, and the likely actions of the kidnappers. Speed and high-quality communication will be vital. It will be important to have a responsible executive in the kidnap country as soon as possible after the event. Experts advise that the company should initially negotiate with the kidnappers, rather than pay out straightaway. Offering to pay straightaway indicates that money is no object.

Executives can minimize the risk of kidnap by taking precautions. Gangs employ spotters to identify possible targets. People whom they identify as wealthy or important then become victims, as do their families. Individuals should avoid standing out. They should dress inexpensively and drive a modest car. Around 90 per cent of victims are kidnapped in transit, so travel patterns should be varied, and dangerous areas avoided.

Murder and execution

In some cases, people are executed for political reasons. The Dutch film-maker, Theo van Gogh, was shot and stabbed to death in seemingly peaceful Amsterdam, before having his throat cut. His murder resulted from a short film he had made, called *Submission*, about the forced marriage of four Muslim women. Lasting only ten minutes, its broadcast caused an uproar in the country when it was broadcast, and van Gogh received death threats from extremist Muslims.

A corollary of such incidents is a rise in racial or religious tension, leading to further violence. After van Gogh was murdered, several fires broke out at a new mosque in Utrecht, thought to have been started in revenge, and Far-Right protesters marched in Amsterdam and Rotterdam in anger at Van Gogh's killing,

Few companies are likely to anger extremists in the way that van Gogh did; but it is conceivable that publishers and TV executives could be targeted for producing material that is deemed to give offence. Sponsoring an exhibition or controversial opera could cause the same effect.

In another case, a businessman, Amarjit Chohan and his wife Nancy, from Hounslow, west London, were murdered so that two villains could take over his freight business, CIBA, importing and exporting fruit, and use it as a front for importing drugs.

However, it has to be said that such attacks are exceedingly rare, and executives are much more likely to die of coronary heart disease or a routine car accident.

International security

Doing business abroad carries increased risks. They comprise:

- *Technical risks*: the problems of running a business far from home, and the lack of technical know-how, supplies and infrastructure
- *Economic and political risks*: the problems of working in an inflationary climate, exchange-rate movements, arbitrary changes in tax, the threat of nationalization
- *Security risks*: kidnap, terrorist attack or extortion (discussed above)
- *Bribery risks*: In some markets bribery is common; in others, it can be difficult to decide whether bribes are actively sought by the individual awarding the contract, or simply offered by the company seeking to win the contract (Chapter 13 discusses the risks of corruption, and how to prevent it).

These risks all stem from political instability, economic underdevelopment, inequality of wealth, or personal greed.

Before starting overseas operations, it is important to assess the future political climate. The former Yugoslavia was once a humdrum part of Eastern Europe, so the current state of affairs is not always what it seems.

Nor is it always a gloomy scenario. Some countries which are conventionally seen as hostile offer major marketing opportunities. Even under the mullahs, Iran has provided British and other western companies with large and profitable contracts. And in many countries with bad reputations, the risks are often limited to specific locations.

The company should therefore assess the likely political developments. Then it needs to assess at a company level the operational risks of doing business in that country. Finally, it needs to be able to manage a crisis, should it arise.

High-risk regions for foreign businesses

Table 9.4 shows some of the world's danger spots, at the time of writing. However, the high-risk areas quickly alter as peace breaks out or fighting is renewed. Before sending staff abroad, the business should get an up-to-date view of foreign risk.

Table 9.4   Risky locations throughout the world

South America

Haiti (political violence, natural disasters, criminal gangs)	Colombia (guerrillas and drug violence)
Venezuela (political instability)	

Europe

Bosnia-Herzegovina, Macedonia, Serbia, Montenegro (ethnic hatred, landmines, unexploded ordnance)

Africa

Nigeria (violence, including by police and army personnel)	Sudan (militias, population displacement)
Central African Republic (armed robbery, civil strife)	Burundi/Rwanda (civil war)
Liberia (armed combatants, lack of police)	Algeria (hostage taking in the Sahara)
Cote d'Ivoire (anarchy)	Guinea (civil unrest)
Congo, DRC (fighting, civil unrest)	Somalia (factional fighting)
Zimbabwe (political, economic and humanitarian crises)	South Africa (rape)
Kenya (anti-western terrorist threat)	

Middle East

Yemen (Al-Qa'ida activity risk)	Iraq (political violence, kidnapping)
Israel (terrorist attacks)	Iran (tension with Iraq, demonstrations)
Saudi Arabia (risk of anti-Western terrorist attack)	

continued

Table 9.4   *concluded*

Asia

Afghanistan (civil war)	North Korea (famine, uncertain political future, tension with South Korea)
Pakistan (potential anti-Western violence)	Nepal (Maoist terror activities)
Chechnya (political violence, war)	Philippines (anti-Western terror threat)

One of the *Wall Street Journal's* correspondents was kidnapped and murdered by a radical group in Pakistan. According to Gabriella Stern of Dow Jones, the newspaper's owner, the 200 journalists in the Middle East and Africa are made aware of the risks they sometimes face. 'But we have to take risks because we want to write about risks,' she says. 'To write about politically risky places, we have to be there. Our customers want to know about risks and opportunities.'

CASE STUDY: MANAGING RISK IN COCAINE'S HEARTLAND

Colombia is the location of one of the world's biggest oil fields. Oil pipelines are vulnerable, stretching as they do over such long distances. Therefore the oil companies have to manage such threats to the pipeline.

Before they start prospecting, the companies need to assess not only the geological risk but also the *political risk*. The damage caused by a country's political instability may outweigh the revenues that accrue from the oil.

Then they need a *plan of action* to minimize the risk. This will involve regular communication with local inhabitants at all levels. Building good relations is important, and local people need to see the advantages of the oilfield, especially through increased employment.

Oil companies also need *defensive measures*, which will include protecting expensive or especially vulnerable parts of the pipeline, such as pumps. Passive defences, using locked enclosures, may need to be augmented by guard patrols.

Like other oil companies, BP explores for oil in some dangerous parts of the world. It has found significant amounts of oil in Colombia, a country with a reputation for drug-related lawlessness. BP hopes to produce up to 600 000 barrels a day from

this field. Because Colombian oil is potentially so important, it has attracted the attention of guerrilla groups such as the National Liberation Army, who want to see BP's work disrupted. The company has a plan for managing that risk.

Security figures highly, and the company receives help from the Colombian military forces. David Harding, BP Exploration's Chief Executive for the southern hemisphere, says that the company invests in staff communications, 'ensuring that they understand the company's policies for handling risks, and training and advising them.'

Only one in five employees are expatriates, and that percentage is continually falling. The company employs Colombian graduates as *local managers* and is forging links with local schools.

David Harding says: 'We're managing our risks in Colombia as we do elsewhere. We're listening. We're maintaining the standards of business that we apply throughout the world. We're building contacts with authorities at all levels. And finally, we're communicating with staff – both Colombian and expatriate – so that they know what we're doing, and why we're doing it. That's the right way to manage risks.'

The Control Risks Group considers a country to be a high risk if it is suffering a civil war, if law and order are breaking down, or if there is a campaign against foreign businesses. Note that many of the risks will be confined to certain regions of a country, for example border areas.

CORRUPT COUNTRIES

Among oil countries, Angola, Azerbaijan, Chad, Russia, Iran, Iraq and Venezuela all score highly on Transparency International's (TI) list of corrupt countries. 'In these countries, public contracting in the oil sector is plagued by revenues vanishing into the pockets of western oil executives, middlemen and local officials,' said Peter Eigen, Chairman of TI.

As can be seen in Table 9.5, Nordic countries ranked highly as being free from corruption. The UK came 11th, while the USA was 17th.

Table 9.5   Most and least corrupt countries (higher numbers represent greater corruption)

Least corrupt		Most corrupt	
1	Finland	137=	Indonesia
2	New Zealand		Tajikistan
3=	Denmark		Turkmenistan
	Iceland	140=	Azerbaijan
5	Singapore		Paraguay
6	Sweden	142=	Chad
7	Switzerland		Burma
8	Norway	144	Nigeria
9	Australia	145=	Bangladesh
10	Netherlands		Haiti

Source: Transparency International

Security services

Not every task can be undertaken by in-house staff. Some jobs are carried out only occasionally, and so they are better performed by an outside firm.

Note that security consultants have different skills. Some are mere locksmiths, while others are a uniformed guard service. You should thoroughly check any consultancy's credentials and experience before hiring the firm. Here are some of the services they might specialize in:

- advice on travel risk
- protective and security services
- emergency support
- kidnap for ransom
- corporate internal investigations
- competitive intelligence
- hostile takeovers
- computer forensics
- financial forensic investigations.

Useful links

Control Risks
www.crg.com

Transparency International
www.transparency.org

UK Foreign Office Travel advice
www.fco.gov.uk

US consular country sheets
http://travel.state.gov/travel/warnings.html

Risk assessment – security

By answering the questions below, you can see how vulnerable your company is to breaches of security. Score one point for each box ticked.

Topic	Question	
Buildings	Does the business have manufacturing or warehousing premises?	☐
	Are the company's premises easily accessible to the public or visited by many people?	☐
Information	Could your paperwork or computer data have commercial value to a competitor?	☐
Espionage	Does the business operate in markets subject to fashion or technological advance?	☐
Intellectual property	Does it have inventions, trade marks or well-known brand names?	☐
Attacks on premises	Does it employ large numbers of people?	☐
Tampering	Does the company sell fast-moving consumer goods (fmcg)?	☐
International	Do your executives travel to unstable developing countries?	☐
	Does the company have assets in unstable developing countries?	☐
Review	Has the company failed to carry out a security review?	☐
Total points scored		

Score: 0–3 points: low risk. 4–6 points: moderate risk. 7–10 points: high risk.

The appendix contains a summary of all the checklists in this book. By entering the results of this one, you can compare your security risk against other categories of risk.

10 *Pre-empting Fraud*

In this chapter we examine:

- *The scale of fraud, and how it happens*
- *Who commits fraud?*
- *Online fraud, telephone fraud, being used for fraud*
- *Minor fraud, competitor fraud, the indicators of fraud*
- *How to carry out a vulnerability analysis*
- *How to set up a fraud policy*
- *How to prevent fraud*
- *What to do on discovering fraud.*

The scale of the problem

The big fraud cases like Enron grab the headlines. But there are countless cases of fraud that don't reach the press, and which can put a company into receivership.

Fraud is surprisingly common. It costs UK businesses more than £40 bn last year – equivalent to £100 m a day – and the problem is getting worse, according to a report by accountants RSM Robson Rhodes.

In all, UK companies lost £32 bn in 2003 through acts such as fraud, embezzlement, corruption and money laundering, and spent a further £8 bn seeking to combat the problem. FTSE 100 companies alone lost an estimated £500 m and all listed companies lost £3 bn. Although the survey confirms that economic crime is now a board-level issue, nearly one in three businesses only discuss economic crime once a year or less, indicating that UK boards are not doing enough to tackle a potential 'business killer'.

The Ernst & Young Global Fraud survey found that 47 per cent of companies had been 'significantly defrauded in the last year'. Other companies had suffered a fraud but not reported it. Twenty-four per cent of companies have suffered a fraud of over £250 000 at least once in the past two years. This indicates that fraud is both widespread and costly.

Ernst & Young believe that companies suffer from other unreported ways:

- loss of impetus in managing the business
- loss of business
- loss of customer and banker confidence
- adverse movement in the share price
- impaired health and performance of the management team.

Why fraud takes place

Sixty-two per cent of companies think that fraud has become more common. It is the nature of their business that makes companies feel they are more vulnerable to fraud, as Figure 10.1 shows.

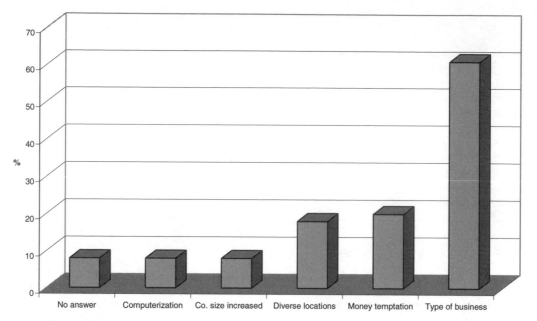

Source: Ernst & Young

Figure 10.1   Reasons why business is more vulnerable to fraud

Fraud can continue for several years before being discovered. Often the accounts tally, and cannot therefore be easily spotted. The thief often understands the principles of double-entry bookkeeping, and therefore the fraud cannot be easily detected. For example, the thief might insert a false invoice into the system and arrange for its payment.

Detection of fraud not only allows the company to recoup its money through legal proceedings, it also stops the losses from continuing, which could be even more costly.

Who commits fraud?

Fraud is so varied that it is difficult to define. In law it is often treated as a sophisticated form of theft, usually involving deception. It can be undertaken by virtually anyone in the organization:

- *Blue-collar workers.* This could be the theft of goods. A security guard may over-record a vehicle's weight, or an operative may stop a meter running.
- *Clerical workers.* Clerical workers handle paperwork, and are often in positions of trust. It is easy for them to falsify or destroy records.
- *Managers.* A lot of fraud is white-collar. Managers can approve invoices from a fake company which they own.

• *Customers or suppliers.* A supplier or customer is often involved, either on their own, or in collusion with a member of the defrauded company's staff. For example, an office worker may issue fraudulent credit notes to a supplier.

About two-thirds of company fraud is committed by directors or senior managers, according to a KPMG survey of British business fraud.

The survey also found that 32 per cent of fraud was committed by longstanding employees who had been with their companies for between ten and 25 years. About 23 per cent of perpetrators had been with the company for between five and ten years, while 20 per cent had been employed for between two and five years. So longevity is no guarantee of loyalty or honesty, and statistically makes fraud all the more likely.

Meng Chih-chung, a director of Taiwan's Directorate General of Telecommunications was jailed for seven years for forging documents and granting illegal favours to Ericsson of Sweden. In the $220 m (£142 m) scandal, five other directorate officials received sentences of five to six years on similar charges.

How fraud happens

For fraud to take place, various preconditions must be in place, as Figure 10.2 shows.

1 *Motive*: The fraudster (often a trusted employee) has a reason for his action. In a recent case, an employee wanted to give his daughter the perfect wedding. Another needed to fund his gambling addiction. The motive may be cloaked in justification. For example, an employee might want to take revenge on the company (for not giving them a pay rise or promotion). This is often simply a justification for theft. Many employees feel aggrieved without stealing from their employer.

2 *Assets worth stealing.* Money is the ultimate desirable object. But products, raw materials, tools and equipment are also worth having, particularly if, as we see below, there is an

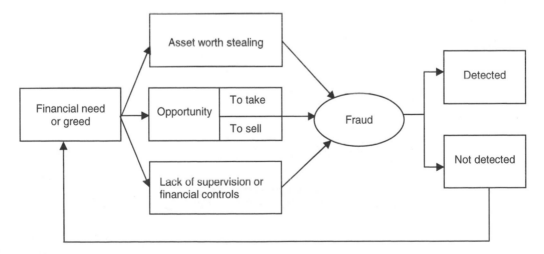

Source: Ernst & Young

Figure 10.2 Preconditions for fraud

opportunity to sell them. Blank cheques are an asset which cost the British Council £520 000, forcing it to cut back its educational programmes throughout the world. An employee simply passed genuine Council blank cheques through the cheque-signing machine. He later filled in the amount and the payee's name.

3 *Opportunity*: The person who loads and drives a van full of equipment has an opportunity. So does a manager who is responsible for approving overtime payments.

   The opportunity must exist for the individual to both steal and sell the goods. In most cases, the fraudster needs an outlet. This might relate to:

   – physically taking stock and knowing someone who will buy it
   – falsifying a document and having an acquaintance in a supplier's firm who will benefit, and with whom they will share the proceeds.

But the opportunity to steal is pointless if the thief can be easily detected and caught. A bank cashier can easily take money from the till, but the bank's systems will soon discover the loss. So the next element (lack of control) must be present.

4 *Lack of control*: The individual must feel able to commit a crime without being discovered. Absence of checks is the way this occurs. The opportunity to steal takes place when an accountant is unsupervised. It also takes place when someone handles both the raising of purchase orders and their payment. This points to an individual who carries out work on their own, and who is in a position of trust, no matter how junior.

The above factors, then, may result in an act of fraud. And if it is undetected, the fraudster will be emboldened and the cycle will repeat itself.

   Companies believe that having good systems and staff make them less susceptible to fraud. As Figure 10.3 shows, this is substantially more important than other factors.

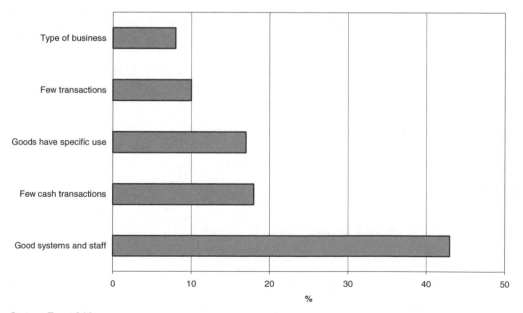

Source: Ernst & Young

Figure 10.3   Companies which are less susceptible to fraud

Restructuring to reduce costs often reduces the level of supervision. This creates greater opportunities for fraud. It is ironic that efforts to save money can actually create greater losses.

CASE STUDY: THE BOOK-KEEPER WHO LAVISHED STOLEN CASH ON HIS MISTRESS

Jailed for four years, Andrew Harpur stole £400 000 from his employer to lavish on his home, his wife and his mistress.

Though he earned only £12 000 as the company's book-keeper, he spent money 'at the rate of someone who had just won the pools', according to Judge Barrington Black.

Over 18 months, he bought a Volvo car with £26 000 in cash, he had helicopter lessons which cost £10 000, and was taking his family and his mistress on flying trips.

'It's amazing that he wasn't caught earlier', said Detective Constable David Hanley who led the investigation.

Harpur had been a warehouseman who re-trained as a book-keeper. He set up bogus companies and siphoned large sums into their bank accounts. The fraud was only discovered when 12 cheques totalling £60 000 were stopped by the company's bankers because the company did not have enough money to pay them.

Types of fraud

Even fake solicitors and accountants are busily at work committing fraud. In UK law, anyone is entitled to call themselves an accountant. However, by taking the time to investigate a prospective accountant's credentials, a company can eliminate any risk that a fraudulent accountant might pose.

ONLINE FRAUD

There has been a huge increase in the scale of online fraud. This generally involves fake or stolen credit cards that are used to buy merchandise which is later sold. Organizations that have sizeable online stores or valuable goods are particularly vulnerable.

Online fraud is thought to run at around two per cent of sales, but in addition retailers are rejecting more orders, resulting in lost sales. According to a survey by CyberSource International, UK merchants decline six per cent of orders on suspicion of fraud, while a further 1.6 per cent of accepted orders turn out to be fraudulent.

Over two thirds of UK retailers responding to this survey accept international orders, with Nigeria being identified as the riskiest source of transactions (35 per cent), followed by the US (13 per cent) and Indonesia (11 per cent).

Address verification and card security-code checking are currently the most widely used methods of managing online fraud in the UK. Online fraud could increase if the 'chip and pin' cards discourage fraud in retail outlets.

Actions that can be taken to reduce online fraud are as follows:

- Accept no order without full address and phone number.
- If in doubt, call the phone number listed on the order.

- Use the authentification service offered by Visa and MasterCard, or a commercial fraud screening service, to verify the card and address.
- Consider rejecting online orders from countries known to have high levels of online fraud, notably Nigeria.
- Consider rejecting any order originating from a free or web-based email address. Ask the customer to provide an ISP or domain-based address that can be traced back to a real person.

TELEPHONE FRAUD

Most businesses are aware of the risk of hackers, but they often overlook one area of vulnerability – the telephone. Ireland's Department of Social and Family Affairs noticed that its phone bill was rising, and found that expensive calls were being made out of office hours, and to Africa and south-east Asia. An investigation found that hackers had gained the password to the organization's PBX system, and were able to make international calls through a part of the system used only for maintenance. These calls cost the department €300 000.

Companies tolerate small levels of abuse from employees making overseas foreign calls, but sometimes this can cost a lot of money. For example, an employee can divert their phone to an international number. At home after work, they dial their office number, which puts them straight through to their friend or relative in Australia or the USA, at the company's expense.

The information security firm Rits recommends barring most lines to international calls, and to restrict the use of forwarding. Companies should also monitor any changes in phone use, especially of out-of-office hours and international calls.

BEING USED FOR FRAUD

The company might simply be a vehicle for an employee's fraud. For example, certain employees might be colluding with those of another firm to defraud it. Or in local government an employee could be receiving money to smooth the path of planning permission.

Other companies are used to launder money. The International Monetary Fund estimates that between $600 billion and $1.5 trillion is laundered annually, equivalent to 2–5 per cent of the world's GDP. The majority of this is laundered through banks but the increased threat of international terrorism, funded through money laundering, has seen stricter controls being introduced.

However, as recently as 2001, the Financial Services Authority rebuked 15 UK banks for their control weaknesses in relation to the laundering of $1.3 billion, stolen by the former Nigerian dictator General Sani Abacha. As banks have got tougher on money laundering, the criminals have shown more variety in their methods. In 1999, Ussama El-Kurd was jailed for 14 years for his role in laundering £70 million through a London bureau de change. At the time it was thought to be the biggest money laundering operation in Europe.

CORPORATE IDENTITY THEFT

While many individuals have had their identity stolen for criminal purposes, the same is now happening to some businesses. Internet users have received emails purporting to come from NatWest, Lloyds TSB, Barclays, Citibank and Halifax. The user is forwarded to a site that looks like the bank's, with the aim of collecting the user's account details and password. This is the phenomenon known as phishing.

Two activists duped BBC journalists into believing that their DowEthics.com website was genuine, and emailed the listed PR contact. The activists then posed as Dow Chemical spokespeople in a BBC TV interview. They apologized on the company's behalf for the Bhopal disaster, and said it would be paying $12 billion compensation to those who suffered. When the news was broadcast around the world, Dow was forced into a 'retraction' and had to explain that it was not going to give money to the victims.

The same 'Yes Men' pranksters had previously angered toy maker Mattel by swapping the voice boxes of Barbie and GI Joe action figures and putting them back on shop shelves. To the confusion of the children, Barbie wanted to go on the attack, while GI Joe suggested shopping trips.

In his book, *Defending the Brand: Aggressive Strategies for Protecting Your Brand in the Online Arena*, Brian Murray suggests the following steps to manage the risk of online corporate identity theft:

1 Get your stakeholders to provide early warnings. Make it easy for employees and customers to report any suspicious emails or websites they encounter.

2 Tell your customers that you never ask for their personal or account details by email or on the phone.

3 Make sure you're easy to find online. Promote your web address and keep it simple – to avoid misspellings. Try not to rely on others to deliver your customers to your site. When customers attempt to locate your site through search engines, partners or spam, it provides an opportunity for others to intercept them before they arrive.

4 Manage your domain registrations, and monitor new registrations that include your company name or trademarks. Register common misspellings of your website address. You can automatically redirect visitors to the correct address.

5 Plan your response to an attack before it happens. Many trade associations have advice on best practice. Also seek advice and establish relationships with the police and other organizations that can help remove fraudulent sites if an attack occurs.

It is not only online that a company can suffer identity theft. For example, employees could order goods in the company's name, and have them delivered to another address.

MINOR FRAUD

Lesser cases of fraud may involve employees doing work on their own account at work (using company tools), or allowing use of corporate facilities (such as the computer). At one firm, the managing director got the maintenance department to build a new mast for his boat. In another, staff mended lawn mowers and sewing machines at work.

Employees frequently take the firm's goods home with them. This ranges from protective clothing and tools to personal computers. Policies should be made and adhered to, so that no one is in doubt about the correctness of their actions.

COMPETITOR FRAUD

The company should check that its competitors are not gaining an unfair advantage, whether by gaining business intelligence or through bribing a customer.

Information about a competitor's activities can be gained from market intelligence, market research, or the trade association. Any evidence obtained should be given to the police.

The indicators of fraud

There are often clues that fraud is taking place. Here are a few of them:

- The physical stock in the warehouse is usually less than that shown on computer records.
- An employee gains sudden wealth, which they claim is from a rich relative's will, or a pools win.
- An employee who never takes a holiday (for fear that their fraud will be revealed). Ensure everyone takes their holiday, and that others do their work while they are away.
- Evidence of fraud involving a supplier: a substantial amount of work going to one supplier; a supplier whose additional costs are regularly accepted; or a supplier who receives multiple orders just below the threshold for tendering.
- Evidence of fraud involving a customer: for example, unexplained credit notes.
- Gaps appear in records, caused by 'computer breakdown'.
- Active accounts are used for samples or guarantee claims. If these do not generate an invoice, they are easier to conceal.

Vulnerability analysis

A company which believes itself to be at risk of being defrauded should undertake a vulnerability analysis. This will assess where and how the company could be defrauded. It will determine what money or assets are at risk, and which functions could undertake fraud. Doing this analysis will help to direct fraud prevention resources to where they are most needed, and avoid wasteful checks in unlikely areas.

The company can undertake a vulnerability analysis either as a routine task once a year, or in response to growing losses whose cause is unknown. A vulnerability analysis will assess:

- what assets might be at risk
- who might take them and who might benefit
- how the thief might take them (the method of theft) and sell them
- how effective the controls are.

ASSETS

The most easily stolen assets are cash and small high-value stocks. Other assets which could be taken include information, raw materials, and plant and machinery.

Items which are at risk include cash, credit card transactions, intra-firm accounts, and credit sales, as well as special items which are not billed to anyone (such as samples or test products).

FRAUD – THE LOCATIONS

Places where fraud occur are:

- locations where money physically changes hands
- accounting transactions (where, for example, fractions of a penny can be regularly posted to a wrong-doer's account)
- locations where documents which have monetary value (such as invoices or expense claims) are issued or received
- places where poor records are kept, or where much short-term activity occurs (such as suspense accounts)
- locations where physical goods exchange hands, such as stock leaving the company's premises
- departments whose costs are difficult to trace (such as a maintenance department where large numbers of people use spare parts)
- computer programs which a programmer can patch to divert money to a fraudster's account.

In its department stores, House of Fraser deploys security tags and uniformed guards, and checks changing rooms for empty hangers – a sign that thieves are operating. But over and above this, the store records activities on video at the point of sale, whereas many retailers video only around the store. This has significantly reduced the level of cash theft, credit card fraud and refund fraud. With its expensive brands, the store believes it will always be the target for thieves. But by presenting a robust and visible deterrence through guards, video recordings and changing-room controls, the store aims to discourage fraud and theft.

WHO MIGHT TAKE THE ASSETS?

As we have seen, fraud can be committed by staff, customers, or suppliers. It can also be committed by organized crime which has a growing involvement in corporate fraud. Fraudulent employees may be those who:

- are addicted to gambling, drink or drugs
- have heavy financial commitments
- have close business or personal links with suppliers or customers
- are involved with handling assets
- display wealth greater than their income would support.

As Figure 10.4 shows, fraud tends to occur in departments where the opportunity for fraud is greatest. The arrows in the table also show that collusion takes places in predictable ways. The table shows common frauds, but does not include all the possible departments involved, nor the full range of frauds. Note that at director or manager level, frauds may involve inflating expense claims, or 'cooking the books', so collusion may not be involved.

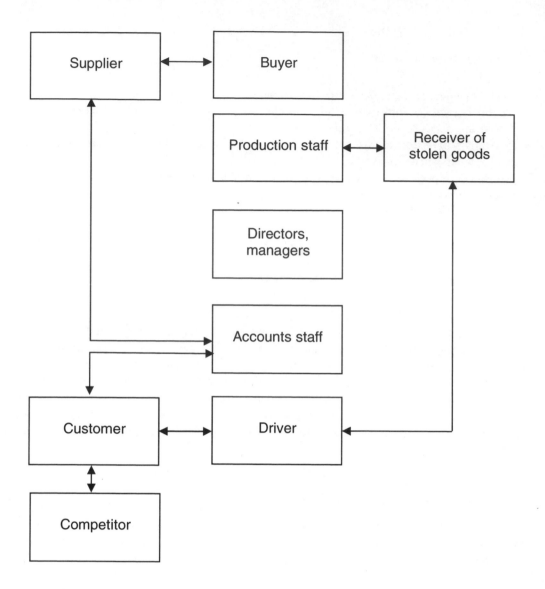

Figure 10.4   Typical areas of fraud

HOW FRAUD IS COMMITTED

Fraud may involve any of the following actions:

- theft of assets
- tampering with equipment or meters to give a wrong reading
- falsification of records (invoices, cheques, stock control records and so on)
- corruption (for example, where a buyer awards a contract in return for a bribe)
- a customer selling 'seconds' as perfect quality products
- using today's colour photocopiers or sophisticated printing equipment, which makes forgery easier
- use of a stolen or fake credit card to make online purchases.

EFFECTIVENESS OF CONTROLS

In analysing the effectiveness of controls, the auditor should examine controls over cash, accounts, purchasing and invoicing. The auditor should also check controls over stock control and production, and supervision of personnel. The checks should assess whether controls are more lax at certain times (such as during night shifts, when the opportunity for theft is greater).

DOING THE ANALYSIS

The analysis should check for losses in terms of money or goods, or for areas where controls are insufficient to prove that loss has not taken place. The check should take place over a set period (such as one week), and should be compared with previous records (see example in Table 10.1).

Treat unexplained deviations from the norm as particularly interesting. In some cases, fraud will cease while the investigation is being conducted. Auditors should be able to compare the results of the investigation period with the period preceding it, to see whether the pattern has changed.

Table 10.1   Vulnerability analysis

Company		Site		
Date of assessment		Auditor		
Vulnerable assets or areas of potential fraud	Who might be involved, and how?	Method of fraud (for example, forgery)	Effectiveness of controls	Level of risk (Low–high)
1.				
2.				
3. and so on				

AFTER THE VULNERABILITY ANALYSIS HAS BEEN DONE

Once the analysis has been done, the company can check to see whether losses are in fact occurring. This will involve various kinds of audits, including:

- data analysis (for example, examining documents, or comparing ratios over time)
- physical checks (physical stock checks, for example)
- surveillance (this can include electronic tagging to track items which are at risk).

CASE STUDY: EVEN SECURITY-CONSCIOUS FIRMS GET DEFRAUDED

The Bank of England is said to have lost £600 000 through theft by employees who were paid to destroy old notes. It was alleged in court that over four years, Mrs Christine Gibson, a team leader, hid bundles of old £20 notes in her locker.

She would take the notes from sealed cages which contained up to £2 million, while a colleague distracted other workers. The cage had two keys, one black and the other white. Mrs Gibson only had keys to the white lock, so her accomplice substituted another white lock painted black.

The fraud was only discovered when Mrs Gibson and her husband paid £100 000 for investment bonds to Reliance Mutual. The couple emptied bundles of notes on to a desk as staff looked on in amazement. Counting took several hours. The police were later called, as a result of routine checks that follow any large cash transaction.

The Gibsons appeared to rely on Mrs Gibson's £15 000 salary. Yet they owned two brand new four-wheel-drive cars, had £32 000 in savings, and a mortgage-free home.

The Bank of England has now installed concealed cameras and extra staff. It claims that a repeat of the crime is now impossible.

Preventing fraud

The most unlikely people are often found to have committed fraud. The prevention of fraud must seek to minimize the opportunity for fraud and to implement proper controls. Fraud prevention starts with a written fraud policy.

INTRODUCE A CORPORATE FRAUD POLICY

The fraud policy should include the following:

- *The company's attitude towards fraud.* The company should make it plain that fraud is a form of theft, and as such it is a criminal offence. Nor will the company condone other activities such as giving or taking bribes.

- *The corporate policy towards giving and receiving inducements* should be stated. Policy on giving and receiving entertainment, gifts and the payment of commission should be spelt out. So should the difference between this and bribes.

- *Methods for controlling and investigating fraud* should be defined. The company should have systems for preventing fraud and procedures for checking against fraud. This should include the reporting of fraud to the statutory authorities, and the recovery of losses. The details of confidential methods of investigation should not be included in the policy.

- *Responsibilities for fraud control* should be defined. The ultimate responsibility should rest with the Chief Executive. This is because many frauds are carried out by senior staff, and because the executive responsible for managing fraud must have sufficient authority.

- *Resources must be allocated to fraud detection.* This is because fraud does not come to light in normal audits.

- *Channels for reporting fraud.* Employees should be told how to report suspected cases of fraud.

- *Policy of dealing with wrong-doers* will include a policy on dismissing and prosecuting wrong-doers, reporting to the police, and references for dismissed employees.

How to minimize fraud

As we have seen, the company should assess where it is vulnerable to fraud, and introduce a fraud policy. Then it should take a series of measures to reduce the likelihood of fraud. They comprise the following points, which we consider in more detail below.

- Improving the recruitment process
- Reducing the fraudster's motive
- Reducing the number of assets worth stealing
- Minimizing the opportunity to steal
- Increasing the level of supervision
- Improving financial controls and management systems
- Improved detection
- Improving record-keeping.

IMPROVE RECRUITMENT

The company can reduce the employees' wish to commit fraud by taking care to recruit honest people. This involves properly investigating applicants' CVs and taking up references.

REDUCE THE MOTIVE

The company should also be seen to operate in a fair and honest manner. What reason is there for employees to behave honourably if their company condones bribery in overseas markets, allows office politics to flourish, or pays its top executives unduly high salaries?

MINIMIZE THE NUMBER OF ASSETS WORTH STEALING

The company may be able to sub-contract certain types of work, or to operate a Just in Time system which prevents valuable raw materials from being available. The company could also make the assets more difficult to sell, for example by marking them as corporate property.

MINIMIZE THE OPPORTUNITY TO STEAL

The company can minimize the opportunities to steal in various ways, such as by having secure warehouses or perimeter fences. This is discussed further in Chapter 9 on security.

INCREASE THE LEVEL OF SUPERVISION

Increased supervision is only necessary in areas of potential fraud. It includes such simple things as requiring all executives to submit expense claims to a superior, or requiring cheques to be signed by two directors. Supervision may also include video surveillance, and employee searches (where this is necessary, acceptable and legal).

IMPROVE FINANCIAL CONTROLS AND MANAGEMENT SYSTEMS

Improved financial controls will ensure that procedures are in place and are properly followed. For example, records should be written up straightaway, and mail might need to be opened by a team of employees.

- As regards auditing procedures, check for adjustments, management overrides and procedural breaches.

- Prevent sole responsibility for complete financial transactions from occurring.

- Ensure that corporate purchases are subject to formal tenders. This includes making sure that sufficient tenders are received, and that they are from genuine and independent companies.

- Ensure a complete audit trail, so that money paid by the company can be traced to the goods or services it bought.

- Introduce mystery shoppers who check that staff issue receipts, hand over corporate goods (rather than their own), and that procedures are observed (such as closing the till after every transaction).

- Make use of business ratios, such as net profit to sales. If profit is slipping, it may be that sales are not being recorded, or that costs are being inflated. Compare your results with the industry average. It is worth noting that the Inland Revenue uses this technique to check that it is receiving enough tax from each business. The company should also make comparisons between branches.

- Ensure that computer programs are verified and their integrity maintained. Do not allow changes to be made. Critical areas where fraud could take place should be examined.

IMPROVE YOUR CHANCES OF DETECTION

This simply means ensuring that staff are regularly aware of auditors in the business, with special audits being undertaken in areas of high vulnerability. This will discourage employees from considering a fraud.

IMPROVE YOUR RECORD-KEEPING

Matching of documents should be required to trigger a payment or the despatch of goods. For example, the warehouse might not be allowed to release goods without first receiving the order form.

Sequential numbering of forms helps to stop employees removing items to cover up theft or fraud. Prominently numbered forms make gaps or additions obvious. Having coloured pre-printed forms, and changing the colour from time to time will also prevent the criminal from photocopying an old form and changing it. Furthermore, a signature should be required on forms wherever possible, though this is not a very effective deterrent.

The company should ensure that accounting systems are explicitly defined in a manual, and should educate staff in adopting the appropriate procedures. This will stop staff from claiming that they were ignorant of methods. It will also speed the auditing process, and help auditors assess whether the system is operating as it should.

What to do on discovering fraud

According to the survey by KPMG quoted earlier in this chapter, only one in four cases of fraud were detected by a management review. Most fraud cases were discovered following an employee blowing the whistle or a tip-off from an anonymous or external third party. This means the organization should make it easy for people to report fraud.

Fraud, once discovered, may be distressing or difficult to handle since it may involve a senior or longstanding employee. That is why the company should have written procedures and should scrupulously follow them. There should be procedures to:

1 Preserve the evidence
2 Freeze misappropriated assets
3 Report fraud to the authorities and shareholders
4 Implement a public relations plan if the company's image is at stake.

What companies do to prevent and report fraud

According to an Ernst & Young survey, 52 per cent of companies have a formal fraud prevention policy, and more than half the surveyed companies had trained their staff in fraud awareness in the past year.

The three best ways to discover fraud (according to the respondents) are, in order, internal controls, whistle-blowers and internal audit. However, external audits were thought to be less effective in detecting fraud than 'by accident'.

This indicates that internal company control mechanisms and audits should be a common and well-managed part of every business. To reduce the cost and improve their effectiveness, the audits should be targeted on suspected areas of fraud. Further, there should be a way for suspicious employees to convey their concerns in confidence, working in tandem with modern legislation which protects whistle-blowers.

Many frauds are never reported. This is because of the time that it would take, the embarrassment that would be caused to the business, and the fact that the money has been recovered. It is estimated that 40 per cent of frauds are detected but not investigated.

Useful links

Association of Certified Fraud Examiners
www.cfenet.com

BDO Stoy Hayward
www.bdo.co.uk

Economic Crime forum
www.financialcrimeforum.com

Fraud hotline – for reporting UK fraud
www.fraudhotline.net

International Fraud Prevention Centre
www.nbs.ntu.ac.uk/depts/ifprc

National Fraud Information Center (US)
www.fraud.org

PWC
www.pwc.com

Risk assessment – fraud

By answering the questions below, you can check to see how vulnerable your business is to fraud. Score one point for each box ticked.

Topic	Question	
Assets	Do you have assets worth stealing?	☐
	Do you have commercial secrets that a competitor would pay for?	☐
Staff	Are certain employees responsible for finance or assets left unsupervised?	☐
	Is any employee addicted to gambling or drink, or do they have heavy financial commitments?	☐
	Do any employees have close links with suppliers or customers?	☐
	Does any employee display wealth greater than his or her income would permit?	☐
	Does any accounts employee never take a holiday?	☐
Systems	Is record-keeping weak in some areas of the business?	☐
	Is there a lack of written procedures in parts of the business where fraud might occur?	☐
	Does the organization fail to conduct fraud audits?	☐

Total points scored

Score: 0–3 points: low risk. 4–6 points: moderate risk. 7–10 points: high risk.

The appendix contains a summary of all the checklists in this book. By entering the results of this one, you can compare the risk of fraud against other categories of risk.

11 *Staying Financially Healthy*

In this chapter we consider financial risks. They include:

- *Pre-empting financial risk*
- *Seven ways to reduce financial risk*
- *Healthy margins*
- *Cutting overheads*
- *Reducing production or operating costs; outsourcing*
- *Offshoring*
- *Unfixing fixed assets; flab.*
- *Unprofitable prices*
- *Bad and excessive debts; substantial borrowings, and vulnerability to interest rates*
- *Selling or closing part of the business*
- *Overseas investment; international finance risks*
- *Financial management and corporate governance*
- *Dealing with a cash crisis; reporting adverse results; the takeover bid; going bankrupt.*

We look at ways of managing the company's finances to reduce the risk. We also examine the steps to take in a financial crisis, and what you can do in the event of an unwelcome takeover.

Pre-empting financial risk

Like all aspects in a business, risk is ultimately measured financially. Where a risk has a low price tag, management tends to place less importance on it. That is why many organizations don't debate health and safety unless a crisis occurs, despite it being potentially a serious risk to the workforce.

Risk has only become a board issue as the penalties – financial and personal – have grown for failure in corporate governance.

Financial risk comes in many forms, such as:

- having insufficient money to meet the company's commitments – this means becoming unprofitable or insolvent
- doing deals which, if they fail, will capsize the business
- being exposed to problems in the market, or being vulnerable to swings in interest rates, or raw materials.

Seven ways to reduce financial risk

The seven ways to reduce financial risk are as follows:

1 *Maintaining a healthy margin.* All things being equal, a higher margin gives a company more room for manoeuvre, and more time to sort out problems. It allows the business to build up greater reserves, to invest, and to acquire other businesses. The nearer the margin gets to zero, the closer it gets to making losses, and the more likely the business will fail. Margins are simply the difference between revenue and costs.

2 *Building financial reserves.* Financial reserves will see a business through a recession, or help it escape from an unprofitable new venture.

3 *Having saleable assets.* This includes profitable divisions which other businesses would want to acquire. Many companies survive a trauma by selling some of their subsidiaries.

4 *Avoiding financial adventures that 'bet the shop'.* This includes acquisitions whose impact on the business could be ruinous. The 'precautionary principle' was originally used in connection with global warming. It states that where there are threats of serious or irreversible damage, lack of scientific certainty should not be used as a reason for postponing cost-effective measures to prevent environmental degradation. This is also known as 'better safe than sorry'. The same principle can also be applied to business risk. If the outcome could be catastrophic to the business, the opportunity should be forgone, or the operation sold. This could be used as an argument against all investments, but it harks back to Figure 1.4 'Determining acceptable risk' in Chapter 1.

5 *Bullet-proofing the business.* This can include reducing its reliance on a few big customers, heavily cyclical markets, or risky processes.

6 *Having a clear oversight of the organization's finances*, having control measures in place, and having effective audits.

7 *Keeping costs low.* The lower the costs, the easier it is to stay in profit. It is especially important to minimize fixed costs, something we discuss later in this chapter.

The need for healthy margins

A strong margin is the cornerstone for a healthy business. There is little point in growing a vast empire which cannot pay its bills. Some businesses are investing in the future or engaging in a 'land grab' mode, so that for a period of time their investors accept losses or operating at breakeven. An example of this is the television company BSkyB which for years struggled to make money; but which ended up profitable. Another example is the 'dot com' era where investors invested large sums of money in new businesses in the belief that they would grow and ultimately be profitable.

Healthy margins are a combination of:

1 Adequately high prices
2 Sufficient volume
3 Low costs.

It is hard to get the first two right – high prices and volume – especially in changing markets. But the third element – low costs – is very much within the company's control. Next we consider the two main elements of cost – overheads and production (or operational) costs.

Cutting overheads

The larger company usually has lower unit costs, due to economies of scale. As demand grows, the unit cost should therefore decline. However, a growing company also adds fixed costs (staff, property and equipment) to help it meet demand. An increase in profit lets the company hire extra computer staff or sponsor the local football team. But, if sales start to fall, these overheads can become a burden, and some of them may be pruned without affecting sales.

Costs are easy to add but, once in place, are difficult to prune. High costs put the company at a disadvantage because they raise the break-even point. While a low-cost producer can survive when sales fall, the high-cost producer reaches a loss situation much earlier, and is therefore less well-equipped to survive.

Reducing total costs and unfixing fixed costs allows the company to make profits on a slimmer turnover. In a time of crisis, the better-run company will survive longer.

Reducing production or operating costs

High production costs create a high selling price, which leads to a loss of business. Alternatively, it can cut margins, which moves the company closer to the danger zone. Benchmarking, market research and feedback from customers will tell the company whether its production costs are excessive.

In Chapter 4 we examined several factors (such as design) which affect production risk and cost. In this chapter, we start by looking at ways of reducing variable costs; through efficiency, automation and order size.

Increased productivity – getting more output for the same cost – is an often neglected way of looking at reducing risk and improving margin. Increased productivity means:

1 Achieving more output with no increase in costs, or
2 Achieving the same output for less cost.

ACHIEVING MORE OUTPUT WITH NO INCREASE IN COSTS

Improved efficiency reduces costs. This may entail better planning so that materials are at hand when needed. It can also involve reorganizing work or payment systems so that the workforce produces more products or fewer rejects. It may also entail removing bottlenecks, and reducing staffing levels.

ACHIEVING THE SAME OUTPUT FOR LESS COST

Reducing variable costs often involves increased automation: replacing people with machines. Companies evaluate the value of the investment by comparing the cost of the machine against the savings in labour and materials.

Small orders are often expensive, because the profit is often outweighed by the cost of fulfilling the order. Such business is sometimes managed better by a wholesaler or retailer. Many businesses are moving towards 'batch of one' production (where every product is different). While this is a laudable marketing aim, it adds cost and therefore risk.

OUTSOURCING

Companies today are outsourcing many functions which are not seen as core skills. They include the vehicle fleet, computer services, premises management and catering. Using outsourcing relieves the firm of capital costs, which are built into the service contract. It can also reduce variable costs, because a specialist firm can often carry out the process more efficiently.

At one time, it was blue-collar jobs that were outsourced, but the 1990s and 2000s saw the outsourcing (and later offsharing) of clerical and then professional jobs.

However, management's view of what constitutes a core competency can change over time. JPMorgan Chase, the financial services group, first outsourced its IT services to IBM for $5 bn (£2.7 bn), and then reversed the deal two years later. JPMorgan said IBM had performed well and had missed no milestones. But the company now regarded technology as a source of competitive advantage. For some firms, dealing with third-party suppliers can't match the ease of working with colleagues in the same organization.

There is evidence that managers who try outsourcing regret it. A worldwide survey by Gallup for Proudfoot Consulting showed that one third of managers said outsourcing had either delivered less than expected or had been a complete failure. And a study by PA Consulting showed that two-thirds of companies were disappointed. But Phil Morris of outsourcing advisors Morgan Chambers said when outsourcing deals fail it is usually because they were badly handled from the start. The complexity of bringing it all back in-house when it goes wrong and transferring staff again means that most companies opt to simply try a different supplier instead. 'There are a substantially greater number of companies that solve failing outsourcing by going to a different outsourcer and opting for a different sourcing and delivery model. We see more re-letting than un-outsourcing,' he said.

Jobs that are most suitable for outsourcing are those that a supplier could do more cheaply and more effectively, and where the supplier specializes in that field. For example, many of Cisco's routers and switches are not made by Cisco employees. The company focuses on doing what it does best – design and marketing.

With 1000 cars and 500 light commercial vehicles operating from 70 sites, one industrial group estimated that by outsourcing the acquisition, day-to-day management and disposal of its fleet it would save £500 000 a year. In their turn, fleet car companies like Avis Fleet Services outsource activities such as public relations, advertising and catering.

OFFSHORING

As a result of globalization and the Internet, many jobs once carried out in the West can be done profitably in low-cost countries such as China and India. The aim is to reduce costs, and there is nothing new about that.

Meanwhile, manufacturers have discovered that low-cost Chinese imports were entering their market, and soaking up sales. As a result, they relocated their production facilities abroad.

The jobs that are most easily offshored are those that are not customer-facing, and that involve routine work, such as data processing. If the job can be done via the Internet or on a PC, or with the use of scanned documents, then it can be offshored. This includes much insurance work, mortgage applications, and so on.

However, organizations have also been able to offshore other white-collar jobs such as accountancy. The research company Gartner reckons that 25 per cent of high technology jobs in the West could be offshored.

The jobs that are more difficult to offshore involve:

- interacting with others, for example, teacher, social worker or security.
- physical jobs such as veterinary surgeon, shelf stacking, cooking, or drain cleaning
- on-site jobs such as firefighter, drain cleaner or receptionist
- 'core competencies', such as engineering or proposal writing (however, design is being regularly offshored).
- strategic 'head office' jobs such as planning or marketing.

Having set up an offshore business process outsourcing firm in India to do its back-office work, General Electric subsequently sold a majority share in it, and raised $500 m. General Electric Capital International Services (Gecis) and its 16000 employees were intended to provide support services for the company, including training financial analysis and administration. Following the sale, Gecis was then able to accept work from other companies, and became a revenue earner rather than an overhead. And GE, in turn, was able to use the $500 m to find new growth areas such as security technology.

Offshoring risks

But offshoring isn't without its risks. According to the *Financial Times*, US companies in 2003 made $8 billion profit in China. And while that sounds a lot of money, in the same year they made $7 bn in Australia, a market of only 19 million people. They also made $9 bn in Taiwan and South Korea, which have a combined population of just 70 million. And in Mexico, a country dismissed by many, they earned $14 bn. So China has not been a source of huge wealth for business as was expected.

Moreover, things can go badly wrong. Telecoms companies used to make money in China until 2001, when local firms started producing cheap mobile phones and destroyed the profitability of the market. Carmakers have done well from China, as have those which face no competition from state-owned Chinese firms, those whose designs cannot be easily copied or stolen, and service companies such as McDonald's.

According to the *FT*, the biggest profits are gained by those who buy from China, such as Wal-Mart, the US retailer, rather than invest in it.

When it comes to offshoring call centres, 28 per cent of people who sought technical support for desktop PCs reported some kind of communication problem, according to a survey in *Consumer Reports* by the Consumers' Union. Six out of ten complainants said that the support staff's English was limited or hard to understand. Dell stopped sending US corporate support calls to India, amid customer complaints. But many of their home users are routed to an overseas call centre, according to *USA Today*.

An alternative to manufacturing in the developing world is to cut costs in western manufacturing plants. This has been seen in Germany, where Volkswagen aimed to cut personnel costs by 30 per cent, by introducing a number of cost-cutting measures. This included a two-year wage freeze and more flexible work rules. In return the company pledged to manufacture certain models in Germany and thus secure jobs at the plants that made them.

UNFIXING FIXED ASSETS

A production line, complete with manufacturing staff, is a virtually fixed overhead. It will continue to produce products unless drastic action is taken. It is not easy to lay off staff, nor recruit skilled workers when business improves. Every time a company commissions a large factory, it is adding a substantial amount of extra risk. Many new factories have huge appetites, requiring large quantities of material every week to break even.

However, some parts of the process can be sub-contracted. This means that the company only pays for what it needs. This is a 'make or buy' type of decision. For example, computer firms often re-badge other companies' printers or disk drives as their own. This extends their product range without requiring the company to invest in production facilities. Many small and little-known electronics firms are kept busily at work assembling satellite TV receivers and DVD players for famous Japanese companies. Large companies sub-contract their manufacturing because of the brief life cycle of such products and because they recognize that their expertise now lies in designing and marketing their products.

You can encourage service functions to become separate profit centres by seeking work from outside the business. An extension of this is to 'privatize' them, whereby they become a separate business and sell their services back to the company.

Buildings

Leased buildings can be sub-let or the lease re-negotiated. Sometimes the company can downsize into fewer buildings, selling off the surplus properties. When a building is jettisoned, many other costs go with it: insurance, repairs, canteen staff, telephone bills, receptionists, gardeners, rates and water rates.

Buildings are often millstones – as Athena found when its high-cost shop leases bankrupted the firm – so a company should be careful about signing long property leases in these uncertain times. The company should avoid the kind of leases that commit the company for 20 years, have upward-only rent reviews, and no facility for sub-letting. It is better to seek a shorter lease which allows the business to vacate the property or pay less in a case of high interest rates. Such contracts are more easily found when the market is at its lowest.

Home working

Firms can reduce their costs by arranging for staff to work from home. The first stage is to disband regional offices and for regionally based staff to work from home. Reducing the number of staff who need desk space allows the company to move to smaller premises. At some companies, staff book a desk space when they arrive at work (known as hot desking), and all phone calls are automatically routed to the telephone number associated with that desk.

Apart from IT staff and sales people, home working is suitable for management consultants, architects and other high-grade professionals. But companies should take care when considering home working. Its disadvantages include lack of supervision and face-to-face contact, and the danger of reduced productivity.

Equipment

Depreciating assets such as equipment should normally be leased rather than bought. This will spread payment in line with the income that they produce. Even existing plant can be sold to a leasing company on a sale-and-leaseback agreement.

Some production-led companies dote on their machines, and often buy shiny equipment which is then under-used. Sometimes equipment is leased before a downturn in demand. WPM Engineers leased three £80 000 machines, only to find that the demand for its products was falling. The company considered allowing the machines to be repossessed, but feared that they would be sold at a very low price. Instead the company has itself sold one machine, and used the money to pay off the outstanding debt.

Care should be taken to avoid contracts which commit the company to extended or onerous payments. Photocopier leases, in particular, have often been found to be usurious.

Stocks of raw materials and finished goods

Excessive stock ties up capital. It also risks being written off if it becomes out of date. This in turn leads to losses. A tight control of stocks can only be achieved if the company has a good production planning system, uses quality suppliers, with which it has a close relationship.

Salaries

When a company is performing badly, it is the staff furthest from the customer and the production line who are made redundant quickest. That often means R&D people, designers, health and safety officers, personnel assistants, training managers, and environmental managers.

As we see below, apart from getting rid of people, the company has other choices. This includes outsourcing (see above), and making salaries more variable by relating them to corporate performance.

Employees' salaries often represent one of the largest costs to the company. Traditionally, the only way to reduce salaries was by making staff redundant. In other cases, management has initiated staff wage reductions.

Employees can also be given fixed-term contracts of employment for one to five years rather than permanent contracts. This reduces management's commitment to the employee, but it also reduces the employee's loyalty. It does not reduce costs in the short term.

Some firms use part-time or seasonal staff to meet peak sales or production periods. In slack periods the firm can reduce its use of part-timers without risking the core staff.

More recently, companies have been making part of their employees' salaries dependent on corporate profit or turnover. This allows employees to earn more in times of profit than they could if their salary was fixed (and less when the company is making losses). These profit-related pay schemes even out the peaks and troughs of the business cycle, and thus reduce the amount of hiring and firing. They are unlikely to be popular in times of poor sales, and may lead to employee dissatisfaction.

Sales support costs

Companies sometimes put sales staff on commission-only payment. This has its drawbacks. It can encourage sales people to go for short-term sales, and to sell products to people who don't need them. It also discourages those activities which don't lead to immediate sales, such as client servicing.

Other firms convert their sales people to self-employment, and allow them to sell the products of non-competing firms. The company is then relieved of salary costs, paying commission costs instead. This has the disadvantage of reduced control, reduced loyalty, and poorer customer servicing.

A similar solution is to transfer the sales function to an agency. Agencies are especially popular in grocery, where a large number of outlets have to be serviced. The advantage of an agency is that it reduces fixed costs. On the other hand, an agency sales force is selling many companies' products, and therefore some firms will lose out.

A better solution is to focus sales effort on key accounts, and to service smaller customers through telesales, which is less expensive. This reduces cost, while often improving effectiveness. It also matches the trend in most markets towards a concentration of buying points.

Transport and delivery costs

Companies whose goods are moved by contract carrier are relieved of the problems of leasing and managing a fleet of vehicles, and paying their drivers. They avoid most of the fixed costs of distribution.

Promotional costs

The cost of promotion can be up to 10 per cent of revenue in some fast-moving consumer goods companies and even higher among mail-order businesses and consultancies.

Companies which are anxious to cut back on promotional spending are often those which cannot see a benefit from their expenditure. Sometimes advertising becomes a symbol of virility, with competitors comparing the size of their annual spends. However, research suggests that companies which cut back on advertising during a recession do less well when the economy picks up.

Computers

Every year the computer industry invents a more powerful computer or an even more dazzling piece of software. A company may easily feel pressurized into buying the latest equipment, but the cost of computing has to be kept under control.

Despite the widespread belief that computers improve productivity, the actual results are still in doubt. A study by Dale Jorgensen suggests that IT development and investment may have been worth around 0.5 per cent per annum in GDP growth in the late 1990s in the G7 countries.

On the other hand, a study by Paul Strassmann of US commercial banks, the industry that spends most on computing, showed little gain in productivity between 1995 and 1999. Strassmann analysed the ratio of payroll spending to revenue and found that, despite the greater amount of IT available to the staff, the bank's revenues did not rise significantly in proportion to the amount it spent on workers.

Some of the problems with IT are the lack of training, lack of management and the lack of control over the use to which IT is put. As a new generation of computer-literate workers joins the workforce, we may find productivity increasing with IT investment but it is too early to predict this confidently.

As we saw above, more companies are outsourcing their IT systems. This gives them professional support, removes the problem of managing IT staff, and avoids capital costs. The bill for outsourcing is not cheap, however.

GETTING RID OF FLAB

Many parts of a business under-perform. For example, if a company instructs its sales force to call on ten customers a day rather than their usual eight, profits could rise by the same proportion, namely 25 per cent.

Some companies' flab can be seen in excessive overheads. Marble walls will not disguise the fact that the company cannot pay its suppliers. A directors' dining room or a fountain at the front of the building will impress no one if the production equipment is held together with string.

The company should avoid having too many layers of management, and many companies have cut out tiers of middle management. Staff should be encouraged to manage themselves, and senior management should run the business rather than managing day-to-day problems.

Unprofitable prices

'Low prices' are attractive words to the consumer, but they can endanger the company's survival. Companies underprice their products for two possible reasons:

1 They lack adequate information about costs.
2 They are (or believe themselves to be) in an overly competitive market.

Obtaining information about direct costs should be easily done, even if the allocation of overheads to different products can provoke debate.

Unilever companies, which make a range of supermarket brands from Persil to Flora, assess the profitability of each major customer. This is particularly useful in cases where the customer is demanding more discounts. From the annual revenue, the analysis deducts the cost of production, cost of discounts, promotional offers, sales support, and advertising contributions. This shows whether the price charged is profitable. It can help the company withstand further demands for price reductions.

Bad debt

Unpaid invoices cost UK business £20 billion per year. Intrum Justitia, a provider of credit management software, estimates that almost half of UK invoices are overdue, with an average delay of 18 days. It also estimates that 1.9 per cent of the amount invoiced in a year is never paid. Recent legislative changes mean that businesses can now claim interest on late payment and 20 per cent of firms have done so, according to the Better Payment Practice Group. Despite this, late payment and bad debts threaten the survival of many otherwise successful companies. There are two elements to controlling debt: prevention and collection, which we turn to next.

DEBT PREVENTION

It is better to prevent bad debts from occurring than spending time chasing them once they have occurred. Prevention is always better than cure, and sound credit management procedures can reduce bad debts by 90 per cent, according to some experts.

For new customers, the company should take up references from credit reference agencies and other traders. The company should be aware of the need to obtain references from genuine suppliers.

Conservative credit management is often criticized by sales people when they see sales opportunities lost because of cautious financial staff. When finance people throw caution to the winds, however, company performance is usually the loser. In the 1980s, the UK banks relaxed their lending requirements, giving 100 per cent mortgages when previously they would have only lent 80 per cent of the value of the property. As a result, many people ended up being unable to afford their mortgage, and the banks were unable to recover their loan. The same occurred in the commercial property market.

In a growing economy, companies often feel they need to join the stampede, for fear of being left behind by their more daring competitors. Corporate policies are overturned, and a new spirit of adventure pervades the firm. This is a risky period, and companies which have sound financial policies tend to survive better than those that don't. It is better to forego risky business, than to see it turn into a bad debt later.

Companies should state payment terms clearly, and charge interest for late payment. They should report outstanding debts, and never let debts rise beyond a predetermined limit. When they do, it is time to collect them, a factor which we consider next.

COLLECTING DEBTS

Insensitive debt collection can cause a company to lose customers. That is why handing the problem to a debt collection agency is not a simple solution. It is often better that a member of the sales force visits the late payer, discusses the situation and tactfully seeks payment. Other ways to prevent bad debts include factoring and credit insurance.

In factoring, the company sells its invoice to a factor (or agent) when issuing it, and gets up to 80 per cent of the value straightaway. The balance is paid when the debt falls due (usually 30 days).

Similarly, credit insurance ensures that the company will get up to 80 per cent of a debt if a customer goes bust. The insurer will usually set overall credit limits for major companies, while new accounts can be opened providing they are less than a specific sum.

Excessive borrowing

Excessive borrowing is caused by three factors:

1 Management rashness
   • Excessive investment in new plant
   • Unwise diversification
   • Mistimed investment
2 Management inactivity
   • Failure to respond to a period of falling sales
   • Failure to prevent sales from falling in the first place
   • Allowing costs to rise excessively, or pricing goods below their proper level
3 Interest-rate rises
   • Leading to larger higher repayment costs and the need for more working capital.

Borrowing has three harmful effects:

1 It adds to the burden of overheads (examined earlier), so that revenue goes to repay loans rather than being invested in the business.
2 The bank or shareholders may lose confidence in the company's ability to repay the loan. Shareholders may sell their stock, while the bank may press for repayment.
3 The company may reach its overdraft ceiling, and be refused further borrowing. At this point, it will be unable to pay its debts. If it cannot find new sources of credit, it either finds a buyer or goes bust.

A highly geared company (one that is borrowing a lot) is where debt is more than half the shareholders' capital (a debt:equity ratio of 50 per cent). When the debt exceeds shareholders' capital, the company is heavily in debt.

For the three reasons quoted above, excessive debt should be reduced. This can be done quickly, by selling assets; or slowly, by making more profit. Much of this chapter is about improving profit, so we next examine the issue of selling assets.

Selling or closing part of the business

Selling off part of the business helps the firm to acquire working capital and reduce interest payments. It is one of the first things a turnaround expert or 'company doctor' will do when trying to help an ailing company survive. It also solves the problem of a loss-making division.

The company can sell a business unit to its management (as a management buy-out), to a competitor, or to a new entrant to the market.

Losses occurring in any part of the business should be stopped before they drag down the profitable parts of the firm. One firm made good profits from making toilet cubicles, but lost money when installing them for clients. As a result it went bust, despite having a full order book.

Closure is logical when no buyer can be found for the loss-making business. There will be one-off redundancy costs, but at least the losses will be stopped.

ABANDONING MARGINAL PRODUCTS

It is worth checking how many people are employed on different product lines. Sometimes unprofitable products employ many people. Abandoning such products can have a substantial effect on profitability. Companies can often improve profitability by shrinking the business. This involves abandoning marginal products and consolidating their operations to fewer sites.

Overseas investment

Chapter 9 examined the security risks of overseas investment and travel. The financial risks of international activities are also a hazard. A.T. Kearney, one of the world's largest management consulting firms, annually surveys the executives of leading global firms to ascertain which markets they find most attractive for investment. In 2003, China strengthened its position at the top of this survey, despite the SARS outbreak. This is largely due to its impressive growth rate, massive labour pool, World Trade Organization (WTO) accession and rising disposable incomes.

Other leading countries for foreign direct investment were the US, Brazil, India, Russia and Eastern Europe and Mexico. Generally, this survey showed a preference for countries with strong growth prospects and emerging markets.

However, before making any overseas investment, companies must consider every potential consequence. Different companies and different industries will have quite different requirements – a business which is looking to benefit from offshore call centres would look for a large, educated and yet cheap labour force, whereas a manufacturer would want to consider transport links, supplier availability and potential local demand for the product.

> When NEC was looking for a location for its new $1 bn microchip plant, it revealed that California was 'a very hostile environment' to set up manufacturing facilities. The company was put off by stringent environmental regulations and labour laws which made staff costs very expensive. NEC was also dissuaded from investing in Japan due to a monetary crisis and the strength of the yen. The company eventually sited its new plant in Scotland. A strong factor was the productivity of the company's existing Scottish plant, which was 10–20% higher than Japanese factories. Regional grants worth 5 per cent to 10 per cent of buildings costs were another factor, as was the growing European demand for microchips.

INTERNATIONAL FINANCE RISKS

Exporters sometimes lose money because, by the time they get paid, the exchange rate has changed for the worse. Toyota's profits fell by almost 10 per cent in the space of three months when a weak dollar made imported Japanese cars less competitive in price.

Exporters (and companies dealing in commodities) often insure against a change in exchange rates by the use of derivatives (futures and options contracts). Some companies only take out forward contracts. This lets them buy a currency at a set rate in advance. It is thought to be cheaper and less risky than buying options, which give the company the option to buy a currency at a set rate at a set time. But unlike forward contracts, buying an option does not lock the company into a potentially unfavourable exchange rate. Used as simple insurance, derivatives are straightforward and risk-free. The problem occurs when companies use them to speculate. In the UK, local authorities lost £600 million by investing in interest-rate swaps.

The most famous case was Nick Leeson of Barings Bank. Leeson gambled on the future direction of the Nikkei 225 and in 1993 was responsible for 10 per cent of the bank's profits. However, by allowing Leeson to essentially be his own guardian, the bank made it easy for him to disguise enormous losses in 1994. In January 1995, Leeson disappeared from his offices and left behind £1.3 billion of liabilities. Although Leeson was later found and prosecuted, the losses led to the collapse of the bank.

Despite this, derivatives trade has grown sharply in the past decade, with the International Swaps and Derivatives Association estimating that the current value of outstanding contracts is close to $85 trillion. This has concerned many experts who give examples such as Enron as portents of impending doom. The US energy markets rely on derivatives trading for most of its deals, despite the sheer complexity of these deals contributing to the Enron collapse.

Speculating in derivatives is attractive because of the huge sums than can be made if the market moves the right way. The average company should recognize its inexperience and the scale of the risk, and restrict itself to insuring foreign revenue on the forward markets.

COMMODITY PRICES

A company which processes a commodity (such as a coffee manufacturer) is at risk from commodity prices. The company can reduce this risk by buying commodity futures. This need not be expensive, but such futures can only produce a temporary cushion. Eventually rising prices must be paid for by the consumer, and excessive price rises will eventually cause them to switch on to substitute products (such as tea or cola, in the case of coffee).

Coffee prices are, at the time of writing, around a fifth of the 1994 value (a drop which has hit hard farmers in the developing world), but in the two years before 1994 there was almost a 400 per cent increase in prices, following two periods of frost in Brazil. This was not an isolated incident. From 70 cents a pound in 1975, coffee prices leapt to 360 cents the following year, again following a frost in Brazil.

Financial management

Effective financial management means having rapid information systems which warn of problems, and holding regular management reviews. It includes keeping a tight rein on money, whether it is spent by staff or owed by customers.

BASEL II

The 'New Capital Accord', known as Basel II, is an international agreement that helps international banks measure and manage risks. Endorsed by the central bank governors and the heads of bank supervisory authorities in the Group of Ten countries, it has now spread to investment companies and other businesses for whom money is a major risk.

Many people believe that the requirements of Basel II will trickle down to other financial organizations, especially through government regulation, and therefore it should not be ignored. Being caught unprepared is not an attractive proposition.

Basel II concerns the need for financial service providers (FSPs) to keep a cash reserve on hand to meet their risks, in order to avoid disaster. Under Basel II, these reserves should amount to eight per cent of the company's risks. And to achieve that reserve, banks must know what their risks are. They must therefore be able to assess their risks. Basel II defines risk as 'The risk of direct or indirect loss resulting from inadequate or failed internal processes, people and systems, or from external events.'

Companies that are concerned with the following need to take Basel II into account: credit risk, derivatives, investment management, insurance risk, foreign exchange risk, energy risks, asset liability management, and commodities. Apart from banks, the accord could also affect asset management firms, insurance firms, energy companies, brokerage firms and corporations.

Basel II has three 'pillars'. They are:

- *Minimum capital requirements*. This requires FSPs to measure credit, market and operational risk, and maintain reserves equal to eight per cent of their value.
- *Supervisory review*. This requires regulatory authorities to ensure that each bank has sound internal processes in place.
- *Market discipline*. This requires FSPs to publicly disclose information about their risks.

To comply with Basel II, many FSPs have instigated IT-based solutions. Forrester research suggested that large European banks on their own would spend € 115 million over five years, in order to comply with Basel II. Through being more efficient and knowledgeable, banks that comply with Basel II should see many advantages, including wider margins, better leverage, and less need for equity capital.

While most banks in the industrial nations have already implemented these ideas, Basel II converts best practice into a regulatory requirement, and expands this exercise across the world.

Some institutions use the Zachman Framework (www.zifa.com) as a way of modelling the enterprise. The framework models the company's processes, and gives a clearer picture of how different functions and processes work together. It asks the question: who does what; why, where and when.

RISK MANAGEMENT FOR FINANCIAL SERVICES

For financial services, good risk management includes:

- *Better transparency*: if errors are spotted and reported early, there is less risk that they will be hidden and multiplied, as happened with Nick Leeson at Barings Bank.
- *A risk management culture*: people need to be aware of the risks that face their department. This requires training.
- *Better supervision*: the financial services industry pays high salaries to high flyers who often work alone. As with Transparency above, better supervision might have saved Barings.
- *Operational risk management*: the organization needs controls in place to prevent overly risky decisions being taken.

What to do if a cash crisis happens

If a cash crisis occurs, the following actions should be taken.

1 Stop cash flowing out of the business. This will include the following actions:
   - Stop all purchases which are not essential to the short-term survival of the business.
   - Put all capital projects on hold
   - Close loss-making operations
   - Reduce costs, especially staff and non-productive sites
   - Sell divisions or assets to raise cash
   - Collect outstanding debts
   - Slow the rate of payment to creditors.
2 Develop a survival plan and implement it.
3 Communicate with the bank and other creditors.

Reporting adverse results

The City expects to see a continued growth in profits, year after year, and any forecast of a fall-off sends tremors through the investment community.

Reporting poor annual results can cause shares in a public company to slide. If the market loses confidence, and the slide continues, the company could be taken over. (Typical targets also include small companies which are doing well, as well as larger companies which are doing badly.)

The markets should always be warned about poor results. Keeping in touch with city analysts and the financial media is essential for companies which want to keep a steady share price.

All public companies can and should invest in financial PR. If the company keeps in touch with investors, if it explains what it is doing and why, it will be in a much better position in the event of a takeover bid. While the City is notoriously lacking in loyalty or gratitude, investors are more likely to trust a management team with whom they are familiar and whose strategy they understand.

Responding to a takeover bid

Strictly speaking, a hostile bid is mainly a risk for the people on the receiving end, rather than the business itself. Takeovers are merely a way for the capitalist system to reward profitable businesses, and allocate assets efficiently.

In the event of a hostile takeover bid, the company should assess the effect of the takeover. If it decides to reject the bid, it should:

- Gather experts in finance, banking, the law, and city PR.
- Tell shareholders why they should reject the offer. Explain the disadvantages of the offer and the benefits of maintaining the status quo. The arguments should be based on finance not emotion.
- Demonstrate conviction and resolution. Shareholders and the takeover firm can sense signs of weakness or vacillation.
- Consider alternatives to outright rejection. This could include mounting a bid for the other company, or making life difficult for it by adopting liabilities.

Reporting risk in the financial accounts

Annual reports often convey minimal useful information about the real trading position of the business. To combat this, and to protect shareholders, accounting bodies are increasingly urging companies to be more open in their reporting.

Companies should identify in their annual reports the risks the business faces. This would include an analysis of:

- the main factors affecting a company's performance and market position
- the risks and uncertainties it faces (including sensitivity to interest-rate rises and currency fluctuations)
- how risks are being managed
- in quantitative terms, the potential impact on results.

According to the UK's Accounting Standards Board, factors liable to affect future results include:

- scarcity of raw materials
- reliance on major suppliers or customers
- self insurance
- skill shortages
- environmental costs.

These should be reported, says the board, irrespective of whether they were significant in the reported year.

See Chapter 13, where we look at the Sarbanes-Oxley Act and the Operating Financial Review.

How likely is the business to go bankrupt?

There are several models that predict business bankruptcy. Springate is one such model, developed by Gordon L.V. Springate. It uses four out of 19 popular financial ratios that best distinguish between sound business and those that failed. The Springate model takes the following form:

$$Z = 1.03A + 3.07B + 0.66C + 0.4D$$

Where:

A = Working capital/total assets
B = Net profit before interest and taxes/total assets
C = Net profit before taxes/current liabilities
D = Sales/total assets

The higher the score, the more financially sound is the company; and the lower the score, the greater the danger of the company becoming insolvent. Where Z is less than 0.862, the firm is classified as 'failed'.

At root, this model simply looks for insufficient liquidity, excess debt, insufficient sales, and lack of profit. There is an online bankruptcy predictor at www.bankruptcyaction.com/insolart1.htm

According to Bankruptcy Action, this model achieved an accuracy rate of 92 per cent using the 40 companies tested by Springate. When a different 50 companies with an average asset size of $2.5 million were tested by another researcher, the model achieved 88 per cent accuracy. A third test on 24 companies with an average asset size of $63 million found an accuracy rate of 83 per cent.

You can also use this kind of predictor to assess new suppliers. Dun and Bradstreet offer a service based on these kinds of statistics to tell you how reliable a supplier will be.

Useful links

Bank for International Settlements (Basel II)
www.bis.org

Bankruptcy Action
www.bankruptcyaction.com

Better Management.com
www.bettermanagement.com

Business Performance magazine
www.bpmmag.net

Chartered Institute of Management Accountants
www.cimaglobal.com

Dun and Bradstreet
www.dnb.com

Society of Turnaround Professionals
www.stp-uk.org

UK Government insolvency site
www.insolvency.gov.uk

Risk assessment – finance

By answering the questions below, you can assess the company's vulnerability to financial risk. Score one point for every box ticked.

Topic	Question	
Financial position	Have sales fallen for two years or more?	☐
	Is any major part of the company making losses?	☐
	Does the company have excessive borrowings?	☐
	Does the company have a large amount of bad debt?	☐
	Does the company have substantial overheads?	☐
	Does the company lack a fast and informative management information system?	☐
Takeover	Is the company vulnerable to a takeover?	☐
International	Does the company export beyond its own trading block (for example, beyond the EU)?	☐
	Is the company dependent on commodities?	☐
	Does the company speculate in derivatives or other high-risk areas?	☐

Total points scored

Score: 0–3 points: low risk. 4–6 points: moderate risk. 7–10 points: high risk.

The appendix contains a summary of all the checklists in this book. By entering the results of this one, you can compare the scale of financial risk against other categories of risk.

12 *Avoiding IT Disaster*

In this chapter, we examine the risks that relate to computers, and we consider how to minimize them.

- *How prevalent is computer disaster? How serious is data loss?*
- *What causes computer failure and data loss? How easy is recovery?*
- *The problems caused*
- *The six main types of risk*
- *How to avoid disaster from theft or unauthorized access*
- *How to avoid infection*
- *Minimizing the effects of hardware failures, user error, and lost data*
- *Spyware; scams; software piracy*
- *Setting a policy*
- *Contingency planning*
- *ISO 17799; TickIT*
- *Outsourcing IT.*

How prevalent is computer failure?

Is computer failure common, and how serious are the losses? What causes them? We start by setting out the facts.

In the last 12 months, according to the UK government's Information Security Breaches survey, two thirds of large businesses suffered an incident where they had to restore significant data from backup (for example, a systems failure or physical theft). Of the businesses that had an incident, roughly half faced major disruption to their business operations, some for up to a month. This clearly demonstrates that computer failure is very common.

Research by Aveco shows 20 per cent of companies will suffer a major computing disaster. The 2003 PC Magazine Reliability and Service survey shows nearly a quarter of desktops require repair in the first twelve months of their life. A survey by research company Ontrack Data (Figure 12.1) showed there are a wide range of disasters that can cause computer failure.

How serious is data loss?

Eighty-seven per cent of businesses are dependent on electronic data to a significant extent, according to the Security Breaches survey quoted above.

Contingency Planning Research estimates that 43 per cent of companies affected by a computing disaster will never reopen and that a further 29 per cent cease operation within two years. A company which has become reliant on its IT system can be brought to a standstill. Large organisations which use real-time processing (such as insurance companies)

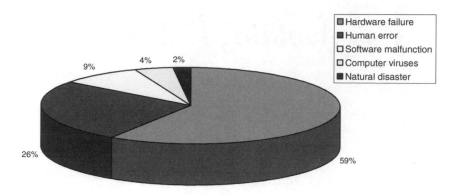

9%   4%   2%

Hardware failure
Human error
Software malfunction
Computer viruses
Natural disaster

26%

59%

Source: Ontrack

Figure 12.1   Causes of data loss

are likely to have a professionally managed system; but medium and small-sized companies should assess their dependence before disaster strikes.

In a study of Canadian CEOs and CIOs (chief information officers) by Ernst & Young, 34 per cent of those surveyed identify computer system failure as the most significant risk to business continuity, ahead of other threats such as recession, commodity prices and exchange rates, disasters and terrorism.

What causes computer failure and data loss?

The majority of computer failures (59 per cent) are caused by hardware problems, according to an Ontrack survey, shown in Figure 12.1. This includes electrical failure and head crash. Human error, such as accidentally deleting files or dropping a computer, caused 26 per cent of the failures.

How easy is recovery?

In the Ernst & Young survey quoted above, 65 per cent of those who said it was critical to restore their systems within 24 hours admitted they could not do it. Therefore, it is clear that many businesses would have trouble recovering from a systems-wide computer failure before it caused significant disruption to their business.

The same survey showed that 26 per cent do not have a business continuity plan; 25 per cent have no computer disaster recovery plan; and 41 per cent have no overall crisis management plan. This reinforces the feeling that data is not easily recovered, and that companies are not taking sufficient steps to ensure survival.

The problems caused

According to a Loughborough University survey, the most common effects of computer disaster are a loss of revenue, cash and goodwill (see Table 12.1). This strikes at the heart of any business.

Table 12.1   Most commonly identified consequences of computer disaster

Consequence	%
Loss of business or customers	24
Loss of credibility or goodwill	21
Cashflow problems	21
Reduced quality of service to customers	18
Unable to pay staff	12
Backlog of work or loss of production	11
Loss of data	10
Financial loss	9
Loss of customer account management	8
Loss of financial controls	7

Source: Loughborough University

CASE STUDY: HOW MUCH AT RISK IS BUSINESS?

A survey by DataFort showed that only 18 per cent of businesses have a comprehensive and secure backup plan. Forty per cent of companies are in the company's 'extreme risk' category, with either no back-ups, or back-ups that would not protect them adequately.

If these companies were to suffer data loss as a result of a virus, technical failure, fire, flood or theft or other incident, the future of the business would be in jeopardy, claims the company.

DataFort surveyed 150 IT-dependent businesses in various markets over a two-month period to monitor backing up habits. They found that an astonishing 83 per cent of companies have an inadequate back-up strategy, and that 40 per cent of companies are at 'extreme risk' of losing data.

Half of those who backed up with tape did not have any way to verify whether the backup had been successful. The survey also found that, once the information had been backed up, 19 per cent of respondents stored it close to their computer systems rather than storing it at another location – an essential precaution against hazards such as an office fire.

DataFort commented: 'Given the recent publicity surrounding backup and disaster recovery, you would think that there would be more people taking this issue seriously.'

If the company merely loses two days' letters, the problem is unlikely to be severe (though it might be disruptive). If, however, the company is unable to carry out customer transactions, or to issue invoices for a month, the loss will be more serious.

More data is now being kept on laptop computers and on desktop PCs, and this poses an additional problem. Companies should check what information is kept on individual PCs, and include them in their recovery plans.

Insurance companies are also getting tough with companies whose computers are stolen. Some companies now have to pay the first £10 000 of any insurance claim for stolen computers. As a result, companies are no longer reporting thefts, because of the conditions that might be imposed on their policies.

However, the cost of the IT equipment is rarely as significant as the impact on the company's processes. Therefore, it is important to assess the value of the company's computer data, and what effect there would be on the business if you were unable to use it. After one year, the data held on a PC is said to be worth ten times the value of the computer itself. Only by recognizing the company's dependence on its data will computer protection be taken seriously. The greater the dependence, the more carefully the data must be managed.

Figure 12.2 shows that the survival of the business was threatened after 72 hours of data being lost. The survey was conducted among people who visited a business continuity website, so it doesn't adequately reflect normal business opinion; but it is nevertheless indicative.

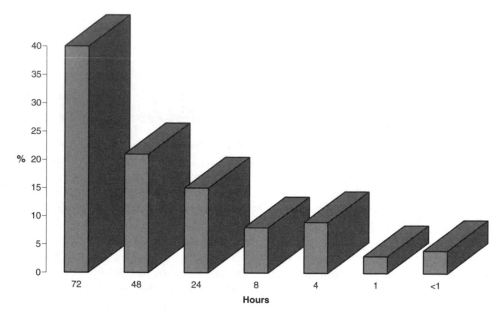

Source: Contingency Planning Research, and *Contingency Planning & Management Magazine* (www.contingencyplanningresearch.com)

Figure 12.2   At what point does the loss of data threaten the survival of the business?

The six main types of IT risk

There are six main computing risks which cause problems. They are:

1 *The theft of computers*. The loss of hardware leaves the company without the ability to process data. The loss of data could mean that the company doesn't know who owes it money, what orders have been received, or what products it is supposed to make. Laptops are especially vulnerable to theft and to being misplaced, as are flash memory drives.

2 *Unauthorized access into the system*. This can take two forms. A member of staff may try to access confidential data, either out of curiosity or malice. An intruder, normally a hacker,

may also try to obtain access to your data. The result is either a loss of company secrets, or the loss of data: hackers can leave viruses on the system. We discuss the problem of wireless networks below.

3 *Introduction of viruses* by employees, from the Internet, personal players or USB flash memory devices. Viruses can be copied on to the corporate network when staff surf the web or download music onto their iPod at work.

4 *Hardware or software faults.* Surveys reveal that computers frequently suffer faults, often when first installed. (In Chapter 8, we also looked at the problems of fire and flood.)

5 *User error.* Staff often delete files accidentally, or lose data by misfiling it.

6 *IT project failure.* IT projects are notoriously prone to failure. This is a problem discussed in Chapter 18.

Next we consider how to prevent these problems from happening.

Avoiding theft

Computers are routinely stolen. A Home Office study showed that computer theft accounted for 18 per cent of non-residential burglary, with the average cost being £2616. Since thieves know that computers are quickly replaced, they often return to steal the replacement equipment. Twenty-five per cent of all computer crimes from commercial properties in the Home Office survey were 'repeats.'

It is extraordinary that such expensive, useful and portable equipment can be left loose on executives' desks. Computers should be locked to the desk: there are several systems on the market for doing this, including laptop locks. The insistent thief can cut through a padlock and wire, but it will deter the casual thief. Computers and printers should also be security marked, and their serial number recorded. Labels which cannot be removed will make the computer less saleable.

Other devices which make burglary less attractive are stickers warning the thief that the computer will not load from the floppy drive, and that the operating system is encrypted. The thief can also be warned that the computer contains a traceable radio bleep, or that it is registered on a national database. Computers can also be alarmed, so that when moved they set off a siren.

Walk-out theft by staff can be minimized by using the procedures suggested above, and by requiring staff to pass a security desk when exiting the building.

Protecting the system against unauthorized access

There are several ways to avoid unauthorized access or theft of data by staff or hackers:

1 Use a firewall, both at the perimeter and desktop level. This will block all computer ports other than those intentionally left open by the IT administrator. Firewalls can provide

an effective defence against many hackers but should not be considered a complete solution.

Wireless network connections are particularly vulnerable. A survey in Dublin quickly found 11 wireless networks, of which only three had any form of encryption. Those encryptions were cracked in less than ten minutes, which meant that a corporate spy or hacker, sitting on a park bench, could have access to the same data as the staff logged into the network at their desks.

2 Restrict the number of computers with removable drives. USB ports are another vulnerability.

3 Restrict access to parts of the computer network which contain confidential data (through, for example, password protection).

4 Keep some computers off the network (for example, those in board members' offices).

5 Adopt closed user grouping, which allows a company to send confidential information down standard telephone lines.

6 Use passwords. They should be unique to the individual and changed often. They should not be a word in the dictionary (see below), nor a birth date. The password should be easy to remember but not obvious to an intruder. This is particularly important for computers which are connected to the Internet, a network which links 20 million users worldwide, including government ministries and the armed services.

Hackers can set up their computer to go through dictionaries until they find a legitimate password. Once inside the network, they can destroy files and damage the company. Companies should therefore monitor the number of failed password attempts to check whether your computer is being targeted by a hacker. The number of tries should be limited, this being a powerful way of protecting the system.

On average, 49 per cent of large companies will suffer a successful hacking or unauthorized access incident in a year.

If a hacker is discovered, they should be locked out by severing external communication links. A hacker who discovers they are under surveillance may instantly take drastic steps to cover their tracks, such as wiping all the corporate data.

It is just as likely that an employee, working from home, will connect to the company's network using a virtual private network (VPN). If the home PC is infected, this gives viruses and worms complete access to the corporate PCs and servers. This means ensuring that each work PC is equipped with virus checkers. Home workers should be given this software too.

How to avoid infection

Many viruses find their way into the corporate system when employees download programs from the Net, from other parts of the network, or when they bring their own program disks to work. The company should stop staff using pirated or 'borrowed' disks, or disks from suspect or unknown origins. A policy, which we discuss later, should be introduced, widely disseminated and actioned.

CASE STUDY: THE DAMAGE DONE BY VIRUSES AND OTHER PROGRAMS

A virus is a self-replicating program, usually intended to cause damage to a computer system. The first was called Brain. Invented in 1987 by two programmers from Pakistan, it was intended not to cause harm but merely to self-replicate.

The Christmas virus was also developed in the same year. It affected 250 000 IBM users around the world, and caused the company's email system to fail for two hours. Started as a prank by a German law student, the virus drew a picture of a Christmas tree, and then duplicated itself to all the names and addresses on users' distribution lists. The lost time caused by the Christmas virus among the first 50 000 users is estimated to have cost $2 million. The virus did not destroy data, but shows how rapidly a virus can spread.

Modern viruses are not so benign. The security firm mi2g estimated the cost of the Netsky.B virus to be at least US$3.12 billion worldwide. This was calculated 'on the basis of helpdesk support costs, overtime payments, contingency outsourcing, loss of business, bandwidth clogging, productivity erosion, management time reallocation, cost of recovery, and software upgrades'.

There are various species of damaging programs, not all of which are (strictly speaking) viruses. Logic bombs are designed to lie dormant in a computer, awaiting a particular date. They then 'explode' by deleting files. Unlike viruses, bombs act only once, though their tasks might be to release a virus.

Worms sit in memory, reproducing themselves. Because they reproduce exponentially, they quickly clog up a computer.

Trojan horses are a species of virus which only start after the user has interacted with them. In the case of the Christmas virus, users were asked to type the word 'Christmas' to get a picture of a Christmas tree. Fifty per cent of UK companies suffered from a virus attack or disruptive software in 2004, up from 41 per cent in 2002. While 93 per cent of companies use anti-virus software, the fact that 50 per cent of companies were infected shows that modern viruses are increasingly sophisticated and capable of avoiding protection software and firewalls.

Companies should be prepared for virus attacks that go beyond the first level of protection that anti-virus software provides.

Companies must check the system for viruses by using anti-virus scanning software. Anti-virus activity used to focus on the perimeter – at the point where emails and Internet came into the system; now it must be done at each desktop. The company should also put anti-virus software on all laptops and give a copy to mobile employees for their home PCs. You may also decide to remove CD-ROM drives or USB ports from vulnerable PCs.

The company should also protect programs from being altered; it can do this through software that stops the computer's registry from being changed. Staff should not be able to alter the programs themselves.

Avoiding access to the Internet prevents users from downloading infected games and other files. Using a stand-alone PC for important work prevents it from being infected by other machines in the company.

Minimizing the effects of hardware failures and user error

Companies should take maintenance insurance for granted as part of the costs of their IT system, unless the costs are borne in-house by the IT department.

Companies need to develop in-house expertise in data management and data recovery. The more that users understand how their computer can fail, the less likely they are to have a problem. This means training staff to avoid problems. Few companies teach staff about taking backups, not pulling leads out of computers while they are working, nor exiting from a program by switching the computer's 'off' button.

Computers should be stored where they cannot be damaged by floods (so don't put them in the basement); food and drink; or accidental movement.

Even when a hard drive fails, or data is accidentally deleted, the data is still in the machine. In previous decades, companies needed to send the equipment to a computer recovery firm, or wait for an engineer to arrive. Now, companies can sometimes recover lost data using a remote recovery service, for example Ontrack.

Minimizing the effects of losing data

All data should be backed up daily, and this should be automatic. The data should be backed up to a separate storage system, so that a failure of the hard drive or mainframe will not affect the data.

Backup data should be kept off site. When a fire engulfed the premises of Forgeville, an engine filter company, the records kept in supposedly fire-proof cabinets were reduced to cinders. The company lost catalogue part numbers, invoices, bank details, VAT receipts, and 20 years of records. Outsiders were unsympathetic: the VAT man said the fire was no excuse for the late submission of tax returns.

It is unwise to assume that staff will carry out backups. Specialist staff should be assigned to do this task. Ideally the secondary storage should be physically separate. A £100 million Friendly Society processes its data at its Leicester head office, but backs up the data to an independent storage facility in Nottingham.

Spyware

The average PC is infected with 28 pieces of spyware, according to a survey by Webroot Software. According to Internet firm, Earthlink, over 80 per cent of the world's PCs contain spyware. Spyware activities include opening harmless but irritating pop-up pages, sending information about the user's online activities to its creator, opening pornography sites, and infecting the PC with harmful viruses. Some spyware captures credit card details, and posts it to the spyware firm.

Spyware is usually downloaded unintentionally, when the user is downloading some other file. For example, the popular file-sharing program Kazaa does this, as does Ezula. The problem occurs, therefore, when employees download files for personal use. Often they don't realize that they are downloading a spyware program – it comes bundled with the software they wanted, and the details of the spyware are tucked away in the middle of the end user licence agreement (EULA). Hardly anyone ever reads the EULA – they simply tick the 'Agree' button.

All companies are vulnerable, but companies that process confidential information such as credit cards are particularly to keystroke loggers. These record each keystroke made on a PC, and can be used by criminals to harvest credit card details.

Every PC should contain anti-spyware software. These check for spyware, in the same way that virus checkers do. Since no one spyware program picks up all items, experts recommend that users put two different programs on each PC. To be of any use, the anti-spyware software should regularly update its list of bugs online.

It is also dangerous to assume that the anti-spyware software will operate without supervision. As with anti-virus software, you need to regularly monitor its activities, and manually check that the system is bug-free.

Scams

Users often receive an email purporting to come from their bank, Ebay or Paypal, asking them to update their credit card details, at pain of losing the use of their online services. This message actually comes from criminals who harvest the information and run up a bill on the user's credit card.

While the sophisticated PC user might be amused to think that anyone would be stupid enough to fall for this trick, which is known as 'phishing', for the fraudsters it's a numbers' game. If they send the email to enough people, a percentage will be fooled. Therefore, you have to imagine the impact of a scam on the least able employee. And while this kind of scam might secure only the user's personal details, there are accounts of phone calls from 'the IT department', asking employees for confirmation of their password to the server. This is a quick way to gain access to company records, and would be invaluable for industrial espionage.

Software piracy

Owning unregistered software may not seem like a big risk, but using copied disks exposes the company to the wrath of Business Software Alliance (BSA), an organization comprising leading software companies.

The BSA pays up to £20 000 to people reporting the use of pirated software, and much of this is thought to come from disgruntled employees or contractors. When individuals are laid off, they may decide to 'shop' their former employer as an act of revenge.

Tullis Russell, a papermaker based in Glenrothes, was taken to court by BSA, for the illegal use of software. Tullis Russell eventually paid BSA £18 000 in an out-of-court settlement. The exercise started after BSA received a call on its confidential hotline. Following enquiries, Tullis Russell was found to be using 154 unlicenced products, including Attachmate, Visio, Symantec and Microsoft software.

Twenty-four per cent of BSA's settlements come from organizations within the IT sector, while construction/engineering and architecture/design together represent 27 per cent of settlements; educational organizations make up 8 per cent.

In the US, the BSA has 700 active investigations at any one time into software piracy across the United States. According to the BSA, corporate and government employees account for 'the lion's share' of the $29 billion in revenue that software publishers lose annually to piracy. According to an IDC survey, 29 per cent of software in use in the UK is illegal.

Since the BSA compares records with leading software companies like Microsoft, it isn't hard for them to determine whether the software is legal. But the BSA says it targets 'egregious' use of pirated software rather than companies that simply suffer from poor record-keeping.

The court can award unlimited damages for software piracy, though the average fine is in the region of £25 000. BSA can also settle out of court. Solicitors advise that companies which receive a questionnaire from BSA should answer it. Unanswered questionnaires are followed by a BSA visit.

The BSA's website has software that helps companies collate information about their licenses.

CASE STUDY: KEEPING WITHIN THE LAW, ACCORDING TO MICROSOFT

- Buy from trusted sources, such as vetted sites and official manufacturers' sites.
- Obtain full details of your supplier in advance. This includes their name, address and telephone number. Do not buy if the seller fails to divulge this information.
- Print out pages containing order and invoice numbers, and keep them until the software arrives and proves satisfactory.
- Watch out for sellers offering 'special deals with the manufacturer', or 'bankruptcy' sales. These phrases make buyers believe that they are getting genuine products that wouldn't otherwise be discounted.
- Know something about the product you're buying. That makes it easier to spot a fake.
- If in doubt, ask the manufacturer what the package should contain.

Microsoft also recommends that companies be suspicious of vendors offering:

- PCs with bundled Microsoft software without the Certificate of Authenticity (COA) included.
- Academic and government versions. Academic products are marked 'academic edition', and proof of affiliation to an educational institute is necessary to purchase this software. It is illegal to sell it under any other circumstances.
- Original equipment manufacturer (OEM) software without a PC. The product packaging for this software clearly indicates 'For distribution with a new PC only'.
- Products at prices and in packaging inconsistent with offerings through legitimate retail channels.
- Software sold solely as a CD housed in a jewel case.

SOFTWARE LICENSING AS A BUSINESS ISSUE

Software licensing is the most important IT issue for organizations, according to research by FAST Corporate Services and Centennial Software. This indicates a move away from security as the traditional top priority in recent years.

Twenty-nine per cent of respondents cited software licensing as the most important IT issue faced by their organization, compared with 27 per cent for risk management/business continuity and 18 per cent for IT security.

Centennial Software chief executive, Andy Burton, wasn't surprised by the results: 'Whether it's fines for non-compliance, over-spending on unnecessary applications or badly-negotiated support deals, the financial and business risks of not having 100 per cent visibility of your software can have a dramatic impact on the bottom line.'

In the same survey, 50 per cent of respondents said they hoped that better IT asset management would reduce their spend on new licences and support renewals.

Setting a policy

Just over half of large companies have a security policy and contingency plans in place. But in some cases the security policies are not strictly enforced.

The company should have a policy on computer data, and this should be endorsed by senior management. The policy should cover:

* lines of responsibility for the IT system
* care of data and backup systems
* anti-virus and spyware procedures
* use of peripherals
* access to internal data by staff
* use of the Internet by staff
* policy on personal emails.

This policy should be supported by written procedures, specifying the action to be taken to protect the data. To ensure that the procedures are implemented, the company should regularly carry out audits.

Contingency planning

IBM believes that companies pay insufficient attention to contingency planning for their computers. Its research shows that four out of five companies don't have a viable contingency plan for computer disaster.

As we saw earlier, many companies lack a business continuity plan, and many organization's backup data is not checked.

All companies which rely on their computer should have a contingency plan, and the plan should be monitored all the time. This means assuming that the computer system has failed. The company should check what would happen if its programs became faulty, its data was lost, or its computers were stolen.

Contingency planning is discussed more fully in Chapter 16.

BS EN ISO 17799

Companies looking for a comprehensive way to manage their IT system could use BS 7799. This is a management system that helps the organization do the following:

* It enables companies to identify the risks facing their information, and introduce controls to protect it.
* It ensures that personal information is kept secure, as required by the European Data Directive 95/46/EC. Organizations with ISO 17799 are unlikely to suffer the scandal of confidential records turning up on rubbish dumps.
* It reassures trading partners that the organization protects and controls their own information and that of the partner.

ISO 17799 involves the following actions. Companies have to:

1 Define the organization's information security policy.
2 Define the scope of the system (what should be included?). This depends on the business requirement, the assets to be protected, the location and the technology.
3 Assess the risk: identify the threats and vulnerabilities to assets and the impacts on the organization.
4 Identify the areas of risk to be managed (risk management).
5 Select the controls that will be used.
6 Document the selected controls.

> TickIT is a version of ISO 9001 (the quality standard), adapted for software developers. It is designed to improve client confidence in software companies' management systems. It also aims to improve professional practice amongst people who audit quality management systems in the software sector. In short, it helps software companies get their product on to the market quickly, efficiently, and bug-free. The use of TickIT could prevent a software company from crises caused by bug-ridden software, delays in getting software to market, and resulting loss of income.

Outsourcing IT

Given the arcane nature of IT, its need for 100 per cent uptime, its costs and the ever-changing technology, IT outsourcing is a serious option.

A Gartner survey showed that 83 per cent of IT costs is spent on upgrading and operating existing applications; while a mere 17 per cent is spent on innovation. Thus a company that uses an Oracle database might get Oracle to maintain its database and add new functions.

Another factor favouring IT outsourcing is globalization. In India and China, the cost of writing software can be as little as ten to 40 per cent of the cost of doing it in the West. So a lot of work has been transferred there; and more could follow. This serves primarily to reduce cost (outsourcing is covered in more detail in Chapters 9 and 11).

Another option is 'utility computing', which means assigning responsibility to another company to supply all your computing needs, including servers and storage. Thus the supplier will provide extra computing power when the business needs it. For example, some businesses have greater computing needs once a month for accounts or payroll; while banks need more computing power at Christmas. Also known as grid computing or, on-demand computing, it works in the same way that a utility firm provides whatever electricity you need, when you need it.

The advantages of utility computing lie in getting rid of redundant backup servers. Since the supplier will be looking after many clients, computing power can be shared. It should also make costs easier to control, and allows the company to respond to unpredictable demands from customers without investing in technology that may never be needed. In addition, it frees the company from seeing IT as an area constrained by budgets, and therefore lets it become more flexible.

However, the disadvantages are you may get locked into a service contract, lose expertise in this area, and become reliant on the supplier. It may be difficult to break out of the contract and retake control of your IT. Moreover, the supplier will want the business to integrate its systems through all departments, and use a standard operating system and storage. This could entail a learning curve as employees get to grips with new methods and applications. However, the company may end up being more lean and effective as a result of this.

Outsourcing companies point out that companies may use 60 per cent of a server's processing power, and none of the backup server attached to it. Therefore there can be a lot of unnecessary capital tied up in IT. According to one estimate, companies use 20 per cent of PCs, 20 per cent of Intel-type servers, less than 40 per cent of Unix servers, and 40 per cent of storage space. If this is shared among many companies, there will be a cost saving.

The companies most suited to utility computing are enterprise-sized organizations, and especially retailers who suffer peaks and troughs in sales – because a utility supplier can provide computing power as needed. Suppliers point out that companies don't have to switch the whole business over to this method; they can start by moving specific departments.

IT PROJECT RISKS

IT projects are discussed in Chapter 18, within the overall context of project risk.

Useful links

Ad-aware
www.lavasoft.de

Business Software Alliance (BSA)
www.bsa.org and www.justasksam.co.uk

Datafort
www.datafort.co.uk

Institute of Internal Auditors
www.theiia.org/itaudit

OnTrack
www.ontrack.com

PestPatrol
www.pestpatrol.com

Risks Digest
http://catless.ncl.ac.uk/risks

Spybot Search and Destroy
www.safer-networking.org

Risk assessment – IT

By answering the questions below, you can assess your vulnerability to IT disaster. Tick all applicable boxes.

Topic	Question	
Computer use	Is the computer used for real-time applications (such as mail order or financial services)?	☐
Impact on the company	Would the loss of computers for two days disrupt the business?	☐
Contingency planning	Does the business lack an IT contingency plan? Or does it have one that has not been recently tested?	☐
Finance	If computer data was lost, would the business know who owed it money?	☐
Accessibility	Can the computers be stolen from their desks?	☐
	Can data be accessed without passwords?	☐
Networks	Are computers linked to an outside network?	☐
Backups	Are backups not taken, or (if they are kept) are they left in the same building?	☐
Projects	Is the company undertaking a major IT project?	☐
Staff	Do many managers lack training in the use of computers?	☐

Total points scored

Score: 0–3 points: low risk. 4–6 points: moderate risk. 7–10 points: high risk.

The appendix contains a summary of all the checklists in this book. By entering the results of this one, you can compare the scale of computer risk against other categories of risk.

13 *Liability, Legal Risks and Intellectual Property*

In this chapter we consider:

- *The risk of litigation, and how to manage it*
- *Product liability litigation*
- *Access for disabled people*
- *Sarbanes-Oxley Act*
- *Operating Financial Review*
- *Turnbull guidelines*
- *Non-executive directors*
- *Diversification, acquisitions and divestment*
- *Intellectual property*
- *Legal risks of email.*

Litigation

RISK OF BEING SUED

The biggest threat to small and medium-sized businesses (SMEs) comes from 'no-win, no-fee' litigation, according to a survey by Axa. Thirty-six per cent of respondents quoted US-style legal suits as their biggest fear, compared with 32 per cent who worried about EU 'red tape', and 14 per cent who feared cheap imports.

But the fear of getting sued is greater than its reality, and more businesses will be damaged by mundane risks such as fire or lack of sales than litigation. Nevertheless, businesses are right to be concerned and should take steps to prevent it. In particular, the existence of no-win, no-fee lawyers increases the risk of your being sued.

SOURCES OF LITIGATION

It is dangerous to focus on any one source of litigation. Companies can get sued by many groups, including the following:

1 *Employees*: wrongful dismissal, harassment, failure to promote
2 *The consumer*: product or service failings, professional failure
3 *Business customers*: failure to meet the requirements of a contract
4 *Suppliers*: failure to pay
5 *Regulatory authorities*: failure to comply (this is typically a statutory fine rather than litigation, but its impact costs and loss of reputation is similar)
6 *Pressure groups*: for failure to abide by its corporate social responsibilities, for example with regard to abuse of suppliers in the developing world.

7 *Competitors*: infringement of intellectual property, such as trademarks.

REDUCING THE RISK OF LITIGATION

The best solution is not to get sued. Here are the steps to take to prevent people from taking action against you:

- *Get good contracts*. Prevent litigation by ensuring that your legal contracts are routinely signed, and that they are watertight. Ensure that employees and customers understand what they are being offered.

- *Human resources*. Manage staff recruitment, disciplinary meetings and terminations of employment by the book. Make sure everything is documented in writing. And ensure everyone is treated equally. Never act hastily, especially when it comes to firing people. And don't ignore bad workforce practices. Never overlook bullying, or fail to adopt safe working practices – these things can come back to haunt you.

- *Don't over-sell or over-claim*. Point out problems or deficiencies in writing before the other side gets committed. People sometimes litigate because their expectations were not met.

- *Keep solid paperwork*. Make sure that sales people keep records and get signatures.

- *Train staff*. Make sure everyone knows what the risks are, and how to manage them.

- *Act ethically*. Treat all stakeholders with respect. For example, don't use others' patents or designs without their approval. Companies that regard customers as no more than ignorant idiots are on a dangerous track.

COUNTERING LITIGATION

Once you receive the solicitor's letter, what steps can you take? Here is some advice:

- *Avoid going to court* if at all possible. Court cases are expensive and time consuming, and their outcome is uncertain. There is no certainty that the innocent party will prevail: a court case is a piece of theatre, with juries being swayed by the rhetoric of barristers, and the lies and half-truths of witnesses. In short, try to settle out of court.

- *Get the CEO to talk directly with the litigants*, if possible. This can result in the parties coming to an amicable arrangement. The CEO is the one person in the business with the authority and flexibility to do deals.

- *Leave your ego behind*. If the litigation becomes a battle of wills, the result could cost you dearly, and may not be in the best interests of the business.

- *Decide how central the litigation is to your business*. If the issue doesn't matter, it may be that you can afford to yield. You may have more important battles to fight. On the other hand, if the litigation goes to the heart of what you do, you will have to face it.

- *Employ legal advisors whose advice you trust.* But take charge of the process. Don't assume that experts know everything. Remember that lawyers make lots more money when cases go to court.

- *Weigh up the strengths of the litigant.* Never fight someone who is bigger or more powerful than you. There are exceptions: Richard Branson has succeeded several times against the much bigger British Airways. But small guys often lose to bigger ones.

- *Some litigants' anger can be assuaged by apologies.* When people go to court, it is sometimes because they have been goaded by the prevarication and elusiveness of the organization. It can be better to make a personal visit, and spend time listening to the complainant. Small amounts of time spent early in the case can prevent years of slow-moving and costly litigation.

- *Use an arbitration service.* This will usually be cheaper and less confrontational than going to court.

- *Learn from the experience.* What caused the litigation? Was it a lack of internal control, a loss of ethics, or a slippery floor? Whatever the cause, ensure that it cannot happen again; and check whether you could get sued in related areas. For example, a weakness in health and safety could indicate a weakness in environmental issues.

If you are worried about the impact of litigation, you can take steps to minimize the effect of future litigation. Two options are as follows:

1 *Reduce your physical assets.* Sub-contracting production or offshoring it minimizes the company's exposure to predatory litigation.

2 *Protect your assets.* By separating ownership of different assets, you can ensure that individuals (notably directors) and assets are protected from being seized in the event of the business being successfully sued. This can include operating from within limited liability status, to having separate ownerships of different assets.

Regulatory controls

PRODUCT LIABILITY LITIGATION

The first big product liability claims were against asbestos. Staff who contracted asbestosis initially received small sums from workers' compensation schemes. Then in 1969, Thelma Borel, the widow of a dead asbestos worker, won $79 000 in a court action against Fibreboard Paper Products, an asbestos firm. The award triggered claims from thousands of other sick asbestos workers in the US. It meant that other asbestos firms were liable for illness caused by their products. It also meant that people could sue firms directly.

The courts also were appalled by the asbestos companies' duplicity in hiding medical evidence. It led to larger and punitive damages, with James Cavett, a retired boiler maker, receiving $2.3 million in 1982.

Apart from asbestos, there have also been big awards against manufacturers of silicone breast implants, against accountants, against pharmaceutical companies, against tobacco firms and against firms which caused pollution incidents. Courts and governments seem increasingly keen to see that firms are made to pay heavily for their dangerous failings. The Dalkon Shield case saw A.H. Robins Co. set up a $2.3bn trust fund in 1989 to pay compensation to the victims of its faulty intrauterine contraceptive devices. They only finished processing claims in late 1999. Even cases such as that pale in comparison to the $255bn being paid by tobacco companies to the US government in compensation for smoking-related health costs.

Product liability occurs in unexpected ways, and in the US it can be expensive. A court in Albuquerque, New Mexico ordered McDonald's to pay $2.7 million damages (later reduced to $480000) because its coffee was 'too hot'. Stella Liebeck, an 81-year-old grandmother, had tried to prise the lid off her coffee cup by holding the polystyrene cup between her legs. The coffee spilt over her legs and she was scalded. The jury said the punitive damages were intended to be a 'serious message' to the fast food industry. Two of the jurors had even wanted to hand out even higher compensation. McDonald's said that its coffee was 'substantially cooler than the coffee you would make at home'.

The upshot is to avoid products and services that are likely to end up in court, and to fully test new products before launching them. After that, you have no more chance of being hit with a headline-grabbing case than any other business.

ACCESS FOR DISABLED PEOPLE

The UK's Disability Discrimination Act requires that businesses make 'reasonable adjustments' to their premises, to make them accessible to disabled people. The fines for non-compliance are up to £50000. Such legislation is also appearing in other countries. In the USA, businesses have been fined $1000 (£560) a day for being in breach of the regulations.

With disabled people ready to assert their rights, businesses need to ensure that their premises, in particular retail outlets, are accessible. Some smaller businesses are reluctant to invest, believing that some of the costs, such as the installation of lifts, are excessive. But some experts say the costs are overstated and that businesses are dragging their feet. The National Register of Access Consultants can provide advice (see further information at the end of the chapter).

SARBANES-OXLEY

Sarbanes-Oxley (known as SOX) is a US law passed in 2002 in the wake of corporate and financial scandals, notably Enron. Named after the two politicians who sponsored it, the law aims to restore investors' trust in companies' accounts, by placing more controls on annual reports and directors' behaviour. It is aimed at accountants and the directors and managers of public companies, and makes them personally responsible. CEOs and CFOs must certify the accuracy of their company accounts, and this means top officers can no longer plead ignorance – they are personally responsible for the integrity of an audit. They can be fined up to $5 million and imprisoned for 20 years for failing to obey the law.

The law also applies to all companies whose subsidiaries are listed on a US stock exchange. This means that if you have US interests, you may have to introduce the new controls into the business.

The requirements of Sarbanes-Oxley are as follows:

* Companies may not make loans to directors and executive officers. This ban may even preclude personal loans and the use of company credit cards and the cash-less exercise of share options. This means that directors can no longer treat the company as their personal piggy bank. Such controls might have prevented the scandal at Hollinger International, the newspaper company that accused its chief executive, Lord Black of plundering its assets. Some of the minutiae included *Jogging attire for (his wife) Lady Black, $140; Exercise equipment for Lady Black, $2083; a leather briefcase for Lady Black, $2057; Opera tickets for Lord and Lady Black, $2785;* and *Summer drinks, $24 950.*

* Companies must have an independent audit committee which will appoint, compensate and oversee the work of the auditing firm, and to which the auditing firm must report directly. Members of the committee may not do other work in the firm.

* The accountancy practice must rotate the partners in charge of a corporate client every five years. This will prevent the relationship from getting too cosy.

* The law bans accounting firms from providing a number of non-audit services. These services include book-keeping; design and implementation of information systems; appraisal or valuation services; actuarial services; management and HR services; investment advisor or investment banking services; legal services and other expert services. This means the accounting firm can't advise on acquisitions, and then approve them in the annual report.

* Section 404 of the law requires the company's annual report to contain an 'internal control report', which assesses the effectiveness of the company's internal financial controls. This will require more stringent internal auditing. And, according to a survey by Financial Executives International (FEI), it will greatly increase the company's costs, including a 40 per cent increase in the fees charged by external auditors.

Some UK and European companies, such as Fugro, a Netherlands-based engineering consultancy, have chosen to avoid floating US subsidiaries on grounds of increased complexity. Other companies have complained bitterly about the added burden that Sarbanes-Oxley imposes. But if the business wants US funds, there may simply be no alternative. Even if you don't have US-listed businesses, the Sarbanes-Oxley act may still have an impact because it is setting a new global standard for 'best practice'. Lenders, accountants, business customers and partners may come to expect it.

Other countries have also been implementing their own reforms of company law, such as Australia's Corporate Law Economic Reform Program, and South Africa's 'King II' report.

THE OPERATING FINANCIAL REVIEW

In the UK, the Operating Financial Review (OFR) plays a similar role as Sarbanes-Oxley. It is designed to give shareholders better information on quoted companies, and give directors a discipline for stating the business's strengths and weaknesses. The review should describe the following topics:

- the company's objectives and strategies
- the resources available to the business
- the risks and uncertainties facing the company
- the capital structure, treasury policies and objectives, and liquidity of the business.

The OFR should also provide information on the company's environmental and social impacts, and its relationships with employees, customers and suppliers. (However, medium-sized firms are exempted from reporting on non-financial indicators in the Review.) As such the OFR looks not only at the past but also the future, and therefore goes beyond the traditional backward-looking annual report.

TURNBULL COMMITTEE RECOMMENDATIONS

The Turnbull Report (formerly the Combined Code of the Committee on Corporate Governance) was published in 1999.

The report recommended that companies should set up a uniform system of risk management across the organization's systems, which will give directors a holistic view of the potential threats to the company and the danger each poses. The processes involve:

- assessment and monitoring of a risk to the business
- the probability of the risk occurring
- the impact to the business should it occur
- the business' ability to avoid or reduce that impact
- whether the costs of preventive action are justified.

Unlike previous guidelines on corporate governance, Turnbull recommends that companies should look at all threats to the business, not just financial risks. These include 'operational risks', any factor that could:

- inhibit the business's ability to operate effectively and profitably
- damage the reputation or share price of the firm or the company's assets
- put the company at risk from legal proceedings.

The Turnbull guidelines are only recommendations and therefore not obligatory, but they are influential. The report brings greater awareness at board level of the importance of taking a holistic view of the company's situation and implementing a uniform system of internal control. More importantly, many business partners will come to expect, or actively require, the company to prove compliance with Turnbull's guidelines.

The London Stock Exchange rules require that a company incorporated in the UK should state in its accounts whether it has complied with the Turnbull guidance. If it has complied, it must do so in a manner 'that enables its shareholders to evaluate how the principles have been applied'. If it has not, it must explain how it failed to comply and 'give reasons for any non-compliance'.

The Institute of Chartered Accountants in England & Wales says the board of directors is responsible for establishing the company's policy for internal control and regularly reviewing its implementation and effectiveness.

The board should consider:

- the nature and extent of the risks facing the company
- the extent and categories of risk, which it regards as acceptable for the company to bear
- the likelihood of the risks concerned materializing
- the company's ability to reduce the incidence and impact on the business of risks that do materialize
- the costs of operating particular controls relative to the benefit thereby obtained in managing the related risks.

THE IMPACT OF GREATER REGULATORY CONTROL

The penalties for failing to comply with regulations can be severe. The Financial Services Authority (FSA) fined Royal Dutch/Shell a record £17 m for misleading the market over the size of its oil reserves. This followed Shell's admission that it had overstated its reserves by 20 per cent. But the company later fought back, claiming that the fine didn't take into account the company's internal and external audits, and that estimating reserves was a matter of judgement. Some have seen these events as a trend towards increasingly combative behaviour by regulators and an unwillingness by companies to meekly accept regulators' judgements.

Non-executive directors

An essential element of good corporate governance is the role of the non-executive director. Non-executive directors should be responsible for monitoring executive behaviour but should also aid the development of company strategy. Thus, the recruitment of suitable non executive directors can help lessen the likelihood of a wide variety of risks. The Higgs report of 2003 into the role of non-executive directors recommended that at least half the board of larger companies should be independent, as should all members of the audit and remuneration committees, and a majority of the committee for nominating board appointments.

As company finances become more transparent and reporting more extensive, it will become more difficult to find experienced people prepared to serve as non-executive directors. The work is now more onerous and serious than it was, and these directors risk being sued if the company goes under. Equally, higher payment to non-execs could undermine their independence. Payments for non-execs is likely to rise. Payments for non-executive directors are now in the region of £50000 a year, with additional payments for chairing a boardroom committee.

Diversification

As we shall see in Chapter 14, the company needs to be in the right markets, and achieving this may involve the firm in either acquisition or divestment.

The passion for diversification in the 1970s and the rise of the conglomerate was quickly dissipated when many conglomerates got into difficulty. Many companies lacked synergy, and the conglomerates, with their wide range of products and markets, were more difficult to manage. 'Stick to the knitting' was the advice given by Tom Peters in his *In Search of Excellence*.

Nevertheless, companies can reduce their risk by operating in more than one market. There may also be strong practical reasons involved: some diversifications are designed to counter seasonal sales troughs. And as we discussed in Chapter 3, businesses can add value through their management skills and capital strengths.

ACQUISITIONS

Company acquisitions are a dangerous area because large sums of money are at stake, and the needs of seller and buyer are completely opposite. Leaving aside whether you're getting value for money, and whether the new business is the right fit, you need to know whether there are problems lurking out of sight.

The term 'due diligence' is often associated with self-preservation on the part of business advisors. But for the purchaser, it is vital to ensure that you're getting what you think you are. The areas to check are the financials, including tax returns, book-keeping and debt. You also need to verify patents and trademarks, especially if they have financial or marketing value. You need to check that the company isn't facing lawsuits. And you should branch out into sales, talking to customers about their view of the company. You should also do background checks on the company's key executives. While some of this work should be left to forensic accountants, it is risky to leave it all to professionals. Personal involvement often reveals information that cannot be gleaned from a balance sheet.

The price tag will reflect the company's value at its current level of sales. The trick, therefore, is to work out how to increase sales. Otherwise, you will face a lean period of many years while the company's profits simply earn back the price you paid. Some businesses are sold by retirees, and these can be good value, especially if the business is solid but has coasted for a while. A new business sold by a young person is more likely to have problems, so discover why they are selling.

The following questions should be asked when an acquisition is being considered:

- To what extent does the acquisition meet a strategic need for diversification?
- How familiar are we with the new market?
- Are there any skills (marketing, financial or production) we can use to gain an advantage?
- Have we researched the market? Is demand set to grow, decline or remain stable?
- Have we spoken to the target company's customers and potential customers? What do they think of the company?
- To what extent do the acquired company's profits and revenue depend on key employees, key customers or ephemeral products?
- To what extent is the company's profit due to extraordinary items, such as revaluation of assets or sale of premises?
- What liabilities might we be acquiring, such as liability for cleaning up contaminated land?
- Are property and asset values reasonably stated?
- Are there any parts of the new business which might be sold off, to pay for the acquisition?

Divestment

Companies need to look at the businesses they own with a critical eye, and ask whether they should keep them. Unsuitable businesses can drain the whole company of resources, and if their problems grow they can put the whole company at risk.

In some cases, farsighted management can see problems on the horizon before they become serious, and can sell the business while it is in good shape. The checklist in Table 13.1 shows the kinds of businesses which should be sold or kept.

Table 13.1   Divestment strategy

Divisions to keep	Divisions to sell
Occupies little of management's time	Occupies a lot of management's time
Geographically close to the rest of the business	Geographically distant from the rest of the business
Has synergy with the rest of the business	Lacks synergy with the rest of the business
Is part of the core business	Is not part of the core business
Is profitable	Contributes little profit, or makes a loss
Its market is growing	Its market is static or declining
Good industrial relations	Poor industrial relations
Competent management	Weak management

Intellectual property

We live in an age of weightless companies, whose manufacturing is often outsourced and the important assets are brand names and the company's knowledge. A good example is Nike, whose products are made by sub-contractors and whose strengths lie in design, branding and marketing.

This makes the ownership of intellectual property (IP), such as trademarks and patents, important. A company's value and its attractiveness to purchasers often hinges on its intellectual property, and where companies are valued more highly than their asset value, the difference includes the value of intellectual property. Intellectual property can also be used to gain a competitive advantage and to keep out competitors.

Globalization means that an unprotected asset can be copied and sold in other countries, leading to a loss of revenue for the asset's original creators. Yet UK companies are not to the fore in acquiring intellectual property, according to the Patent Office. In 2003, no UK company was in the top 25 most active applicants for UK patents, as can be seen in Table 13.2. This suggests, says the *Financial Times*, that domestic companies are lagging behind international rivals. The highest placed UK organization was the Ministry of Defence in 28th place. The Patent Office believes that UK companies view patents defensively, and highlight their expense. It is thought that the country's poor showing also reflects the prominence of electronic and automotive sectors where the country is no longer strong.

Using intellectual property actively and wisely is also essential. BT discovered, buried among its 15 000 global patents, one that it reckoned would allow it to own the principle of the hyperlink. Filed in 1977 but not issued until 1989, the patent was designed for use in text-based information services such as Prestel and Viewdata. Success in the courts would have

Table 13.2   Number of UK patents granted

2002 Rank	Organization	No. of patents	2003 Rank	Organization	No. of patents
1	NEC	188	1	NEC	209
2	Motorola	149	2	Hewlett Packard	196
3	Samsung	126	3	Samsung	177
4	Bosch	117	4	Schlumberger	172
5	IBM	109	5	IBM	171
6	Ericsson	100	6	Baker Hughes	120
7	Baker Hughes	91	7	Ericsson	115
8	Schlumberger	87	8	Motorola	113
9	Rover Group	81	9	Visteon	112
10	Hewlett Packard	79	10	Ford	100

Source: UK Patent Office

meant every software and computer company in the world paying rights to BT. In the end, a US judge threw out the application in 2002 on the basis that it related to dumb terminals (1970s' technology) rather than between computers (the structure of the Internet).

INTELLECTUAL PROPERTY

All of the areas below require proper assessment and active management.

- *Patent*: gives an inventor ownership of an invention.
- *Trademark and service mark*: a symbol or brand owned by the person who created it (for example, the famous Coca-Cola trademark is owned by the Coca-Cola company).
- *Internet domains*: Not just part of the organization's branding, but for many an integral part of its marketing and selling and distribution operation.
- *Geographical indication*: products whose production is limited to a specific place. Roquefort cheese is protected, but cheddar is not.
- *Copyright*: the exclusive rights to written, musical, photographic and other artistic material. Films, records and books are protected by copyright.
- *Trade secrets*. These can be protected through employment contracts and confidentiality or non-disclosure agreements, as well as injunctions and litigation over their breach.

INDUSTRIES WHERE IP MAY NOT SEEM A PRIORITY

In some industries, such as retailing, IP appears to be less relevant. Retailers exist to split bulk materials into smaller quantities suitable for end users. And so their strengths and risks lie in achieving the right ranges, store size, and store location. Their core skills also include logistics – getting the product on to the shelves in a timely manner – managing stocks, and low prices.

But retailers who are merely efficient lack a competitive advantage – which means that the consumer has little to distinguish them from competitors' stores. The answer lies in developing their own brands. Since these are available only in their stores, own brands create additional store loyalty.

Other service industries, such as banks, insurance companies and solicitors, might also claim that IP isn't important. They often see client servicing and location as their critical success factors. But there are important areas of intellectual property that service companies sometimes overlook. For example, software that might be developed through a software firm, which might in turn start selling it to competitors.

To give themselves a competitive edge, service companies develop exclusive products and services, and business processes. If competitors copy and use them, you lose that advantage. Therefore you need to investigate the extent to which you can protect such processes and services from use by others.

There are also financial issues at stake. After the city of Munich decided to convert its 14 000 computers from Windows to Linux, its hand was stayed over patent issues relating to Linux and open source software. It feared that companies holding software patents could issue a 'cease and desist' order to Munich's city hall, which would shut down the city's computer systems or force it to pay license fees.

The legal risks of email

In the USA, one in five employers (21 per cent) has had employee email and instant messages (IM) subpoenaed in the course of a lawsuit or regulatory investigation. Another 13 per cent have faced workplace lawsuits triggered by employee email. This indicates the risks of email. Legal risks include the following:

- *Legal liability for emails sent by employees.* In the UK, Norwich Union was forced to pay £450 000 in an out-of-court settlement, after an employee sent an email stating that a competitor was in financial difficulties. Sexually offensive emails may also be the source of litigation from offended employees.

- *Court-ordered retrieval of emails.* Email records are increasingly used in lawsuits since they tend to contain important evidence. For instance, you may be required to provide all emails about someone who alleges they were bullied. According to epolicy.com, a court ordered a US top 500 company to hand over any email that mentioned the name of a former employee who was suing the company for wrongful dismissal. The company faced the prospect of searching more than 20 000 backup tapes, containing millions of messages, at a cost of $1000 per tape. The total potential cost for that electronic search was $20 million.

Other risks include:

- *Confidentiality breaches.* Employees may send confidential information about the business either intentionally or unintentionally to other firms or individuals. With the large number of questions being posed by customers in emails, there is a big risk that someone will send out confidential information.

- *Lost productivity.* Companies can lose productivity due to employees spending time on personal email and Internet use.

- *Viruses from downloads and opening attachments.* Ever more sophisticated fraudulent emails and spyware risk infecting the company's network with viruses.

- *Network congestion.* Emailing large picture files or mp3 files can slow down the company's computer system.

- *Loss of reputation.* In the USA, a Federal Communications Commission (FCC) employee inadvertently sent a rude joke entitled Nuns in Heaven to 6000 journalists and government officials on the agency's email list. This created bad publicity for the FCC. A badly written email, or an email containing unprofessional remarks, can also give a bad impression of the company. At UK law firm Norton Rose two of their employees started the 'Claire Swire' email, a sexually explicit email that was read by over 10 million people around the world. Since the company in question was a law firm, this email could have damaged the company's reputation.

SET AN EMAIL POLICY

Email-policy.com recommends setting a comprehensive email policy. Some topics you might include are as follows:

- *Safe use of Internet and email*: Employees should be told not to open attachments from unknown emails, to be suspicious of all attachments, and not to download files from the Net. They should also be told that visiting some popular websites can cause spyware to be installed on to their PC.

- *Netiquette*: Give employees advice on writing emails, in order to maintain the company's reputation and deliver effective customer service. Any email sent from the company could end up on an Internet forum, and so discretion should be maintained at all times.

- *Personal use*: Employees should not make excessive personal use of the company's email system or Internet access, nor use company computers for their own business activities. You may want to set an Internet Acceptable Use Policy (AUP).

- *Offensive content*: The email system should not be used to create or send offensive or derogatory messages. Emails are highly public messages.

- *Confidential data*: Employees should take extra care not to divulge confidential information or trade secrets.

- *Reporting abuse*: Employees should be given an email contact to refer abuse.

- *Privacy*: Employees should be told that their emails may be monitored.

Other steps to take:

- *Train staff*: Many more staff work on email customer service desks nowadays. You should train them to answer emails effectively, rather than assume they can do it. Product knowledge is also essential.

- *Use standard replies*: Programs such as Answertool allow companies to paste pre-written answers into emails or other documents. This reduces the risk that the wrong information or inconsistent messages will be sent.

- *Permanently delete emails*: Unless the business does not have a statutory requirement to keep records, emails should be automatically deleted after a fixed period. This will preclude the business from having to search for, and hand over, old emails. On the other hand, some emails need to be kept, and these should be saved to a different location.

- *Use an email disclaimer*: Adding a disclaimer to the bottom of an email may protect the business against legal liability, negligent mis-statement, entering into contracts, and liability for spreading a virus.

- *Monitor emails*: Email monitoring programs can check for abusive words or people's names in stored emails. It thus warns the company of abuse, though it doesn't stop them being sent.

- *Monitor Internet usage*: If the business is concerned about staff wasting time on the Internet, it can install software that records the websites visited by staff, and the time taken on each site. To avoid invasion of privacy litigation, you must tell employees that their Internet viewing habits will be monitored.

- *Keep confidential information safe*: The business should keep confidential information from any server that is accessible to the average employee. This includes personnel records, company accounts, new product development information, and survey data.

Useful links

Businesses for sale
www.businessesforsale.com

BizBuySell
www.bizbuysell.com

Department of Trade and Industry (DTI)
www.dti.gov.uk/cld

Disability Discrimination Act
www.disability.gov.uk

Email Policy
www.email-policy.com

Epolicy Institute – electronic legal risks
www.epolicyinstitute.com

IP Menu
www.ipmenu.com

The Law Society
www.lawsociety.org.uk

National Register of Access Consultants
www.nrac.org.uk

Sarbanes-Oxley.com
www.sarbanes-oxley.com

Sarbanes-Oxley forum
www.sarbanes-oxley-forum.com

Treasury and Risk
www.treasuryandrisk.com

UK government – intellectual property
www.intellectual-property.gov.uk

UK government – operating financial review
www.dti.gov.uk/cld/financialreview.htm

UK Patent Office
www.patent.gov.uk

World Intellectual Property Organization
www.wipo.int

Risk assessment – legal risks

By answering the questions below, you can check to see how vulnerable your business is to liability, litigation, and intellectual property problems. Score one point for each box ticked.

Topic	Question	
Litigation	Has the organization been sued in the last 12 months?	☐
	Is the business at risk of litigation from customers through product, service or salesforce weaknesses?	☐
	Is there a possibility of litigation by pressure groups?	☐
Employees	Is it likely that the organization could be sued by employees for wrongful dismissal, unsafe working practices or bullying?	☐
	Has the company failed to implement best practice for disabled employees and customers?	☐
	Are employees largely unaware of the risks posed by emails?	☐
Reporting	Has the company failed to implement best practice in internal financial control and transparent reporting?	☐
	Has the organization failed to institute the requirements of the Operating Financial Review?	☐
Intellectual property	Has the organization failed to maximize the value of its intellectual property, for example through licensing?	☐
	Has the company failed to discuss IP issues with its lawyers in the last 12 months?	☐
Total points scored		

Score: 0–3 points: low risk. 4–6 points: moderate risk. 7–10 points: high risk.

The appendix contains a summary of all the checklists in this book. By entering the results of this one, you can compare the risk of fraud against other categories of risk.

14 *Market Leadership through Risk Management*

In this chapter we show how marketing problems can lead to declining sales, a loss of distribution and an impaired corporate image. We examine the following elements, and consider how improved marketing pre-empts many areas of risk.

- The causes of marketing failure
- Problems caused by government policies
- Problems caused by changes in the market; new entrants
- Problems caused by price wars; pricing strategy
- Counterfeiting and mimicry
- Internal marketing failure: weak product performance
- Poor promotion
- Branding problems
- Effective innovation
- Over-reliance on a few customers
- Distribution failures
- Product performance
- Loss of corporate reputation.

Strategic marketing vision

We start by considering how the business needs to attain a strategic marketing vision.

There is no shortage of marketing threats. Faced with one problem or another, companies often try to win business tactically by cutting prices or spending more on publicity and sales promotion. While this can help the healthy business return to profit, it may compound a weaker company's difficulties, leading to a downward spiral of declining profit.

A more strategic approach is required. Figure 14.1 shows the marketing vision the company should adopt. The organization must have a clear marketing vision. It has to be determined to be in the right market, and to have superior products or service. Strategic marketing vision goes beyond simple brand maintenance. Strategic action is required to realize that vision, whether through acquisition or new product development.

Being in the right market

Being in the right or wrong market is often a matter of historical accident, and does not guarantee future success. Many of today's companies are in existence because they were offering the right product ten years ago. To stay in business, companies have to offer products that are right for today's customers.

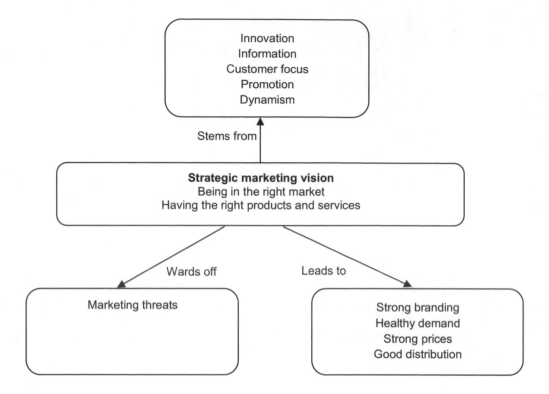

Figure 14.1   Strategic marketing vision

It is easy but dangerous for a company to focus on the products it sells rather than the needs of its customers. This blurs its understanding of its purpose (which is to make profit). The ideal market would:

- be large enough
- be growing
- be profitable
- have a high cost of entry (to dissuade others)
- require skills not easily imitated
- not be subject to excessive cycles, or be vulnerable to government policies
- not be unduly controversial or unpopular (such as the nuclear industry).

Within its market, the company should:

- be large enough to compete effectively
- be able to achieve growth (by increasing its market share or market penetration).

If the company market fails to conform to these two points, the firm should be seeking new products and markets in which to make money.

The causes of marketing failure

Falling sales, reduced market share, and lack of distribution are all signs of marketing failure. Lack of profitable sales is a major threat because sales revenue pays the company's bills. If the company cannot maintain profitable sales, every other part of the business (such as production or R&D) is threatened.

Marketing failure comes about because the company is suffering from one or more of the marketing hazards. They can be classified into the following categories.

1 **Market problems**
   - Changes in government policy
   - Changes in the market
   - New entrants into the market
   - Price wars
   - Counterfeiting and mimicry.

2 **Product and corporate problems**
   - Weak product performance
   - Poor promotion
   - Branding failure
   - Failures of new product development
   - Over-reliance on major customers
   - Distribution failure.

Problems caused by government policies

Some companies are vulnerable to change in government policies. The EU steel industry suffered when the US government imposed tariffs of up to 30 per cent on steel imports in 2002. The same action is also estimated to have cost the US economy 200 000 jobs in industries which required steel, due to increased steel costs. And sales of Geest's Caribbean bananas suffered when general agreement on tariffs and trade (GATT) agreements allowed South American bananas to be sold more widely in Europe.

Some companies are vulnerable to change in government policies. Macro-economic factors which can harm a company take two forms:

1 Increases in tax, interest rates or inflation, leading to a fall in demand.
2 Regulatory changes (for example, the banning of a product, curbs on waste disposal, or new health and safety policies).

For example, estate agents are directly affected by government policies because house sales fall as interest rates rise. House purchases are often discretionary: people who are trading up to a larger house can postpone their move.

Many industries are affected by the business cycle; but some firms manage it better than others, thanks to effective planning and responsive systems.

One management consultancy relied on a government-funded consultancy programme for its business. Its clients could get from the government half the cost of gaining ISO 9000, the quality standard. Eventually the government stopped this programme, and the consultancy found that these lucrative jobs dried up.

The Swiss chemical firm Sandoz has come under pressure as governments tried to halt rising healthcare costs by reducing the drugs bill. Governments do this by reducing the level of payment for drugs, by de-listing some drugs, and by encouraging the use of generic drugs. Sandoz has sought to counteract this squeeze by launching new products, by controlling costs, and by more efficient marketing.

Problems caused by changes in the market

Markets which are subject to fads or fashion (such as toys or clothing), and those which have a short lifecycle (such as information technology products) are difficult ones in which to sustain success. In these markets, companies suffer sales swings.

Since its birth in 1981, the Swiss company Logitech has dramatically changed course several times. In the space of a few years, its computer mice went from being leading-edge products for engineers to mass-market commodity items, and their retail price crashed from $120 to $20.

From a small plant in Switzerland, Logitech moved its manufacturing to a big factory in California and then to low-cost bases in Taiwan and China. Seeking to escape its reliance on mice, the company launched into new markets such as webcams and speakers.

Logitech now distributes its products in over 100 countries and has strategic partnerships with most IT manufacturers. Today it is the market leader in cordless peripherals, which look set to replace the old technology. Daniel Borel, the company's co-founder, admitted that the upheavals were emotionally draining.

In 2004, Ilford called in the receivers. For photographers, the 125-year-old company was an icon, and had a 60 per cent share of the black-and-white film market. But the switch to colour photography and digital cameras led to a 26 per cent fall in sales of its monochrome film in just six months.

Most companies expect small changes in the market, but they are rarely prepared for major discontinuities. Often a small firm or an overseas company introduces the major change.

CHANGES IN CHANNELS – GROWTH OF THE INTERNET

The Internet has wrought the greatest changes, often bringing suppliers and end-users together and displacing the intermediary. This is the process known as 'disintermediation'.

CASE STUDY: SKY TELEVISION

When Sky launched in 1989, it boasted new movies that would not be shown on terrestrial television for years. But now the film companies are distributing these films as DVDs soon after their run in the cinemas and before they appear on Sky. In addition, the price of DVD films has dropped by 30 per cent in five years, making them more attractive to consumers, while penetration of DVD players has risen to 61 per cent of UK households, according to research group Screen Broadcast. Now rental clubs such as Lovefilm.com and Netflix have emerged which rent out DVDs by post and with no late payment charges.

All this has eroded part of Sky's unique selling proposition (USP), and while 5 million viewers take Sky's premium-priced movie channels, 2 million Sky subscribers do not. The company's fee-paying subscribers could further decline with the arrival of Sky's free service and the growth of Freeview. The most ironic aspect of this change is that competition has unexpectedly come from a technology of the 1840s, namely postal delivery.

Companies which once sat in the background, such as insurance underwriters, have developed direct sales strategies, with the results that brokers have in some cases disappeared, such as Norwich Union's Hill House Hammond chain. A survey by Mazars (www.mazars.com) found that brokers regarded direct insurers as the number one high-level threat.

According to the *Financial Times*, many high-street retailers are lagging when it comes to online sales. With online shopping expected to rise above ten per cent of total sales, the high-street retailers are failing to invest in this area. Some major retailers have invested 'next to nothing'. These include BhS, DFS, Hennes and Mauritz, House of Fraser, JJB Sports, Matalan, Monsoon, Safeway, New Look Group, Primark, Selfridges and Somerfield. In some cases, the retailer feels that online shopping doesn't fit their strategy. Many feel that having a store in every high street gives them adequate coverage. But in other cases, retailers such as WH Smith stopped investing just at a time when e-tailing was beginning to burgeon.

STAYING IN THE SAME MARKET TOO LONG

Some companies are in the wrong market. The last 30 years has seen the decline in the West of big smokestack industries, like iron and steel, along with shipbuilding and coal mining. Other industries have risen in their place, such as electronics, computers and retailing.

Companies can alter their destiny by forecasting what the future will bring, and altering their corporate strategy accordingly. We discuss scenario planning in Chapter 16.

GIVING CONSUMERS TOO MUCH OF WHAT THEY WANT

Companies can also become the fall-guy for meeting customers' needs. Food companies, restaurants and supermarkets are now in the firing line for giving consumers food that makes them fat.

In 2001, 23 per cent of women and 21 per cent of men were obese, compared to 8 per cent of women and 6 per cent of men in 1980. The International Obesity Task Force has warned that over 40 per cent of the UK population could be obese within a generation.

The food industry believes that consumers have to take responsibility for their own nutrition and exercise, that sedentary lifestyles are equally responsible, and that small quantities of processed food won't harm anyone. However, pressure groups are quick to criticize the industry for providing 'junk food'. McDonald's, the most prominent fast food restaurant, featured in the documentary, 'Supersize me', in which the presenter ate in McDonald's three times a day for 30 days, and was duly made ill.

Many food companies are working to meet the challenge of better nutrition. PepsiCo's Frito-Lay removed all trans-fatty acids (linked to cancer and heart disease) from its cooking oil. This included modifications to 187 production lines at 45 plants.

Leading companies in the industry are at risk of being sued by single-issue campaign groups. Not all of these lawsuits succeed – the courts rejected a claim by New York teenagers that eating McDonald's made them fat.

The optimum solution is for companies to produce – and consumers to adopt – healthy foods. But while some companies can make improvements, the consumer often chooses foods that are less healthy. This is because we are drawn to food with extra salt, sugar and fat, and in larger pack sizes. We are also drawn to 'hand-held' food. Food companies say it is pointless to make their foods nutritionally attractive if the consumer then refuses to buy them.

NEW ENTRANTS

Life is hardest for the market leaders, because they have a market to defend. This leads to defensive behaviour that protects the status quo. New competitors, by contrast, look for innovative ways to dislodge the market leader.

In the 1970s IBM held a seemingly impregnable position in the computer market with its System 360 mainframe computer. But it lost control of the market to the upstart PCs that took computing power away from the IT department and put them on to the desks of line managers. Although many people expected them to disappear, mainframes still produce revenues of $4 billion for IBM, and are said to hold 70 per cent of the world's data.

Insurance brokers are often worried by bancassurance – the name given to banks that sell insurance through their existing branches. This is a good example of an outsider deciding to attack a new market. However, the banks have often failed to be successful outside the narrow confines of their traditional banking operations.

Problems caused by price wars

A price war can break out due to various factors:

1 There is excess production capacity in the industry.
2 There has been little innovation in the market.
3 One business adopts an aggressive marketing campaign based on lower prices.
4 There are few suppliers (an oligopoly). Examples include newspapers, soap, beer, washing powder and cigarettes.

A beer price war in the USA in 1997 saw profits fall for the two largest US brewers, Anheuser-Busch and Miller Brewing. In response to falling beer consumption (largely due to health awareness), Miller, the smaller of the two companies, reduced its prices at a time of year when Anheuser-Busch, the manufacturer of market leader Budweiser, traditionally increased its prices. It initially saw a two per cent increase in market share, but Bud soon struck back. A year-long price war saw revenues-per-barrel fall by a significant amount.

In contrast, Coors, a third brewer, refused to enter the price war and saw its revenue-per-barrel increase by over $1.50 in the period. It seemed that the price war had served only to cheapen the well-known brands, despite intensive advertising, causing many consumers to trade up, despite the higher prices.

Price wars rarely benefit the manufacturer, and often take the place of innovative marketing and product development.

WAYS OUT OF A PRICE WAR

The same problem hit the global market for computer chips in 2001. Poor consumer demand for computer processors and poor performance from PC manufacturers meant that the industry leader Intel sought to keep its expensive factories moving by lowering the prices of its chips, some by as much as 20 per cent. The price cut immediately sparked price reductions from the major PC manufacturers and PC sales recovered. However, most chip manufacturers were unable to respond to the price cuts. On the same day as Intel's pricing announcement, six competitors gave profit warnings. Having a competitor leave the market is one of four possible 'solutions' to a price war.

The situation only resolves itself when:

1 One or more competitors leave the market.
2 Companies scale down their output. New facilities are sometimes mothballed.
3 One of the companies innovates its way out of the problem.
4 Demand starts to grows sufficiently so that there is enough business for all the firms.

Often, several of these factors combine to pull the market out of the doldrums.

WHEN FALLING PRICES ARE A SIGN OF HEALTH

Falling prices do not always signal a problem. This is especially true if points one and two above do not apply. When technology or mass production reduces production costs, the consumer price falls correspondingly. This happens in IT markets, and can be a sign of healthy marketing.

Sometimes a price war can benefit the market leader by knocking out weaker competitors. UK supermarkets continue to build new and larger superstores, but the consumer is spending no extra money. This puts pressure on supermarkets to win sales, and they do this by dropping their prices. The smaller supermarkets and those which are carrying debt will fail first, leaving the biggest operators to emerge victorious.

EuroTunnel initiated a price war with cross-channel ferry operators. With strong performance in other sectors of the company, P&O was able to withstand the competition but not without reducing its Dover–Calais capacity from eight to seven ships. This forced reduction in competition will obviously benefit EuroTunnel.

PRICING STRATEGY

The company should estimate what levels of sales and profit would result at a given price level. This knowledge will help it respond strategically to competitors' price moves, rather than follow in a knee-jerk reaction.

Some markets grow when prices fall; others are relatively inelastic. Failure to raise prices in line with inflation often leads to sharp falls in profitability. The company should therefore adopt a confident and consistent pricing strategy. It should make small but regular price increases, these being less visible to the customer. Price increases are often best made after the peak sales period or before holidays, so that the rise is less noticeable.

Grocery brand manufacturers such as Unilever and Procter & Gamble have found it hard to maintain market share in supermarkets as consumers find cheaper own label products as effective (see Table 14.1). This is partly attributable to the rise of 'the hard discounter' stores, such as Lidl, initially in Germany but also found in France and other European countries. As a result, the companies have had to spend more money promoting their products, which reduces profits.

In some categories the consumer finds an emotional benefit which serves to keep them buying the branded product. For example, young men continue to buy Unilever's Lynx deodorant (also known as Axe) because it promises to make them more sexually desirable.

Table 14.1   Fastest growing private-label categories

	% private-label growth	% private-label share
Drinking yoghurt	38	8
Sports energy drinks	33	6
Lipstick/gloss	26	2
Facial cleansing	21	6
Baby food	20	1
Face moisturisers	20	2
Complete ready meals	20	51
Eye shadow	19	3
Cooking oil	16	21
Flavoured milk	13	14

Counterfeiting

In Paris's *Musée de la Contrefaçon* are the world's earliest fakes. Dating from 27 BC and found in Arles, southern France, they consist of four wine bottles marked with the stamp 'MC Lassius' – a leading wine brand of the time. However, three of the stamps are fake. Evidently the counterfeiters wanted to present their wine as the real thing, and make more money as a result.

Counterfeiting has been with us for a long time, but globalization has turned this problem into a serious issue. According to the museum, a kilo of fake goods is worth eight times more than a kilo of cannabis, so the rewards are clear.

According to the International Chamber of Commerce (www.iccwbo.org), seven per cent of the world's trade is in counterfeit goods, valued at $350 billion. Industries affected include manufacturers of software, automobile and aircraft parts, pharmaceuticals and fast moving consumer goods (FMCGs) such as foodstuffs, beverages, tobacco, clothing and personal-care products. Counterfeiting is a particular risk for companies with strong brands that sell in South America, Eastern Europe and South East Asia. But the problem can also arise in Europe and the USA. The latter is a major producer of counterfeit goods.

The victim company risks losing not only its revenue, but also its reputation, for many counterfeit brands are of poor quality.

Software and record companies suffer a similar problem over copying. According to the IFPI, the organization which represents the world's record companies, music piracy was worth $4.6 billion in 2002, up seven per cent on 2001. It was estimated that one in three discs was a pirate copy.

Software piracy is at least as common, with the Business Software Alliance (BSA) estimating that the illegal copying of business programs costs the US software industry around $11 billion. The BSA has also found that over half of all web users have downloaded software illegally, often using 'Peer to Peer' (P2P) programs such as Kazaa. The Napster court case of 2001 was thought to be a major victory against such illegal file-swapping programs but their use has not abated, with an estimated 300 million Kazaa users worldwide. While the music and software industries are now aggressively pursuing the pirates, a reduction in use does not seem imminent.

One of the worst offenders for counterfeiting is China. According to its Development Research Centre, a research institution affiliated with the Chinese State Council, counterfeiting in China is a $16 billion industry. Other offenders are Pakistan, the Philippines, Eastern Europe and North Africa.

CASE HISTORY: BEATING THE COUNTERFEITERS

100 000 bottles of Smirnovskaya vodka were destroyed in St Petersburg, following a successful court action by Grand Metropolitan. Grand Metropolitan continually takes legal action against counterfeiters which produce vodka bearing the crown, shields and other designs of Smirnoff, and with names like Selikoff and Romanoff. In a single year, the company can take action against 50 pirates.

Johnnie Walker, the United Distillers whisky brand, is often imitated by brands calling themselves Johnnie Hawker, Joe Worker and Johnny Black, generally with similar red and black labels.

According to United Distillers, the fake Johnnie Walker whisky can be 3 per cent Scotch, with the rest being 'local spirits of dubious origin'.

Companies such as Grand Metropolitan, Allied Lyons and Guinness now share information about counterfeiters, in an effort to cut their losses.

Mimicry

Counterfeiting (see above) is illegal, but in most countries mimicry is not. Supermarkets produce own-label products which mimic the brand leaders. According to a survey by Verdict Research, over half (57 per cent) of UK consumers rate own-brand quality as highly as leading brand equivalents. Leading brands complain that supermarkets are parasites which have not invested in creating brands. The supermarkets argue that they are offering the consumer choice and lower prices, as well as powerful own brands. No one, they say, forces the consumer to buy own label products.

Yet, as *The Grocer* magazine points out, Tesco's own-label brands clearly mimic leading brands. Walkers objected to the company's Sensations crisp range which contained the same livery and same image cues such as potatoes set against a rural background.

NOP research has found that one in five consumers had bought own label by mistake. The British Brands Group, which represents brand owners, is seeking a change in the law to protect brands from copycats. And in Europe, brand owners have successfully brought prosecutions against own-label copycats for slavish imitation or 'free-riding'.

In other markets, an innovation introduced by one firm is soon matched by competitors. Much pharmaceutical R&D is designed to develop drugs which match existing competitors' products.

Brand names need to be jealously guarded. In 1998, the US Federal Trade Commission ruled that US grown rice could be labelled as 'basmati,' partly because Indian petitions against the move were somewhat lacklustre. Indian rice growers now fight more vigorously to protect their product, which they believe is a specialist, aromatic rice and something that has a specialist market position resulting from its sub-continental origins. The US ruling is in contrast to UK and Saudi Arabian laws which declare that only specific varieties of Indian rice can be called 'basmati.' Now, the Indian growers must hope that the World Trade Organization (WTO) changes international legislation to prevent basmati becoming a generic term. This example shows that companies (and even countries) can lose their exclusive right to brand names if not rigorously protected.

A US appeal court has ruled that 'Swiss army' knives can come from any country. This has cost the Swiss manufacturers Wenger and Victorinox a lot of revenue. More than half of US consumers who buy a pocket knife with the famous red cross think they are getting a Swiss product. In fact, they are probably buying a poor quality Chinese knife which costs one-fifth of the price, and outsells the original by three to one.

Internal marketing failure – weak product performance

The problems we have examined so far are caused by external forces. They can affect even a company which is excellent at marketing.

Later in this chapter we shall see how these risks can be pre-empted. However, many marketing problems occur as a result of the company's own marketing mistakes. It is these problems we examine next, starting with weak product performance.

Customers buy the product that offers the best performance. In the end, the product with the best performance becomes the market leader. Performance means different things in different markets. It might mean cleaning power, speed of operation, reliability or customer service.

DEFINING COMPARATIVE PRODUCT PERFORMANCE

As Figure 14.2 shows, many markets have three price bands: low price, mid price and premium products. Customers get better performance at the premium end of the market, but not everyone wants premium performance. Many people are content to drive a small Fiat rather than a big Mercedes. Low price is what created the budget airline market, with carriers such as Ryanair and easyJet.

The thick diagonal line in Figure 14.2 shows average market performance. Product A is offering better value for money, as is any other product to the right of the solid line. Product B is offering worse value, like any other product to the left of the line.

Performance improves over time (shown by the dotted line), so that next year's models will be better than this year's, giving the consumer better value for money. A company which was once a leader can quickly become a laggard.

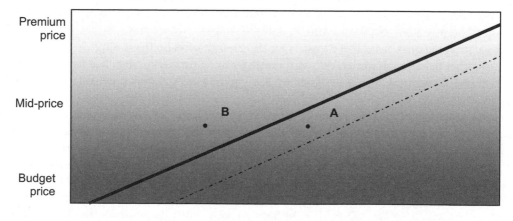

Figure 14.2   Price versus performance

WORDPERFECT: HOW A LEADER BECAME A LAGGARD

It is hard to believe that the market leader in word processing software was once WordPerfect, with over 40 per cent of the market while Microsoft Word had less than 20 per cent. That was 1990. Two years later, their positions were reversed, thanks to Microsoft's introduction of an easy-to-use icon-based word processor.

Microsoft leapt ahead with Word for Windows by offering users greater ease of use and by automating tasks. Users no longer had to memorize arcane lists of keystrokes to format their work – they simply clicked an icon using a mouse. This move was hardly unexpected. Microsoft had borrowed the technique from Apple, which in turn had learnt it from Xerox.

WordPerfect then introduced a bug-ridden WordPerfect for Windows. The company also lacked an Office-type bundled suite. In addition, Microsoft withheld the Windows code, which stopped competitors from linking their word processors into the operating system. Some commentators also alleged that Microsoft played tricks to beat the competition. They said its operating system would make non-Microsoft software crash or send it false error messages, making users think that they needed to use Microsoft products on their PCs.

Finally, an even greater mistake was for Novell to buy WordPerfect for the huge sum of $1 bn in 1994, at a time when WordPerfect sales were plummeting. Two years later Novell sold the program to Corel.

This story has many lessons. It reminds us that innovation can upend a market, that the gatekeeper can control the market, and that a product must work properly to retain even loyal users. It also tells us that a determined innovator can wreak havoc among its competitors, by fair means or foul.

Poor promotion

Service companies tend to stop promotional activity when its staff are fully employed. Marketing takes place when the principals see that long-term projects are ending. This produces 'feast and famine' marketing activity. The same can be seen among engineering companies when they experience a decline in orders.

Promotion should be constant. New customers coming into the market need to be made aware of the product, and existing customers should only change their purchasing behaviour with reluctance. The bigger the price tag, the longer it takes to win the customer, and the greater the need for long-term promotion. And where competitors are promoting their products, the company has to maintain an adequate 'share of voice' if it is to prevent customers defecting.

HOW TO AVOID RISK IN PROMOTIONAL ACTIVITY

Companies put themselves at risk in their promotional activities by:

- over-claiming – this leads to disappointment, hostility and possible action
- dumping good advertising executions just when the customer is beginning to recognize them
- failing to be single minded and consistent about the brand's offer
- failing to understand the needs of the customer
- developing ads that win awards rather than customers

- failing to test and measure the advertising, so the company doesn't know whether the campaign is successful, and which media work best
- failing to use all the available media, including online and viral marketing.

Branding problems

For an industry which preaches the virtues of promoting strong brands, advertising agencies are notorious for their failure to promote themselves. Other than Saatchi and Saatchi, few big agency names can be recalled by more than 25 per cent of big advertisers, according to research.

The same is true of many industrial markets; and in the construction market, where there are thousands of suppliers making everything from roof tiles to carpet tiles, buyers only know the brand leaders' names.

Failure to recognize a brand name is usually due to poor promotion or weak product performance (discussed above). But a strong brand name alone is not enough to make a company immune from marketing problems, as the case history below shows.

CASE HISTORY: WHEN A BIG BRAND WAS SAVAGED BY AN UNKNOWN COMPANY

Every consumer knows Coca-Cola, but few have heard of Cott. The latter makes private-label soft drinks for supermarkets. In 1991 the company began to launch a series of supermarket sub-brands in Canada. Since then, Cott has gained 20 per cent of the Canadian grocery soft drinks market. Coca-Cola has been relegated to third place.

In the UK, Coca-Cola has 60 per cent of the supermarket sales, well ahead of Pepsi Cola which has 20 per cent and supermarket labels which have 10 per cent. Not surprisingly, Cott has sought to attack the lucrative UK market.

Sainsbury's, the UK's top supermarket, adopted the Cott approach. It launched Classic Cola, which it claimed to be a better-tasting drink than traditional supermarket brands and which sells at a higher price,

though cheaper than Coca-Cola. Sainsbury has made substantial gains with Classic Cola. Overall, however, Coca-Cola has suffered little damage because supermarkets account for only a small proportion of its turnover.

Nevertheless, it shows that it is dangerous to rely too heavily on intangible benefits, such as a brand name or advertising skills. If customers find that another firm provides similar performance at lower price they will desert the brand leader. McKinsey, the management consultancy, claims that consumer marketing has grown ineffective and needs to be radically re-thought.

Equally, 42 per cent of Cott's sales come from one customer, the giant Wal-Mart, which makes Cott vulnerable, and something we examine later in this chapter.

Effective innovation

In any market, there are two types of company: leaders and laggards (see Table 14.2). The leader is constantly trying out new ideas, launching new products and looking for new ways to attract the customer. The laggard usually imitates the leader some months later, but it is easy to see who is driving the market. The laggard, by its intellectual failure and its lack of vigour, usually slips further behind.

Table 14.2   Leaders and laggards

Leader	Laggard
Innovates	Follows
Makes news	Makes imitative 'me-too' products
Concentrates on strategy	Concentrates on tactics
Manages for the future	Manages for the status quo

Markets, even the most conservative ones, are constantly changing, even if only because they are affected by the business cycle of growth-inflation-recession. While the elderly Kellogg's Cornflakes is still a brand leader, it is now surrounded by own-label products, new mueslis, and new breakfast foods, many of them made by Kellogg's.

Kellogg's, unlike most market leaders, has stayed on top. Others are less successful. Large airlines now struggle to compete with easyJet, and Marks & Spencer paid heavily for offering outdated products. Market leaders usually stick to what made them successful. They try to protect the 'rent stream' that flows from their big-selling products. This makes them easy prey for the innovative smaller firm.

Sometimes products succeed because they offer new advantages. In the washing-powder market mentioned above, consumers might like faster washing, the ability to shed dirt, or bactericidal action.

Product age is usually a good indicator. If more than half of the company's turnover comes from products which have not changed in the last five years, change is overdue. As Figure 14.3 shows, new product development (NPD) stems from market research, and requires extensive market research input.

NEW PRODUCT DEVELOPMENT

The management consultancy discussed earlier in this chapter was dependent on just one product: ISO 9000. Management consultants sell fashionable management ideas, and the demand for any product always declines eventually. As the demand petered out, the company found it had no other product to sell.

Companies should devote substantial efforts to ensuring that its product remains state-of-the-art. New materials or techniques should never be ignored. Static or mature markets are particularly vulnerable, as we saw with Coca-Cola.

For nearly 20 years Milk Tray chocolates were associated with James Bond imagery. Cadbury then boldly decided to abandon this image, and sales rose by 13 per cent. This demonstrates that taking risks is sometimes the only way to rejuvenate a brand or win new business.

Innovation isn't always easy. For years, Woolworth, one of the world's biggest retailers, tried to find a winning formula to replace the declining 'five-and-ten cent' variety store on which it was founded. As long ago as the 1960s, Woolworth sought to develop speciality stores, eventually succeeding with its Foot Locker sports shoe outlets. In 1997, the company finally closed its remaining 400 US Woolworth department stores, and today the chain operates 2000 Foot Locker stores around the world, selling sports shoes to its 12–20-year-old customers. In the UK, the Woolworth name, sold by the parent company in 1982, lives on with 806 high-street variety stores.

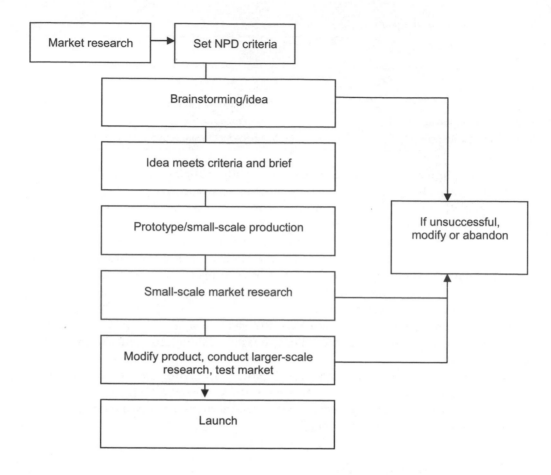

Figure 14.3   New product development strategy

New product development errors

It is easier to fail than succeed in new product development. Errors come about because companies develop products which the consumer does not want. This happens when insufficient research is carried out. The most famous failure of this kind was Sir Clive Sinclair's C5 battery-powered trikes. Consumers found that the trikes were unsafe for use on the road, being slow and too low.

Even major companies suffer. When Lever Brothers added manganese to its Persil washing powder, and called it Persil Power, rumours circulated that it rotted clothes. The Good Housekeeping Institute withdrew its endorsement, and eight independent laboratories agreed that the powder did indeed damage clothes. Lever Brothers reduced the level of manganese content by 80 per cent, but the episode reduced Unilever's profits by £57 million. This was in addition to £200 million spent in development and launch costs. The long-term impact on the 85-year-old Persil brand remains to be seen.

Faults in new products must be detected before they reach the market. Intel, the chip maker, admitted that its Pentium chip had 'a subtle flaw' which affected the accuracy of its long division. The fault would not be noticed by the average user, but the company had forecast annual sales of seven million copies of the chip, which indicates the scale of the problem.

CASE HISTORY: THE TRIUMPHS AND FAILURES OF BARON BICH

Even the most successful innovators sometimes fail. Baron Bich was famous for his disposable Bic lighter, his disposable razors and especially the throwaway Bic ballpoint pen, of which 15 million are sold every day. When he died in 1994, his company had a turnover of £650 million and owned (among other businesses) the largest lingerie business in France and Italy.

But Bich also had his share of failures. He tried and failed to sell inexpensive Bic perfume through supermarkets, newsagents and petrol stations. He eventually withdrew it, after three years of losses totalling £15 million.

His venture into fashion, with the purchase of Guy Laroche clothing, lost £25 million in one year alone. Expansion into windsurfing boards also cost the group profit.

Some products took a long time to come right. Though Bich bought Waterman, the US pen firm, in 1957, the company did not make profits until 1965.

Bich accepted a degree of failure as the price of innovation. He was also unwilling to rest on his laurels, and strived continuously to stay ahead.

Over-reliance on a few customers

Many companies are over-dependent on a few major customers. In some firms 80 per cent of sales often come from just 20 per cent of the customers. The UK grocery market is dominated by five major supermarket chains, so the food processing industry is particularly vulnerable to having its brands de-listed, especially in favour of the supermarket's own-label goods.

In another case, a UK advertising agency got half its work from one US client. When the client sold its UK business, the new owners decided to spend less on promotion, and the agency nearly went bust.

The rating agency Standard & Poors (S&P) says that many European banks are over-dependent on important clients. This is especially true of banks in Germany, Italy and Portugal. In Germany, the top 20 clients accounted for 14 per cent of the average bank's equity, while in Italy and Portugal it is 10 per cent. On average, eight per cent of the equity of the top 100 European banks rests on just 20 clients, according to S&P and this represents 40 per cent of net operating income. The banks most at risk are those catering to particular industries, and those that are oriented toward wholesale and corporate banking. If some of these customers got into difficulty, the banks would be vulnerable.

According to S&P, the current regulatory regime, which requires banks to set aside ten per cent of capital, is inadequate.

Distribution failures

Large branded-goods companies generally know all the outlets that stock their products. Other companies are not always so advanced. Many businesses operate regionally, despite having a product suitable for the country as a whole. Others think nationally, when their product could be selling globally. There are many ways a company can expand: through additional sales people, agents or through exporting. One solution is franchising, which we consider overleaf.

FRANCHISING

Franchising offers several benefits to a company with a strong brand name and a standardized way of doing business. The company can increase its revenue without adding overheads. The franchisee pays for premises, equipment, vehicles, employees and stock.

The more successful the franchisee, the more royalties they pay, and the more product they buy from the franchisor. The franchisee works harder than an employee because they own the business. In bad times, the franchisee shoulders the burden of falling sales. But there are also disadvantages. The company loses the management of its distribution, and franchising may be a less profitable way to do business. The same principle applies to alternatives, such as appointing licensees and agents.

DIRECT SALES AND CHANNEL CONFLICT

Many companies have chosen to sell direct, having learnt that in bypassing the retail trade they don't have to pay out the retailers' margin, and earn higher profits. And while this works for many, it can cause problems.

Apple Computers faced a backlash from its long-serving dealers when it set up a chain of company-owned stores. One retailer says he had to close his flagship store when Apple opened up nearby. According to *Inc* magazine, some dealers launched suits against the company case alleging over-billing and ignoring orders for popular products such as the iPod. The problems originally surfaced when a list of the resellers' email addresses was accidentally despatched to them. This led them to compare notes and discover a pattern of common complaints. However, consumers have been queuing up to get into the stores.

Such conflict is perhaps inevitable. The growth of the Internet has made it possible for an increasing proportion of customers being able to buy goods directly from the manufacturer.

Superior performance

A superior product outperforms its competitors on the important factors. It provides the customer with greater satisfaction. The performance factors for a DIY superstore might comprise:

- Location
- Range and type of products stocked
- Car parking and access
- Opening hours
- Brand image
- Checkout speed
- Store size
- Information and promotion
- Services offered
- Staff attitude and knowledge
- Prices
- Store layout and ambience

When all the leading DIY superstores are offering these benefits, the market has matured. The company with strategic marketing vision has to decide how to create a competitive advantage. Being market leader is not in itself enough. Being market leader results from decisions taken five years ago; and the market leader is vulnerable to attack by small competitors whose size allows them to be opportunistic or entrepreneurial.

The company has to ensure that its brand continues to offer greater benefits than the competitors. Otherwise its performance will eventually be matched by a low-priced competitor (as with Coca-Cola), or surpassed (as Hoover found when Dyson launched its revolutionary vacuum cleaners).

The company knows it is being successful when its prices set the market rate, when it has a sizeable (but not necessarily the biggest) market share, or when it has new products which are growing strongly and which promise to be popular. Even if the market is not as perfect as it might be, the company can minimize the risks. For example, companies in unpredictable markets can keep their costs at a level which matches a bad year.

Several factors create a superior product. They include innovation, information, customer focus, and good communication. We consider those factors next.

Loss of corporate reputation

When a crisis occurs, one of the first casualties is the corporate reputation. As Figure 14.4 shows, the public believes that many corporate offences are as serious, if not worse than, violent street crimes.

The survey, conducted by the National White Collar Crime Centre (which questioned over 1100 members of the US public), found that fraud and product defects were rated worse than street theft and armed robbery respectively. The public were found to be particularly angry in situations where the corporate offender abused a position of authority. Attitudes on what constitutes a serious offence may change over time, but the authors of the survey felt that there has been a hardening of opinion on corporate crime in recent years.

The book as a whole is dedicated to preventing the company from losing its good reputation. In Chapter 17 we consider in more detail how companies can manage their corporate reputation in times of crisis.

ARTHUR ANDERSEN'S FALL FROM GRACE

A railway director burst into the small office of Chicago-based Arthur Andersen in 1914, demanding that he approve the company's annual accounts. The company had inflated its profits by failing to properly record day-to-day expenses. Arthur Andersen replied that there wasn't enough money in Chicago to make him change his mind. Later the railroad company went bankrupt, and the firm of Arthur Andersen became known for its probity. This reputation for stern integrity continued until the 1980s.

But by 1994 two-thirds of Andersen's $3.3 billion in US revenue was coming from management consulting. According to the *Chicago Tribune*, the firm's Professional Standards Group that gave advice on tricky ethical and regulatory issues began to be ignored. Finally, in 2002, it was convicted for obstructing a federal investigation into Enron, its leading client. The company sold off its audit division, and became Accenture.

This wasn't Arthur Andersen's only failure. In 2001, it was fined $7 million by the Securities and Exchange Commission (SEC) for 'improper professional conduct'. This included overstating the earnings of their client Waste Management by $1.4 billion. In the same year, Andersen also paid $110 million to Sunbeam shareholders to settle lawsuits stemming from its inflated earnings statements, according to the US Public Broadcast Service (PBS). The firm had also moved its base from Chicago to the tax haven of the Bahamas. The following year it paid Enron investors $40 million to settle claims against its non-US divisions.

Arthur Andersen's role in the Enron scandal led to the USA's Sarbanes-Oxley Act, which has placed much tighter controls on company accounts and their auditors.

Which is more serious: armed robbery causing serious injury, or neglecting to recall a vehicle that results in a serious injury?

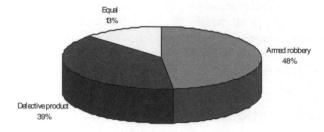

Which is more serious: armed robbery causing serious injury, or allowing tainted meat to be sold which results in one person becoming ill?

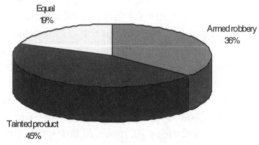

Which is more serious: a street thief or embezzler who steals $100?

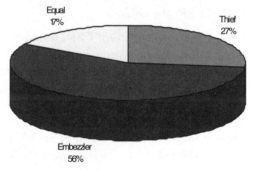

Source: US national survey on white-collar crime

Figure 14.4   Public views on white-collar crime

Information

At a strategic level, good information relies on effective forecasting. Some companies use scenario planning, which is discussed in Chapter 16. This means ensuring that the company is aware of any threats and opportunities on the horizon.

Research should identify the key issues in the market. It should find out what prevents people buying, and how the customer can be helped to buy. Discovering the critical factors for success (which are discussed in the section on benchmarking, below) will help the company become more competitive.

Sometimes, whole industries seem oblivious to the consumer, with products failing to work as the consumer would wish. In much UK sanitaryware, the water flows into the lavatory cistern from underneath. The connection is submerged in several litres of water, and leaks are common. Yet manufacturers show no interest in changing their products.

After listening to feedback from their female guests, many hotels have introduced bedrooms designed for the female executive, which have more feminine decor, feminine toiletries, and added safety features. These rooms are so popular that even men ask to stay in them. Aware of women's needs for privacy and security, some hotels have also introduced new procedures for the lone female in their restaurants.

REDUCING RISK BY BENCHMARKING

In benchmarking, the company decides (preferably through research) what makes a superior product. That could be price, customer service or product design. The company then decides the best companies to compare itself with, and the best units of measurement. It then gathers the data for its own business and its competitors. A benchmark exercise is shown below in Table 14.3. Once it has been undertaken, the company should determine how it could achieve a lead over its competition.

Focus on the customer

Customer focus means caring about the needs of the purchaser. It involves being flexible, and giving customers what they want. A request by one or two customers often represents the feelings of many.

The customer-focused company welcomes customers' ideas and complaints, and listens to them. Customer focus also means breaking down the barriers between marketing, sales, production and research. Everyone should be working to meet customers' needs, and in some companies integrated 'category' teams provide a better solution. In markets where retailers are important, trade marketing and product development need to work closely. In markets where service is important, the marketing and customer service departments may be amalgamated.

Table 14.3   Benchmarking exercise – small electrical goods

Critical success factor	Company to benchmark	To be measured	Method of collecting the data	Action
Customer appeal	Braun	Market share	Published data	Do analysis
Price	All	Consumer price, trade discounts	Price lists	Establish profit margins
Distribution	All	Depth and breadth of stocking	Own survey	Brief salesforce
Functionality	Black and Decker	Warranty cost, comparative tests	Function testing, *Which*? reports	Set up programme
Service response time	Philips	Number of days	Survey	Commission research

COMMUNICATING PROPERLY

Good promotion is *informative*, telling customers something they did not know. It should *seek a response*, especially the urge to buy the product being advertised. It should communicate a *brand image*, one which appeals to the target market. Good promotion is *regular*, because customers are always dipping in and out of the market. It may be *entertaining*, *dramatic*, or *confrontational*, to break the 'glass case of indifference' that surrounds the consumer.

Good promotion does not harangue: it should be the customer's confidant and best friend. It seeks to converse with the customer at different times of day and in different ways, whether conversationally by direct mail or grandiloquently using 48-sheet posters. It talks about the customer's needs and interests, not those of the advertiser.

Companies need to communicate with all their audiences. Despite the fact that he led Shell, the oil company, to its best-ever annual figures, few investors mourned the departure of chairman Sir Phillip Watts in 2004. He had a reputation for failing to communicate with the company investors, most obviously demonstrated when he failed to turn up to the crisis press conference at which Shell announced it had overstated its reserves by several billion barrels. This disastrous lack of communication suggests one reason why the Shell share price jumped 13.5p on his departure.

Useful links

Advertising Association
www.adassoc.org.uk

Institute of Direct Marketing
www.theidm.com

Institute of Marketing
www.cim.co.uk

Institute of Public Relations
www.ipr.org.uk

Market Research Society
www.marketresearch.org.uk

Marketing Society
www.marketing-society.org.uk

Risk assessment – marketing

By answering the questions below, you can assess your vulnerability to marketing risk. Tick all relevant boxes and add up the number of points ticked.

Topic	Question	
Macro issues	Is the company vulnerable to changes in government policy?	☐
The market	Does the company operate in fickle or fast-moving markets?	☐
Sales	Have sales been static or fallen during the last two years?	☐
Dependency	Is the firm dependent on a few customers?	☐
Promotion	Does the company fail to consistently promote its products?	☐
New product development	Is there a lack of new product development activity?	☐
The customer	Is the firm weak in maintaining good customer relations?	☐
Price	Is a price war possible?	☐
Counterfeiting and mimicry	Does the company sell famous brands which can be copied?	☐
Acquisition	Is the company seeking to acquire another firm?	☐
Total points scored		
Score: 0–3 points: low risk. 4–6 points: moderate risk. 7–10 points: high risk.		

The appendix contains a summary of all the checklists in this book. By entering the results of this one, you can compare the scale of marketing risk against other categories of risk.

15 *People Risks and Corporate Ethics*

> In this chapter, we examine the risks which result from management and human resource failings. We consider how to:
>
> • *Strengthen weak top management*
> • *Avoid dissatisfaction among key workers*
> • *Manage industrial relations*
> • *Minimize the risks of stress and bad health*
> • *Maintain corporate ethics and prevent loss of corporate reputation.*

Often it is not business risks that bring down a company, but the management which fails to manage them. A company is at risk if the management is weak. The risks include:

- A board that brings bad PR to the business by agreeing unmerited pay rises or excessive perks to directors.
- A chief executive who lacks leadership or common sense, or who is weak in a crucial area such as marketing or finance.
- Having a weak finance director, or even a non-existent one in smaller firms.
- Being slow to respond quickly to changes, such as new technology, falling sales or increased debt.
- Lack of corporate structure, especially in smaller firms which fail to allocate responsibility for key functions. Often the Chief Executive manages sales or finance on a part-time basis.
- Companies that devote their time to company politics. In one firm, the marketing manager spent his time plotting against the R&D department. R&D, in turn, never attended meetings with marketing people.
- Managers who base their decisions on hunch rather than on fact. Some boards never see or call for research reports, financial data or sales figures.

Quality of the board

Directors' pay awards and perks have been controversial for some time.

- Ross Johnson, CEO of RJR Nabisco, once sent the company jet to transport his dog, Rocco, from Palm Springs, California to New York. He named it 'G. Shepherd' on the passenger list.

- The Securities and Exchange Commission accused Tyco CEO Dennis Kozlowski of looting the company of $600 million. This included a $2 million Roman-themed birthday party for his wife. At the party was an ice sculpture of Michelangelo's *David* whose penis streamed Russian Stolichnaya vodka into crystal glasses.

- Twenty years ago, according to the US Internal Revenue Service, CEOs earned 40 times more than the factory floor worker. In 2003, it was 400 times more, and is now climbing to a multiple of 500. While average incomes shrank two consecutive years, down 5.7 per cent, median CEO pay rose 15 per cent in 2003.

- In the course of a divorce between Jack Welch, former boss of General Electric, the US's largest company, and his wife, it emerged that despite having retired, he was entitled to unlimited use of the company's Boeing 737 (value $291 000 a month) and a Central Park apartment, as well as a $9 million pension.

Undue perks damage a company's profits. David Yermack, an economist at New York University, looked at the 200 largest American companies between 1993 and 2002, comparing those that let their CEO use company jets for personal purposes with those that did not. Even after accounting for other factors, Yermack found that the long-term stock-market performance of perk-rich companies was dramatically worse than that of their peers. This cost shareholders hundreds of millions of dollars a year.

THE NEED FOR STRONG BOARD

A weak board can cause serious problems because it allows the firm to drift, missing opportunities, creating inertia, stifling initiative, and causing good staff to leave.

The chairman and non-executive directors should ensure that the boardroom seats are occupied by people of true merit, and should seek to remove those who fail to demonstrate results (while avoiding short-termism). It is important to distinguish between results that stem from adverse external conditions, and those which arise from poor management. More than one chief executive has been removed while battling in difficult trading conditions.

Appointing non-executive directors and setting up a remuneration committee may give the business an independent outlook that could save it from copying some of the self-indulgent and damaging decisions that have been reported in the newspapers in recent years.

Managing succession

Some companies face strategic risks through the lack of corporate management or succession. A family-owned business sometimes suffers discord among family members as to the future direction the company should take. This affected Clarks, the shoe company, when some family members wanted to sell the business. It also affected the 264-year-old Pedro Domecq, which eventually sold out to Allied Lyons (now Allied-Domecq) for £739 million.

The situation is also likely to affect the public sector. In a 1996 survey of federal US agencies and public-sector organizations, 27 respondents indicated that only 28 per cent had, or planned to have, a succession management programme, despite 56 per cent of the same respondents indicating they believed their organization was seriously short of leaders to meet emerging changes in their organizations.

HOW TO DESIGN A SUCCESSION PLAN

To prevent a vacuum developing at the top, leading to a stagnation and future crisis, the business should adopt the following steps:

- Obtain management buy-in for succession planning
- Identify the future leadership needs of the organization
- Conduct staff reviews to acquire feedback, identify problems and opportunities, and identify competencies
- Identify high-potential talent
- Recruit external future leaders, where appropriate (for example, graduate management trainees)
- Give staff experience of different departments and roles
- Create opportunities for people to grow within the company
- Implement training, mentoring and coaching programmes, both formal and informal.

Key worker risks

Many businesses depend on key workers – namely, senior managers and board members – who are responsible for creating change, managing businesses and keeping customers. If they defect to a competitor, the firm may be at risk from their knowledge and contacts, as former employees can poach customers or key members of staff, set up in opposition, or pre-empt the company's strategic plans.

Some advertising agencies are dependent on a well-known creative director. If that person leaves, the agency may lose existing and potential clients. If the individual's name is on the agency door, this poses added problems.

To manage the risk of losing key workers, companies can adopt both defensive and aggressive solutions. Defensive solutions include contracts stopping ex-employees from working with the agency's clients for a period of time. But this is, at best, a short-term solution. A better plan is to give the key executives rewards which encourage them to stay. This will include:

- Financial incentives (salary and profit sharing)
- Managerial responsibility (or freedom from this kind of work)
- Lifestyle benefits (giving them the respect and credit their egos require, or the lifestyle they like).

Managing people

Over the next decade, demographic changes will make it more difficult for companies to recruit staff. In many parts of the West, there will be a decline in the number of young people and a gradually ageing population, as the 'baby boom' post-war population ages.

The median age of a UK citizen has increased by four years in the past 30 years to 38. This is predicted to rise to 43 by 2031. With low population growth rates, the actual number of people of working age in the UK will drop. This will lead to wage pressure, skill shortages and more flexible working patterns. With these factors in mind, the company needs to ensure it adopts good working conditions for its staff. This will include:

- A more open and equitable management style, as well as common conditions and rewards for all employees
- A culture that values teamwork and excellence, and conditions that assist female (as well as male) employees, such as flexitime, childcare facilities and part-time working
- Training and re-training, to develop a workforce capable of producing products and services which will change rapidly (the willingness of the workforce to accept rapid change will be higher in well-managed firms which have the trust of the labour force).

A company that cares for its workforce will be typified by its willingness to listen and to learn, and to implement changes which improve workforce conditions. Sharing corporate information with the workforce, including sales and cost figures, and involving the workforce in decision-making will be a hallmark of the successful company; and this will include long-term decisions concerning corporate strategy and staffing levels.

Welfare problems frequently cause crises. They include staff anger over unfair dismissal, perks, maternity arrangements, withdrawal of canteen facilities, and unsafe working conditions. Many of these topics will seem unimportant to management, but they quickly spark a dispute.

CASE STUDY: A MEMO FROM CLIFFORD CHANCE

A leaked memo from junior lawyers at Clifford Chance, the world's biggest law firm, claimed they were under unacceptable pressure to bill 2420 hours a year, leading them to overstate their billable hours. The story duly entered into the world's media.

Senior partner Stuart Popham instructed partners to call all clients, rather than wait for them to ring up and ask what was happening. Despite this, a survey among US lawyers placed Clifford Chance bottom out of 132 law firms in terms of where people would like to work. A similar survey in a UK legal magazine ranked Clifford Chance 44th out of 50 firms in London.

The company subsequently debated whether to investigate morale among the firm's 2200 junior lawyers. One partner explained the risk, saying: 'If the firm doesn't poll associates on pay and working conditions, they will make their views known through another medium.'

EFFECTIVE RECRUITMENT

Recruiting a poor performer adds greatly to the risks to which a company is exposed. Yet recruitment is still poorly managed in many firms. This is partly because judging personality and effectiveness is notoriously difficult. Simply measuring IQ does not identify whether the candidate will perform well. In Europe, many firms have adopted graphology, yet research shows this is equally flawed. Companies can minimize their risk by being methodical. This includes:

- preparing a job specification
- creating a personal specification, outlining the required experience, abilities and qualifications
- undertaking the right method of recruitment, whether through head hunting or through advertising

- training managers to be effective interviewers
- checking CVs and taking up references.

Some companies hire MBAs; and while this adds rigour to corporate thought, there is a risk that company thinking becomes overly structured and planned, with less importance placed on intuition, creativity and risk-taking. *The Scotsman* has unkindly described today's 60 000 UK MBAs as 'corporate civil servants'.

STRUCTURING FOR MAXIMUM EFFECTIVENESS

Many companies are reducing entrepreneurial risk by ensuring that as many of their staff as possible meet their customers. Some companies are merging their sales and marketing departments, and re-structuring to provide 'category management'. In this way, companies are recognizing that old boundaries may no longer be the most effective way of managing the business. In Chapter 14, we consider the relationship between consumer marketing, selling and customer service.

RISKS OF BEING SUED BY EMPLOYEES

In the US, according to a survey by Chubb Group, one in four private companies has been sued by a current or former employee. What's more, 44 per cent said they expected to face a claim in the future. The costs of meeting such a claim is large, fuelled by increases in legal costs. A survey of educational institutions by Tillinghast-Towers Perrin found that the average cost of settling an employee discrimination claim at a private institution rose from $60 000 to $175 000 between 1992 and 1997. Public institutions' costs rose from $40 000 to $100 000 in the same period. The survey noted that many institutions seemed ill-prepared to manage the risk. Thirty per cent of the institutions surveyed operated without formal, written policies on critical employment issues. A further 15 per cent have policies but don't review them regularly. This suggests that managing employee relations is a risk area, and receives less attention than it needs. This area is covered further in Chapter 13.

PREVENTING WORKPLACE BULLYING

Cantor Fitzgerald, the US broker, had to pay a £912 000 damages award, later reduced by £116 000, to a former employee who claimed he was subjected to a 'culture of bullying and abuse'. In another case, Credit Suisse bank settled another alleged bullying case for £200 000 when a Pakistani-born trader claimed he was treated like a slave by colleagues, and warned off dating white women.

Lawsuits like these are the tip of the iceberg, and can often damage the company's reputation. In the 9/11 tragedy 658 Cantor employees died, and there was massive sympathy for the firm. But much of this evaporated when the world heard about the company's behaviour towards its staff.

The costs imposed by tribunals are small compared with the time and money involved in recruiting new staff to replace those who leave. According to bullying.com, 15 per cent of employees feel they are bullied, and a fifth of people who witness the bullying also leave. Contrary to myths, bullies can attack popular and effective employees as well as the more obvious shy or retiring victims. Nor is it exclusively bosses bullying subordinates. Clients can bully professionals, juniors can bully superiors, and one colleague can bully another. Sexual harassment and demeaning comments about the victim's race, gender, disability or age are also forms of bullying. Each can have potentially explosive results in the way of resignations and compensation claims.

Other kinds of bullying include verbal assault, shouting and offensive language. So too is belittling the victim's opinions, constant criticism, overwork, isolation, and jokes about the victim's appearance.

CASE STUDY: BULLYING AND ITS AFTERMATH AT ROYAL MAIL

A Royal Mail internal inquiry concluded that supervisors drove one of its employees Jermaine Lee to kill himself at the Birmingham Mail Centre in Newtown, Birmingham.

An inquest ruled that his superiors were blameless. But Royal Mail set up two action groups in the wake of the eight-month investigation, described as 'one of the biggest ever conducted in our 350-year history'.

The Royal Mail set up a 'shop-a-bully' hot-line. It also introduced its 'dignity at work' policy, and within 12 months had trained almost a quarter of its staff in issues relating to diversity. 'It was common knowledge that bullying and harassment was widespread in Royal Mail,' says Satya Kartaria, the company's director of Diversity and Inclusion. 'We wanted to turn that round, make it a great place to work. It was a very macho culture and we knew that in the past no challenges had been made to unacceptable behaviour. We recognized

that training managers and all employees would be crucial in challenging the existing culture.'

To prevent bullying requires a change of culture. Royal Mail now has an active training programme, and has appointed 20 anti-bullying investigators. As a result of the inquiry, Royal Mail sacked a senior executive, and suspended six managers and supervisors; and an area manager resigned.

Five years after Jermaine Lee's death, chief executive Adam Crozier said the company had 'still not beaten the bully boys, with cases of alleged harassment still a cause for concern'. But he said great strides had been taken to stop the bullies and the group was determined to stop workplace harassment. 'We started with the worst record of any company in Britain,' he said. 'But this is something we are absolutely determined to stamp out. This is a real priority for us. We now follow up every case very, very closely and quickly.'

You can prevent workplace bullying by:

- implementing and promulgating an anti-bullying policy; specifying that bullying is unacceptable
- instigating training for all staff on what constitutes acceptable behaviour at work
- establishing systems for investigating and dealing with conflict – this should start with counselling and mentoring, leading to conciliation and arbitration if unresolved, and finally disciplinary action
- informing staff what actions they can take, and ensuring no victimization takes place when bullying is reported
- investigating complaints quickly, maintaining discretion and confidentiality, and

protecting the rights of all individuals involved – to make an effective case, you need detailed written records over time
- appointing a discrimination and bullying advisor.

Stress and bad healthcare

Stress at work accounts for 13.5 million lost working days in Britain according to the Health and Safety Executive. One in five workers rated their jobs as 'very' or 'extremely' stressful. Stress is now recognized as a major cause of heart disease, which in turn produces 21 per cent of male absences from work.

Absenteeism is an indicator of an unhappy workforce. In Britain's NHS Trust hospitals, four out of ten employees have fallen ill or felt unwell from work-related stress, according to the 2003 staff survey. This was due to their workload and was exacerbated by poor management, with two-fifths of respondents noting that they had too many conflicting demands on their time.

Stress of work leads many people to take time off. The Unscheduled Absence Survey, provided by leading employment law firm CCH, found that 11 per cent of all unscheduled absences were due to stress. Dissatisfaction with work can exacerbate these figures. Workplaces with 'poor' or 'fair' morale found that on average 14 per cent of unscheduled absences were due to stress, as opposed to 9 per cent in more positive working environments. The annual per-employee cost of absenteeism is estimated at $645.

Employees can take legal action over stress. In 2000, a record amount was paid to a teacher for the stress which led directly to her retirement on the grounds of ill health. Despite several complaints to the employers, from both herself and her union, Jan Howell was left in sole charge of a riotous class of largely non-English-speaking pupils, 11 of whom had special needs. Despite suffering one breakdown, nothing was done to ease the difficult situation and Mrs Howell suffered a second breakdown, resulting in her retirement. The Local Education Authority was forced to admit liability and pay £250 000 in compensation.

In Tokyo, Japan Tobacco Inc. paid out £246 000 to the bereaved family of Saburo Sanada, a 54-year-old manager who suffered karoshi – sudden death caused by overwork. Saburo had been working 400 hours a month, supervising the construction of a hotel. Karoshi is a major issue in Japanese business (there were 143 reported deaths in 2002); and some believe the phenomenon affects overworked western workers too, such as junior doctors.

Signs of stress are:

- Headache
- Tiredness
- Eczema
- Muscle tics
- Stomach problems, diarrhoea, constipation
- Anger, frustration, violence, aggression
- Anxiety
- Increased use of alcohol, tobacco, drugs or sleeping pills
- Depression
- Feeling powerless
- Irritability with customers or co-workers
- Problems at work, such as forgetfulness
- Absenteeism.

In the longer term, stress manifests itself in heart disease, cancer, ulcers and other diseases.

Employee ill-health endangers not only the employee but also the business itself and other people. The 1988 Clapham rail crash which killed 35 people was allegedly caused by faulty work done by a technician who had taken only one day off in the previous 13 weeks. There are currently several compensation cases in the courts which allege that mistakes made by overworked and stressed doctors were to blame for a patient's death.

HOW TO REDUCE WORKPLACE STRESS

Employers now need to manage the whole working environment, not just the use of equipment or the type of work. This starts with a concern for people. Solutions for reducing stress and absenteeism (as well as ill-health and industrial disputes) include the following:

- Undertake an audit of employee attitudes and stress levels
- Provide clear job descriptions and lines of reporting
- Ensure regular upward and downward communication, and ensure employees' opinions are heard
- Make work more fulfilling (for example, cell production which lets a group of employees complete an entire task rather than just part of it)
- Increase the amount of control that employees have over their work (for example, overtime and pace of work)
- Ensure that workloads are managed and balanced
- Increase employees' technical work skills
- Give employees better coping strategies, such as improved diet or exercise, or strategies for dealing with abusive customers
- Improve support and supervision
- Enhance working conditions (noise, breaks, fumes and so on)
- Implement a fair reward system, perhaps avoiding piece work
- Increase job security and career development
- Increase flexibility in working arrangements
- Introduce stress management training, as well as substance-abuse training
- Improve ergonomics, for example for employees working at computer screens.

Industrial relations and disputes

The hazards associated with industrial disputes are clear: lost output, bitter industrial relations, and loss of reputation among customers, the city and other important stakeholders. Most disputes can be foreseen, as relations between management and unions gradually deteriorate. Grievances can grow over many years, and a workforce that believes it has been treated unfairly is more likely to take industrial action.

The company should have mechanisms to ensure that grievances are heard and treated seriously. Management must make efforts to communicate the reasons for changes and gain the acceptance of the workforce before they are implemented. The company should assess the probability of a strike, consider what damage it could cause, and analyse how it could be pre-empted. The best solutions are to ensure that the company is seen to act fairly and honestly.

RESPONDING TO A LABOUR DISPUTE

The company should assess the needs of the union or workers. It should recognize that a demand for a pay rise could be masking another grievance (such as bad industrial relations). During the dispute, the company should maintain a dialogue with the union, irrespective of how impossible a solution may seem. It should also identify the outcome of different results, in terms of impact on profitability or future negotiations. The company should get a matching benefit for any concession. It should avoid giving any undue concession without a corresponding concession from the union. Management should be consistent in its dealings with the union. It should at all times demonstrate commitment to its course of action.

The business should also require staff to obey the law. In some countries, legislation prevents walkouts or wildcat strikes. The company should respond to lawbreaking by using whatever remedies are available (for example, seeking a restraining order or damages for lost revenue).

Management should give corporate financial data to the unions, because it should have nothing to hide. The wages bill is frequently the company's biggest cost. You should also give information on competitors' costs, if it demonstrates that yielding to demands would make the company uncompetitive.

The company should give regular briefings to the media, emphasizing the risks that agreeing to union demands would bring (for example, job losses).

The firm should seek to communicate directly with staff; for example through notice boards or public meetings, or even letters to the workers' home address (though this can be seen as threatening and invasive). It is wise to avoid actions that may produce short-term solutions but will store up trouble in the future, such as strike-busting through bussing in non-union workers. The company will have to continue operating after the dispute.

To bring the dispute to an end, the company may need to identify face-saving concessions for the union, which will enable both sides to leave the dispute with honour. However, if a dispute seems inevitable, the business may need to:

- build buffer stocks
- move production to other plants
- sub-contract work to competitors.

Ethics

Ethics is increasingly recognized as a major business risk. Damaging newspaper reports and court cases involving bribery and other forms of dishonesty have serious consequences for the corporate reputation and future profits.

At the time of writing, if you type 'Coca-Cola UK' into the Google search engine, four of the top ten websites are hostile to the company. Two of them allege that Coca-Cola bottling plant managers in Colombia encouraged paramilitary death squads to murder trade union leaders, a claim Coca-Cola strenuously denies.

In this Internet age, an activist in their bedroom with a PC has as much clout as the biggest company in the world. All of which goes to show that businesses have to be ethically sound – and be able to prove it.

CONFLICT IN BUSINESS

There are many conflicting issues in business. Companies seek to minimize their costs and maximize their price. If taken to extremes, this will mean providing the cheapest product or service for the highest price. The enticements are greater where competition is imperfect or absent, or where the customer is weak or lacking in knowledge. Thus 'cost-plus' defence contracts have resulted in poor value for money, and pharmaceutical companies have overcharged for drugs. For example, Schering-Plough agreed to pay $346 million in fines and damages to settle charges that it overcharged for drugs sold through the US Medicaid, the US government's health programme for the poor.

Several factors encourage companies to neglect ethics. The need to win contracts can make firms bend the rules. A feeling of 'us against the world' can lead managers to believe that 'the end justifies the means', with a resulting loss of honesty. According to a survey in *Le Monde*, 64 per cent of French company chiefs believe that corruption is endemic in business.

CHANGING THE CORPORATE CULTURE

Companies often profess to act honourably but behave unethically. For many corporate cultures, winning is their most important value. This means that ethical behaviour comes to be seen as an impediment.

Managers who preach the importance of good ethics may be seen as naïve, negative, obstructive, standing in the way of progress, or suffering from divided loyalties. They may be passed over for promotion, or be made redundant when the company is downsizing. This is particularly true when a company is not making profits, or when the economy is in recession.

Until the corporate culture changes, the company cannot set about developing an ethical position. If top management regards themselves as ethically neutral, and for ethics not to be a boardroom issue, the company is at risk from unethical corporate behaviour. If senior management regards ethics as an academic or political issue, rather than something fundamental to the business, the firm risks being damaged by corporate malpractice.

DAMAGE CAUSED BY ETHICAL FAILURES

If discovered, unethical activity can do irreparable damage to a company. Customers may cease doing business with that company and in a market with few customers (such as aerospace), this could be a major problem. Or the company may be entangled in embarrassing or expensive lawsuits and may end up paying heavy fines.

Illegal activity also undermines the company itself. It infects an otherwise honest organization, leads to the creation of secret accounts, and to people turning a blind eye to illegal behaviour. It lets individuals in the company claim exemption from internal investigation due to their work for 'special' clients. Staff will not be loyal to a dishonest company.

It is also difficult to keep unethical activity secret because of the existence of forces opposed to it; in particular:

- 'whistleblowers' – employees who inform on the company
- the media, which likes nothing more than a corruption story.

However, some behaviour is more borderline, and since it does not constitute a criminal offence, it is more difficult to manage or stand up to. Below are listed the main categories of ethical failings, following which we examine how the business can forestall them.

1. Relations with government

Examples of corrupt relations with governments include:

- tax evasion; operating false transfer pricing
- excessive payments to political parties
- failure to obey the law
- selling to tyrannical overseas regimes.

Adhering to government regulations is increasingly important for firms. In the UK's heavily regulated financial services industry, the Financial Services Authority (FSA) polices compliance. It fined Carr Sheppards Crosthwaite £500 000 for failing to 'keep fully up to date with regulatory developments'. Since 2003, the FSA has banned the use of insurance policies for the payment of fines.

Excessive political contributions are wrong because they can undermine the democratic process and because they can corrupt politicians. Companies can be accused of giving donations in order to win public contracts rather than assisting democracy. Although it is difficult to prove a link between political donations and favours for business, the scandal that surrounds suspicious cases is particularly harmful. The damage is done not only to the business involved but also the political party. For instance, some British airports have come under scrutiny for a suspected link between political donations and airport expansion plans. The Labour Party received a £60 000 cash donation from Manchester Airport Plc, which itself is 55 per cent controlled by the Labour-controlled Manchester City Council. Another example is the donations made by Enron subsidiaries to political parties around the world. These were only uncovered in the wake of the Enron collapse, as most of the donations were made before countries tightened the regulations governing the declaration of political contributions.

Some companies have recognized the potential risks associated with political involvement and withdrawn from the practice: BP now has a no-donations policy.

2. Attacks on competitors

Examples of unethical attacks on competitors include:

- illegally obtaining information about competitors (for example, by luring away or bribing their staff)
- making false allegations about competitors, for example through the sales force.

3. Unethical alliances with competitors

Cartels are against the interest of customers and are banned throughout the world. Suppliers are prone to indulge in price fixing, and are increasingly being found out. For example, the European Commission fined four sorbate manufacturers €138 million in 2003 for their part in fixing the prices of the food preservative. The cartel met twice a year between 1978 and 1996 to agree prices, which meant, according to the EU's competition commissioner Mario Monti, 'European consumers paid more for many everyday products than if the companies had competed against each other.' The largest fine of €99 million was levied on Hoechst of

Germany, with smaller fines going to Daicel Chemical Industries, Ueno Fine Chemicals and The Nippon Synthetic Chemical Industry Company.

The commission can fine companies up to 10 per cent of their annual worldwide turnover, and new legislation also allows them to offer immunity to whistleblowing companies. Its record fine came in 2001, when it fined eight companies €855 million for fixing the price of vitamins. Mario Monti called that case 'the most damaging series of cartels the commission has ever investigated'.

Individual governments are no less stringent. The UK Office of Fair Trading (OFT) imposed a record £22 million fine on Littlewoods and Argos for fixing the price of Hasbro toys. Although it had been part of the cartel, Hasbro's potential fine of £15 million was waived because it had provided crucial information and instigated the investigation. This was despite the £4.95 million fine which Hasbro suffered just three months earlier for its part in a different price-fixing case.

4. Products

Ethical product failures include the following:

- producing products which are environmentally unsound (for example, cutting down rainforests)
- testing non-medical products on animals
- selling products or services which are poor value for money, or which could harm people (for example, cigarettes or weapons).

Some of these issues are discussed in Chapter 5. Unethical behaviour can damage the company because if it sells sub-standard products, it may not receive repeat orders.

The converse is also true, that honesy boost business. A life salesman said, 'Honesty is my best weapon. When people know I'm being honest with them, it gives me a big advantage, because customers are desperate to know that they aren't being cheated.'

Companies that sell harmful products (such as the asbestos companies or cigarette firms) are playing a dangerous game. Sooner or later a disgruntled customer or a regulatory authority is going to win a law case that could mean the end of the business.

The many ethical investment trusts have reached a broad consensus on what contravenes ethics. Their policies preclude them from investing in companies which:

- trade extensively in countries which have repressive regimes
- sell tobacco, armaments or gambling (some also exclude alcohol)
- exploit animals.

The ethical investment trusts, which are set to grow, also seek companies that have a good record in labour relations and environmental protection.

5. Staff

Excessive payments to members of the board, especially those who are sacked, is a topic discussed at the start of this chapter. When it comes to other staff, health and safety is a crucial area for ethics. The company should avoid taking short-cuts which might produce short-term benefits but entail danger to the worker. For example, safety procedures should be followed while the plant is running. Downtime will be increased if a machine has to be electrically isolated before cleaning begins, but it also avoids the risks of injuring an employee.

Overseas staff are a particularly important area, especially in the developing world. Companies that relocate production to third world countries are often viewed suspiciously by pressure groups, trade unions and the public. Low pay and bad working conditions are seen as exploitation and the cost of any resulting public relations crisis can damage the brand image. This sort of risk has affected sportswear manufacturers over the past few years, particularly Nike and Adidas.

By contrast, Reebok has prided itself on its human rights program, particularly its own human rights production standards. This ensures that workers making Reebok products around the world have good conditions of work and are treated fairly. As well as helping young people in US inner cities, the company also has an international award scheme which recognizes outstanding young people for their human rights work.

6. Suppliers

The problem partly lies with the drive for lower prices, which results in cheaper supplies. Ethical companies have to face this problem, and recognize that being the cheapest sometimes means being the least ethical. It also means that companies have to emphasize their ethical credentials, to justify their prices.

Acting unfairly towards suppliers causes its own problems. A company that extracts large discounts from a supplier will find that it gets poor quality products or service. Eventually, if it cannot make a profit, the supplier will go bust. If it doesn't go bust, the supplier will look for more profitable customers, and cease doing business with its original customer. In either case, the firm has to continually look for new suppliers. Other examples include:

- using corporate strength to obtain goods at excessively low prices (as opposed to simply applying economies of scale); and exploiting people in developing countries
- using child labour in the developing world (an issue discussed in Chapter 9)
- entering into illegal agreements with suppliers' staff to dishonestly obtain goods.

CASE STUDY: DIAMOND SMUGGLING

Illegal diamond smuggling has paid for wars in Africa and is thought to finance terrorism. For this reason the United Nations has a programme to clean up the industry, and there is a voluntary pledge for retailers that guarantees the origin of all diamonds sold. But retailers are 'largely unable to provide consumers with meaningful assurances that their diamonds are conflict-free' says a report from Amnesty International.

Forty-eight companies, including Asprey, Debenhams, Kmart and TK Maxx, failed to respond to the survey. And the vast majority that did respond failed to provide details of how their policy works in practice. Random visits to 579 stores in the USA and UK found that fewer than half have a policy on conflict diamonds; while only a tiny minority provide a warranty confirming that the diamonds come from legitimate sources.

---

7. The environment

Examples of ethical failure include failing to take precautions against damaging the environment; or knowingly causing damage (for example, by illegal disposal of waste). As discussed in Chapter 7, environmental protection has only become a management issue in recent years; and many companies have been left a legacy of dirty plants and unsatisfactory methods of waste disposal. Many companies are in a dilemma because their products are both essential to modern living and cause environmental damage. For example, paper making has a record of environmental damage. But the industry has taken steps to minimize the damage, with the result that some companies and some papers are less polluting than others. A company must seek to be at the head of its industry, and constantly improve its methods.

8. Customers
Ethical failings towards customers include:

- giving bribes to customers in return for business
- doing businss with criminals.

The Japanese Financial Services Authority (FSA) ordered Citibank to close its private banking operation in Japan, following the discovery that it had done business with organized crime and money launderers. Some managers provided investigators with 'responses that differed from the truth', according to the FSA. It also said the bank had 'amassed illegally ... large profits'. Citibank decided to close down its investment management and real-estate advisory units there, as well as its private bank. Japan's FSA found that the problems stemmed from lack of internal control and lack of US oversight.

In New York, Citibank was also fined $250 000 for 'inappropriate sales literature', by the National Association of Securities Dealers, an allegation the bank neither admitted nor denied. Citibank also put aside $5.2 bn to cover other legal actions, and apologized for disrupting the electronic European bond market. The company has since upgraded its compliance systems, installed new management, amended lines of reporting, and added more independent auditing.

9. Giving misleading information
Prudential was forced to set up a £1.1 billion compensation fund for victims of the personal pensions scandal. Along with other providers, Prudential mis-sold pensions to millions of customers who would have been better off if they had remained with their employer's pension schemes.

10. Withholding information
Few salespeople voluntarily proffer information that could lose them a sale. But in a society that increasingly values full disclosure, this is increasingly what companies have to do. Thus financial service companies have to show their client how much money their intermediary is making from the sale of a service such as life assurance.

In 2004, GlaxoSmithKline agreed to pay the state of New York $2.5 million to settle its lawsuit alleging that it concealed problems of efficacy and safety in its drug Paxil. It also agreed to publish summaries of all its trials in a registry. Drug manufacturers have been criticized for seeking to publish in medical journals only favourable information about their products. According to the *Wall Street Journal*, New York attorney general Eliot Spitzer says he is continuing to seek information from other drug companies.

11. Bribery
While most bribes are secret, a few come to the public attention, such as the Statoil case. The Norwegian oil company was found guilty of paying $15.2 million in illegal 'consultancy fees' in return for securing contracts in Iran's lucrative oil industry. The company was fined

$3 million, despite there being no evidence that the bribe had any effect – many experts believe that the level of corruption in the oil industry is so high that $15 million would not amount to much influence at all. However, the effect on Statoil may be considerable, especially as corruption carries a high level of stigma in Norway.

Another case was the Lesotho Highlands Water Project (LHWP). Masupha Sole was the chief executive responsible for overseeing the construction of two dams, both funded by international development agencies such as the World Bank and the EU. Sole received at least 18 million South African rand in bribes from at least four companies involved in the construction. Lahmeyer International, the largest engineering consultancy firm in Germany, was fined 12 million rand for its crimes; Acres International, a Canadian engineering firm, was fined 13 million rand; and Schneider Electric, a French electrical company, was fined 10 million rand. Other cases are pending. For his part, Masupha Sole was jailed for 15 years.

Another example was in healthcare. 'I bribed and corrupted doctors to prescribe Glaxo drugs', said a former Glaxo sales representative, according to a newspaper report. The report accused the company of giving GPs gifts and entertainment. It was on the understanding that the doctors would prescribe Glaxo's drugs to patients. This is not the only occasion on which Glaxo was said to be involved with bribes. Flavio Maffeis, President of Glaxo SpA, the company's Italian subsidiary, was named in a corruption scandal, in which the company was alleged to have paid £100 000 in bribes and paintings to a senior government health official in return for favours.

Accusations of malpractice by government staff are not uncommon. In the USA, two former Pentagon officials were each recently jailed for 24 years for soliciting bribes in exchange for government contracts. UK government officials were said to have secretly linked aid for building a dam in Malaysia to the purchase of arms by that country.

In some countries, bribery is seen as an essential prerequisite to doing business. But companies cannot condone illegal behaviour in one part of their business, and not expect the corruption to infect other parts. It cannot adopt one set of standards in, for example, developing countries, and a different moral code elsewhere.

New UK government regulations designed to prevent bribery in export sales ran into trouble when major UK exporters refused to agree to some of the rules. In particular, they were unwilling to sign anti-corruption warranties covering the employees of any other party to a deal, such as joint venture partners. The government had imposed these new rules on the Export Credit Guarantee Department (ECGD), a body that supplies credit on overseas deals worth £3 bn a year. But other elements of the regulations remain in place, such as:

- Firms have to show they have anti-corruption systems in place.
- The ECGD has the power to inspect documents to check payments to agents.
- Companies must sign a document stating that they will not engage in corrupt practices, and will take action against employees who transgress.
- Allegations of bribery and corruption will be referred to the National Criminal Intelligence Service.

DEALING WITH UNETHICAL COMPETITORS

Companies sometimes justify unethical behaviour by saying, 'Everyone else in the market does it. We'll lose out if don't.' Taken to extremes, this is the same argument as selling heroin to children 'because other people are doing it'.

If competitors are acting illegally, the company should report the fact to the authorities. In the long run, unlawful activities will be found out and punished. The ethical company should seek to present moral leadership, not follow the worst example. It should do this because illegal activities will eventually come back to haunt the perpetrator.

UNDERTAKING AN ETHICS AUDIT

The company should carry out an ethics audit, using the criteria listed above. The audit should find out whether the company undertakes illegal activity. The auditors need to be sufficiently senior to demand honest answers, and they will need to interview the most senior members of staff, and those in key positions (such as accountants and purchasing managers). Senior management should put its support behind the audit, to prevent employees from simply denying any immoral activity. The audit will represent a 'smoking gun', because any evidence of illegal activity discovered in the audit could make senior management liable. For example, if illegal activities are not reported, senior officers could be guilty of withholding evidence about a crime.

In practice, senior management will already be aware of any major illegal activity, such as bribery. Assuming that the company has halted this activity, if it ever existed, the company should then turn its attention to lesser wrongs, and especially those which, while not necessarily illegal, constitute a grey area. This is the area which, if discovered, could give the company a major PR problem.

ISSUING AN ETHICS POLICY

The company should issue a code of practice that will clarify individual responsibility and alert people to malpractice. The code should cover illegal or immoral activity towards customers, competitors, suppliers, other members of staff, and the public. It should lay down guidelines for the giving and taking of bribes, incentives, gifts and hospitality. It should also cover jobs outside work. There should be an ethical filter for new product development.

There should be a means for staff to report ethical failures. This mechanism should ensure that whistleblowers are not victimized. The policy should be rigorously enforced. If it is not, staff will quickly learn that it can be ignored. Enforcing the policy means that staff who transgress it must be disciplined, which for gross breaches means terminating their employment. See also the fraud policy in Chapter 9.

Communicating the policy

The CEO should launch a policy, perhaps by email or letter to all members of staff. Table 15.1 contains a sample code of conduct.

Table 15.1   Code of conduct structure

	Section outline
1. Letter from chief executive	• Presents top management's message of the importance of integrity and ethics to the organization
	• Introduces the code of conduct: its purpose and how to use it
2. Goals and philosophy	• Considers the entity's: – culture – business and industry – geographic locations, domestically and internationally – commitment to ethical leadership
3. Conflicts of interest	• Addresses conflicts of interest and forms of self-dealing
	• Speaks to personnel and other corporate agents and those activities, investments, or interests that reflect on the entity's integrity or reputation
4. Gifts and gratuities	• Deals with giving of gifts and gratuities, setting forth the entity's policy, typically going well beyond local law
	• Sets standards and provides guidance regarding gifts and entertainment and their proper reporting
5. Transparency	• Includes provisions dealing with the organization's commitment to complete and understandable social, environmental and economic reporting
6. Corporate resources	• Includes provisions dealing with corporate resources, including intellectual property and proprietary information – whom these belong to and how they are safeguarded
7 Social responsibility	• Includes the entity's role as a corporate citizen, including its commitment to human rights, environmental sustainability, community involvement, and environmental and economic issues
8. Additional conduct-related topics	• Includes provisions regarding adherence to policies established within specific areas of company activity, for example: – Employment issues such as fair labour practices and anti-discrimination – Governmental dealings such as contracting, lobbying and political activity – Antitrust and other competitive practices – Good faith and fair dealing with customers/competitors/ suppliers – Confidentiality and security of information – Environmental practices – Product safety/quality

Source: Coso

Useful links

About.com – HR
http://humanresources.about.com

Business Ethics
www.business-ethics.com

Chartered Institute of Personnel and Development
www.cipd.co.uk

EthicsWeb
www.ethicsweb.ca/resources

HRM guide
www.hrmguide.net

Inc magazine
www.inc.com/articles/hr

Institute for Business Ethics
www.ibe.org.uk

Workforce
www.workforce.com

Risk assessment – people and ethics

You can assess your vulnerability to people and ethical risk by answering the questions below. Score one point for each box ticked.

Topic	Question	
Management	Is the chief executive lacking in foresight, creativity or leadership?	☐
	Is a strong finance manager lacking?	☐
	Is the board weak or divided?	☐
Industrial relations	Are industrial relations poor?	☐
Ethics–customers	Do you sell large equipment to governments and major organizations?	☐
	Are incentives, gifts or bribery an accepted part of doing business?	☐
Ethics – competitors	Does the company spread false information about competitors or conduct 'dirty tricks' against them?	☐
Ethics – suppliers	Does the company take advantage of its buying power to force prices down excessively?	☐
Ethics – staff	Do you expose workers to danger?	☐
	Does the work cause undue stress to managers or staff?	☐

Total points scored

Score: 0–3 points: low risk. 4–6 points: moderate risk. 7–10 points: high risk.

The appendix contains a summary of all the checklists in this book. By entering the results of this checklist, you can compare the scale of people and ethical risk against other categories of risk.

16 Contingency Planning, Crisis Management and Business Continuity

In this chapter, we consider:

- The sources of crisis
- Slow-burn versus sudden catastrophe; caused by management or the unexpected; crisis by industry
- Taking steps to prevent a crisis
- How to carry out scenario planning
- How to prepare an emergency plan
- How a crisis develops
- Dealing with disaster
- How to handle the media
- Communicating with customers
- Re-starting the business.

Despite the greatest precautions, things can go wrong. A disaster may strike at any time. Therefore the company should have a contingency plan for each of its main risks.

Companies can usually forecast the kind of crisis they will suffer, because each industry has its own problems. In retail, for example, potential problems include unsafe products, fire, kidnap and ransom, armed robbery, staff theft and shoplifting (including wrongful arrest).

A large employer which is steadily reducing its staff may suffer worsening industrial relations. This can lead to an industrial dispute or strike. In this case, the company needs to decide how it could prevent a strike. This might involve improved communication and negotiation. It might want to forecast the possible causes of the strike, and develop a strategy for forestalling them.

Sources of crisis

As shown in Table 16.1, the biggest sources of crisis are in white-collar crime, defects and recalls, and mismanagement, according to the US-based ICM survey. This is based on cases reported mainly in the US media, with a database totalling over 90 000 individual cases since 1990.

Types of scandal come and go. At one time, people were concerned about the corporate theft of people's pensions, or about the mis-selling of pensions.

Table 16.1   Crises reported in the media

Crisis categories (% of total crises each year)	% 2001	% 2002	% 2003
White-collar crime	8	14	17
Defects and recalls	15	13	14
Mismanagement	6	11	12
Class action lawsuits	23	20	10
Labour disputes	12	11	9
Casualty accidents	5	4	7
Consumer activism	2	2	5
Discrimination	3	3	5
Workplace violence	12	11	5
Catastrophes	5	4	4
Financial damages	5	3	3
Environmental	2	2	2
Executive dismissal	1	1	2
Sexual harassment	1	1	2
Hostile takeover	1	1	1
Whistleblowing	1	1	1
Total	**100**	**100**	**100**

Note: Totals do not add to 100% due to rounding.

Source: ICM

Slow-burn versus sudden catastrophe

According to ICM, 71 per cent of all crises are the slow-burn smouldering type, rather than a sudden crisis. They start small, and take days or months before they get out of control. In other words, management knew about the problem long before it hit the media. Twenty-nine per cent were sudden crises, including industrial accidents, workplace violence, and natural disasters such as storms and floods.

ICM believes that many of the sudden crises were really smouldering ones that were ignored or unrecognized before they blew up. If management had paid attention or acknowledged that a small problem could become a crisis, the problems might have been averted. This includes health and safety problems.

The causes: management or the unexpected?

ICM also believes that management is responsible for more crises than employees or the environment. Terrorist activities and natural disasters are responsible for few corporate headlines. Corporate scandals, white-collar crime, defects and recalls, and other management issues are, however, responsible for half of all crises.

Crises by industry

The most crisis-prone US industries are shown in Table 16.2. The industries vary year by year. For example, commercial banking featured prominently in the top ten crisis-plagued industries from 1995 to 2002, but has been less prominent recently.

Table 16.2   Most crisis-prone industries (USA)

| | Most crisis-prone industries (ranked by percentage of database) | |
	2002	2003
Securities and commodities	4	1
Supermarkets	–	2
Gas/oil production	9	3
Investment banking	4	4
Restaurants	–	5
Aerospace industry	–	6
Telecommunications	1	7
Accounting/audit services	–	8
Discount/variety stores	–	9
Electric power generation	8	10

Source: ICM

Taking steps to prevent a crisis

Having identified, with the help of this book, the most likely area of crisis, the company should then plan to minimize the impact of such a crisis. The main steps to be taken are listed below:

- Carry out scenario planning; identify the risks
- Develop a written emergency plan for each potential crisis area
- Nominate an emergency planning manager
- Assign other roles and responsibilities
- Test the plan: practise emergency procedures
- Implement a management system
- Manage the media: build a good long-term rapport.

CASE STUDY: IS BUSINESS CONTINUITY MANAGEMENT (BCM) JUST ANOTHER PART OF RISK MANAGEMENT?

Some organizations have an advanced BCM culture, while others regard it simply as one element in their overall risk planning. To a degree it depends on the company's products, markets and history. Some industries lend themselves more to BCM. They include businesses that are dependent on their technology; those with large, well-known brands; and those operating in risky environments. However, this could just mean they need good risk management.

BCM implies that the organization is liable to suffer a crisis. Therefore companies in uneventful markets such as wholesaling, agriculture or plastics manufacture might not find it relevant. By contrast, a utility company would be concerned about leaving a city in darkness. So, to an extent, the BCM's usefulness depends on the impact of the crisis on the public or customers. But while they might not have the drama of TV cameras and a switchboard jammed with callers, ordinary companies can suffer their own smaller, but no less important, emergency. So it is worth planning for the worst.

Forecasting and scenario planning

Once-successful companies fail when they stay with the formula that helped them grow, and don't notice the trends or forecast the changes that are likely to reduce the sales of their products. IBM stuck with mainframe computers for a long time and overlooked the growing importance of desktop computers.

Some management gurus believe that, in this age of uncertainty, forecasting is bound to be wrong, and makes companies over-reliant on faulty assumptions. That is why scenario planning is a better solution. As the name implies, it gets the company to plan for several different future possibilities. It is a 'what if' exercise. It asks questions such as:

• What if the price of raw materials doubled?
• What if we lost our biggest two customers?

Scenario planning has traditionally been used to plan markets. For risk management, it can be applied to all potential hazards, and makes the company confront unpleasant possibilities. At Whitbread, they say 'every possible scenario is documented.'

Scenario planning helps the company think the unthinkable, and has helped companies overcome threats if they occur. Scenario planning also encourages staff to challenge long-held assumptions, and to act in advance of change. Table 16.3 has some examples.

Scenario planning will fail if you:

1 **Assume that the future will be an extension of the past** (the future never goes in a straight line).
2 **Opt for the scenario that management prefers**. This is the triumph of optimism over reality.
3 **Choose the scenario that suits your company**. For example, assuming that customers are inherently loyal has sunk many a business.
4 **Build your business around your chosen scenario**. What happens if the future turns out to be different?

Table 16.3   Planning scenarios

Topic	Examples of event
Social	Social unrest disrupts the market
Economic	Inflation rises substantially
	A recession occurs
Political, legal, regulatory	The government bans an important raw material, or imposes restrictions on a product's use
Cultural	Buyers' or customers' criteria change
Demographic	Loss of population from the area causes severe skill shortages
Technology	A new material provides better performance. This material cannot be used at the company's existing production plant
	High-cost plant is needed to remain competitive
Costs	Wages growth, or low-cost competitors make the company unprofitable
Energy	Energy prices rise greatly
Customers	Customers start buying a different type of product, for example, consumers might switch from frozen to fresh or chilled products
	Markets splinter into niches of ever-reducing size
	The market matures, and sales falter
Distribution	New distribution channels emerge, through which new competitors sell their products
	A leading retailer decides to de-list the company's products
	Leading retailers decide to offer cheaper, private-label versions of your product
Competitors	Pacific Rim competition introduces an innovative and low-cost alternative to your product
	The market moves to no-frills, low-cost products
	Excess capacity grows in the industry
Suppliers	Important raw materials become scarce
Pressure groups	Consumer movements attack the business
Extortion	An extortionist tampers with the company's products
Fire	Fire destroys the company's production facilities
	Fire burns down the head office, together with all records
Workforce	A strike halts production for ten weeks
IT	A virus wipes out the company's data
	An extortionist launches a denial-of-service attack on the company's website, making it inaccessible to customers for several days

BBC director general Greg Dyke lost his job and the company was thrown into a crisis following a radio news report critical of the government. In all the BBC's scenario planning, he said, that outcome was dismissed as 'simply unbelievable'.

How to prepare an emergency plan

The company should have an emergency plan to cover all probable eventualities. This may be known as the contingency plan, emergency plan or disaster plan (depending on corporate culture and the extent of plain speaking).

The plan should be put in writing. It should be discussed with all members of staff who will be involved. And it should be regularly tested and updated. The plan will have separate sections dealing with each type of crisis, including:

- product quality failure
- environmental pollution
- health and safety accident
- fire and explosion, including loss of buildings, telephones and so on
- security failure, including extortion, kidnap and ransom
- fraud
- financial crisis
- it or internet failure
- industrial relations problem (and the ensuing lack of production)
- problems specific to the business (some examples of which are discussed below)
- other unforeseen problems affecting the corporate reputation, for example ethical failure.

SCOPE OF THE EMERGENCY PLAN

The emergency plan will set out:

- strategies to be executed before a crisis occurs to reduce the likelihood of its happening
- actions to be undertaken in the event of a crisis, including roles and responsibilities of individual managers and members of staff (for example, the telephonists)
- authorities to be informed (especially where harm or loss in involved) – this will include lawyers if compensation or liability is in question.

The plan should analyse a range of outcomes for each type of crisis, ranging from minor problems to major catastrophes. This will encourage a response which matches the severity of the situation. The plan should have an escalation process or flow chart that maps the scale of the problem to the people responsible. That is, the more serious the problem, the higher up the chain of command should go. As Figure 16.1 shows, by identifying the scale of the problem, you can determine who should take control of it.

EMERGENCY PLANNING MANAGER

The company should nominate an emergency planning manager. This might be the risk manager or a line manager (for example, the production director). A board director will need overall responsibility, to ensure that the plan is carried out. A large company will need several people to be involved, with each risk having its own emergency planning manager. Roles and

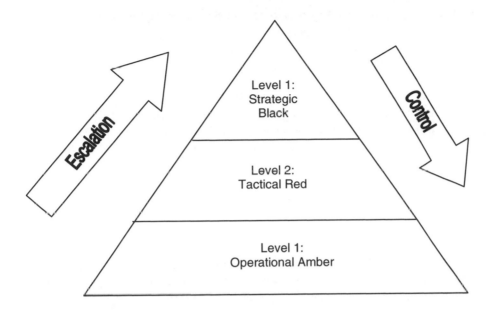

Source: With acknowledgments to the Business Continuity Institute

Figure 16.1 Escalating the response

responsibilities must be defined in writing so that, if a crisis occurs, the chain of command is clear.

The emergency planning manager must have a detailed knowledge of all crises for which they would be responsible. They should also be involved in the risk assessment and will be responsible for drawing up the emergency plan. Either the emergency planning manager, or someone nominated by them, should be available 24 hours a day, 365 days a year. The system must take into account the emergency planning manager's holidays, sickness and absence on business. Crises happen when people least expect them.

ASSIGNING OTHER ROLES AND RESPONSIBILITIES

Staff should be trained on what to do in the case of an emergency. Some staff will have specific jobs to do in an emergency. Telephonists may have to handle many more callers than usual. Engineering staff may have to initiate a crisis plan.

The telephone number of the emergency contact should be prominently posted, and staff should know to whom they should report, and what their function would be during a crisis.

Many crises will result in legal action against the company. A lawyer who understands the nature of corporate crisis should be involved in the whole process of risk assessment, policy-setting and risk management.

TESTING THE PLAN: PRACTISING EMERGENCY PROCEDURES

An emergency plan is useless if not regularly tested. Companies should carry out regular fire practice, not just the testing of alarm bells. If the drill is not regularly carried out, deaths could result.

Similarly, emergency procedures should be carried out to test other crises, preferably at an inconvenient time, such as Saturday evening, to see whether the plan works. Testing the plan will uncover unforeseen problems. Key personnel may be on holiday or simply unavailable, leading to problems such as locating important keys.

The scale of the practice will depend on the potential disaster. Major airlines practise jamming their own switchboard with calls from 'distraught relatives' following a simulated air crash.

It is vital that emergency procedures can be implemented without delay. Recent disasters have demonstrated the importance of being able to respond instantly. Failure to act swiftly increases the scale of the disaster and the level of criticism directed at the company.

Emergency procedures should be posted on noticeboards throughout the site. Staff must know what to do and whom to contact.

IMPLEMENT A MANAGEMENT SYSTEM

A management system provides written procedures for staff, so that they know what actions they should take. We looked at management systems in greater detail in Chapter 4. Procedures should be written for all areas of the business which are at risk, and for all contingency plans. The procedures should then be regularly audited, to make sure staff are complying with them. Trigger levels, discussed below, should be set.

BUILD A LONG-TERM RELATIONSHIP WITH THE MEDIA

A good relationship with the media will ensure that, should a crisis ever occur, the company can expect a fair hearing. It also ensures that journalists will expect the best rather than the worst, when it comes to news about the company. If the company builds trust with the media, they are less likely to write damaging articles if a crisis occurs. Journalists will find it difficult (though not impossible) to write accusing articles if they have only ever received useful, honest and accurate information over a long period.

Later in the chapter we examine how the company should deal with the media if a crisis occurs.

How a crisis develops

A crisis often passes through quite predictable phases (with the signals gradually becoming more and more clear). Management's response is equally predictable, often beginning with incomprehension and a refusal to face facts.

The future success of the company depends on management's efficiency in dealing with the unfolding crisis. The main features are listed in Figure 16.2, to show how the stages can be identified, and how the company can manage them.

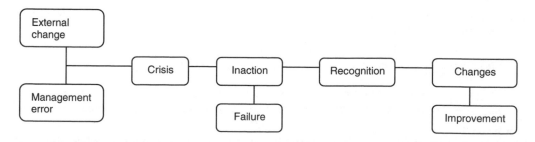

Figure 16.2   Stages of a crisis

ERROR, CHANGE AND CRISIS

A crisis results from an error which can usually be foreseen. It could be an internal problem, such as management's failure to innovate. Or it could be an external act, such as new legislation. It may be a combination of both. Whatever the cause, the crisis often has the same disastrous effect.

It is useful to have a management information system which warns the company of an impending crisis. There will be different triggers for each area:

- In finance, certain ratios will turn negative.
- In the environment, meters which monitor effluent levels will exceed a given toxicity.
- In health and safety, there will be a maximum number of minor accidents.

REJECTION AND INACTION

Management often fails to take action when the crisis first occurs, it often refusing to believe that there is a problem. If managers accept that a problem exists, they often believe that it is not a real crisis. The company also hopes that sales will improve or that the bank will change its mind.

Managers believe that life can go on as before, often with minor changes. This leads to a period of inactivity. If this continues for too long, the company fails. It either goes bust or is bought. The initial delay is often fatal.

RECOGNITION

Eventually (and this may take days or even years) management admits that there is a problem. This can lead to panic. Different views emerge as to how the problem should be resolved. The views on public admission polarize, with PR people proposing openness, and corporate legal advisers cautioning silence. The company's failure to comment at a time of mounting information about the scale of the problem leads to increased press speculation.

CHANGE

The company faces the problem and takes decisive action. This may include withdrawing from a project, admitting to the world that it faces huge write-downs, or making staff redundant. In doing so, it sheds the burden of debt or stops the flow of cash from the business. Now it has a chance of survival.

Good often comes from this process. The company may emerge fitter and more aware of the dangers. Management and staff want to avoid a repetition of the crisis. The company will be more competitive, and less complacent. Changes that were once unthinkable now take place.

Dealing with disaster

We have examined how the company should prepare for an emergency. Next we consider what to do if the emergency actually occurs. The activities are shown below.

- assess whether a crisis exists
- set up a crisis centre and recovery work area

- get the information
- assess the scale of the crisis
- manage the crisis
- communicate with customers, the media, the workforce and others
- re-start the business.

ASSESS WHETHER A CRISIS EXISTS

When the company is facing major problems, it may be difficult to determine whether a crisis really exists. Therefore the plan should define a crisis. Apart from the trigger levels discussed above, a crisis might entail:

- a threat to the long-term reputation of the business
- a potential cost equal to a proportion of annual turnover (say, 25 per cent), whether in sales decline, the costs of a recall, or in clean-up costs
- the risk of widespread litigation
- an interruption of business of a given period of time (say, a week).

SET UP A CRISIS CENTRE

The company should set up a crisis centre, which should be insulated from the day-to-day running of the business. The crisis centre should be equipped with all relevant information, including contact names and phone numbers. It needs secretarial support, with photocopying, fax and other equipment. The business should remember that in the case of fire or bombing, the head office may not be available.

Senior management must break out of the routine of standard meetings and reviews, switching into a disaster mode instead. Regular work is predictable and therefore comforting, but wrong at this stage. However, at the same time, one or more senior managers must be released to carry on the business. This will ensure that ongoing work is not neglected.

The company may need to publicize an emergency number. Like everything else in crisis management, this should have been discussed with the telephone company in advance. The emergency number will then have to be manned with staff who, in turn, will need to be trained and briefed.

RECOVERY WORK AREA – OR DEDICATED MIRRORING OPERATION

A bomb, explosion, flood, storm or other disaster may render your work area unusable. In such cases, you will need alternative premises to work from. For many organizations, their call centre, order entry operation or trading floor is critical to their continued success. If they fail, the business continuity management (BCM) plan needs to get them running again quickly.

Companies can rent work areas from third-party suppliers, or use alternative buildings of their own. Third-party suppliers can bring in fully equipped IT and telephone equipment and desks that will recreate the business. Options for business recovery include:

- Dedicated (where the offices are permanently available for the business

- Syndicated, available from within 8–24 hours from the call for critical processes, and 24–72 hours for other services. These are sometimes rented on a 25:1 ratio, that is, each desk is rented out to 25 clients. You should ascertain the ratio, and find out who else is renting the desks. The question must be asked: what happens if the site is occupied by another firm when you 'invoke'; that is, when you require the service?

- Mobile, where the recovery firm brings mobile recovery trailers to you. If so, there must be parking facilities, and these must be accessible. Police have been known to move such vehicles on.

The third-party organization should be involved in any rehearsals or testing that you carry out. There is a risk that the recovery operation may not work when the time comes, because of differences in IT and telephony systems, and the use of older or newer software. Your staff may be unfamiliar with the recovery company's switchboard. It may take several hours for technicians to iron out the glitches in the system. At the very least, there will be hold-ups and some facilities will not be available.

Given the always-on nature of today's business, speed of recovery is essential. Businesses that use real-time data processing, such as banks or e-businesses, require 'never-fail' or non-stop dependability. A recovery that takes 24 hours is simply unacceptable for these services, and so you may need a data mirroring operation in an off-site location, along with standby computing and telecommunications services. These cost considerably more than conventional recovery services.

The BCM plan should assess the impact of lost services, and determine what delays are acceptable. This is turn will dictate what work area recovery plan is chosen.

GET THE INFORMATION

In a crisis, news is often muddled. It is important to obtain accurate information. To achieve this, the company needs a form that will gather the information for each kind of crisis. A typical form is shown in Table 16.4.

ASSESS THE SCALE OF THE CRISIS

Having established that a crisis exists, the company should evaluate its scale. It can do this by undertaking an impact analysis, as shown in Table 16.5. In the example shown, the company is undergoing a huge increase in demand which, while attractive to the finance director, is likely to pose major future problems with customers.

The timescale of the problem is short, and helps to concentrate the directors' minds. The company has little control over the disaster, except for a degree of financial freedom to determine its own future.

There are several options, for both the short- and medium-term, with the most important issue being to get more finished stock into the warehouse.

COMMUNICATING WITH THE WORKFORCE

An emergency notification system can send a pre-determined message to hundreds or thousands of people almost instantly. This automation means that there is one less job to do; and it lets companies test their staff's preparedness.

COMMUNICATING WITH CUSTOMERS

It is easy to overlook customers if the crisis does not directly affect them (for example, in a health and safety problem). But customers will see the newspaper or television reports, and

Table 16.4   Sample emergency form

Environmental incident form	
Division/department	
Description of the incident	
Injuries or deaths	
Damage caused	
Spillages and so on	
Witnesses	
Reported to police or other authority (time and date)	Police report no.
Response of police	
Corporate legal department informed (name, time, date)	
Corporate legal department's opinion and recommendation	
Reported to insurance company (date/time)	
News media's interest	
External affairs opinion and recommendation	
Nominated spokesperson	
Work phone number	Home phone number
Strategy to be adopted	
Report completed by	Date

will be concerned. Uppermost in the mind of wholesalers and retailers will be the company's ability to continue supplying its product. Salespeople should therefore be taken off their daily routine. They should speak to all major customers, reassuring them that supplies are not threatened. In some cases the work could be given to a telemarketing agency, because customers can be contacted rapidly.

CRISIS MANAGEMENT

A crisis management system includes lists of email addresses, interactive checklists, and can be activated from anywhere. It is likely to be web-based, and will be independent of the business's Internet or email system. It lets people from different sites keep abreast of what is going on. The department store group John Lewis developed its own Internet-based crisis management system after failing to find a suitable product on the market. Named Crisis Commfile, it provides real-time communication between multiple locations during an emergency, allowing those responsible for resolving the crisis to view current and past dialogue.

We have now seen the general steps that management should take in a crisis. Next we consider the specific areas of risk and how they can be managed. We look at the problems of faulty products, pollution, health and safety incidents, fire, security and fraud, financial crises and computer failure. We also consider how to deal with the kind of problem which is unexpected but which could harm the company's reputation.

Table 16.5   Impact analysis

Problem	Competitor has gone into liquidation, resulting in demand for our product exceeding capacity by 30 per cent
Scale of the problem	Important customers will get increasingly irate
	Customers may start to buy from overseas competitors
Timescale	The problem is urgent
	Some patterns are now out of stock, with production planning quoting three months for delivery; other patterns will run out in 5–30 days
	Installation of new equipment would take six months
Control	Future solutions are under our control
Choices	*Short term*
	1 Buy product from overseas competitors
	2 Ration supply
	3 Add extra shift
	4 Increase productivity
	Medium term
	Equipment can be leased or bought
Action Agreed	Initially, ration supplies, giving priority to best customers
	Boost productivity – assign engineers to maximizing output, possibly by allocating more forklifts and other equipment to speed up materials handling
	Assess costs of extra shift
	Review problem in one week

Product quality failures

A product quality failure is relatively simple if contained within the factory gates. Once it is in the distribution chain, the problem becomes more complicated. The first task is to return the faulty product to the factory and destroy it. For the makers of branded goods, this becomes a major task, but one which has reduced in scale with the growing concentration of retail power.

Subsequent actions may be strategically more important. In the USA, Tylenol survived and even prospered as a brand despite a contamination threat, due to its management's media handling and prompt action. Other brands have lost substantial brand share when faced with similar problems.

Pollution

Pollution is likely to be caused by human error or by bad housekeeping. The first job is to stop the pollution from continuing to flow. This may involve shutting off a tap, or even stopping an entire factory.

The company must inform the regulatory authorities immediately. Then it has to define the extent of the problem. (How serious is it? What is the impact on wildlife?) Then the company should identify the possible solutions. This may involve a clean-up operation. A company which has the potential to pollute should have emergency pollution control plans carefully prepared, and those plans should be regularly practised.

Health and safety incidents

Health and safety incidents are often traumatic for the company, its employees and the local community if they involve the injury or the death of a worker. Many incidents need never happen. Workers get careless, and management does not insist on adhering to standards.

In health and safety incidents, the firm should adopt a contrite posture, apologizing for the incident (without necessarily implying liability), and offering sympathy to the family. Flowers and financial assistance may also help.

The company should stop all work that involves the process or machine which caused the accident. A report should be written, new procedures adopted, and lessons learnt.

Fire and explosion

Fire is the one threat that most companies are prepared for. But planning often stops at the point where staff are safely outside the building at the assembly point. Companies also need to plan for the loss of the building, stock, telephones and computers. Specialist firms provide business recovery services, including:

- waste management firms to clear debris
- power supplies, perhaps involving portable generators
- temporary accommodation.

Fire often destroys plant and equipment, work in progress, finished stock and records. This prevents the company from delivering goods, invoicing and chasing money.

After a fire, the task is to start production, possibly in temporary premises or through sub-contractors. It is also imperative to talk to all customers, especially major ones, and explain how and when their orders will be delivered. If customers are aware of the problem, they are much more likely to be tolerant of delays in delivery.

Security failure, including extortion, kidnap and ransom

Extortion, kidnap and ransom are serious threats for companies which trade in the world's danger zones. It is therefore dangerous to send staff abroad without reviewing the arrangements for their safety. The world's danger zones shift as politics change, so it is important to stay abreast of changes.

Fraud

When fraud is uncovered, companies find it difficult to believe that a trusted company servant has behaved so dishonourably. Yet, all too often, the fraud could have been prevented by taking the steps outlined in this book.

The company should have a clear contingency plan for fraud. This involves preserving the evidence, and informing the authorities. Levels of fraud vary in severity, and some sensitivity should be adopted when dealing with it.

In one court case, a woman about to give birth was jailed for stealing a small sum of money, despite the fact that she had replaced it before the fraud was uncovered. Though the sentence was outside the company's power, it brought the firm some hostile headlines.

Financial crisis

Financial crises are ones which no management would ever want to plan for. Nevertheless, the company should know what cuts could be made in the company's costs if sales fell below a given point.

Likewise, the company which could be threatened by a takeover bid should not wait until a hostile bid materializes before deciding what to do. There are many strategies which it can adopt and which would make it less attractive. Likewise, it should have its PR machine ready to run, should the bid occur.

Computer failure

Computer failure occurs, as we have seen, for all kinds of reasons, ranging from a flooded basement to a hacker. Companies which are especially at risk should define the nature of their computing risks and take appropriate action. The company should assume, for planning purposes, that its computers are unusable, and then decide how it would survive without them. Its action might include getting loan machines and duplicate software from the computer supplier or a computer recovery firm, or moving into third-party business continuity offices.

Industrial dispute

In the case of an industrial dispute (discussed earlier in this chapter), the company might lessen the impact of the crisis by having built buffer stocks or having more than one production plant. A more positive approach would be to actively manage industrial relations so that disputes do not arise.

The crisis phase of the plan should cover areas such as contacting customers, and reassuring them about delivery of products. It should also cover communications with staff about the company's policies and plans. The question of maintaining production must also be addressed.

Other unforeseen problems

Sod's law will ensure that the problem that affects the company will be none of the ones for which it has contingency plans. The company should therefore have a general contingency plan for handling PR problems (for example, an ethical failure).

How to handle the media

Throughout the crisis, the company has to tell people what it is doing. Customers are often the most important group, but many other groups are often reached via the media. Successful handling of the media has many benefits. It lets the company tell its side of the story. It gets the public, customers or shareholders on the company's side. It can even help to create a tide of opinion against a perceived aggressor (whether the aggressor is a company planning a takeover, or a regulatory authority intent on taking the company to court). The first stage is to create an emergency PR plan.

DESIGN A PR EMERGENCY PLAN

A PR emergency plan should incorporate many of the points referred to in the previous pages. The PR emergency plan should include the following points:

- nominate a spokesperson
- media contact list
- lists of internal contacts
- access to workspace, especially off-site
- practise most likely scenarios.

In a crisis, the PR person will be responsible for managing the media. Therefore nominating a spokesperson is critically important and we consider this next.

Nominate a spokesperson

It is best to adopt an open attitude towards the media. If the company fails to answer media enquiries, they will write their version of the story, which will lack any mitigating facts that the company might provide.

The company should therefore ensure that a company spokesperson is nominated to handle press enquiries. The representative may not be the PR person. The words often sound better coming from the chief executive. This spokesperson must be authorized to talk to the press. That authorization must allow him or her to make statements without having to clear them in advance. Otherwise, the company will spend too long debating the wording of an emergency press statement. Equally, the spokesperson must have access to the chief executive for briefings and debate.

INVEST IN MEDIA TRAINING

The company should institute a media training programme. This will involve a training day (or half day), in which a media specialist plays the role of a journalist investigating a crisis. The training should include television training, using a video camera to record the executive's answers and body language. Practice in answering questions will help the executive respond effectively to questions concerning admission of liability, compensation and remedial activity.

Managing the media interview

The rules for managing an interview (especially on TV) are as follows:

- Lean forward in your chair (sitting back makes you look disinterested).
- Look at the interviewer, not the camera. Don't look at the ground: you will seem shifty. Keep your hands still.
- Be primed with the answers. Be ready to counter false statements. If the interviewer says, 'People say your plant has a history of accidents', say 'That's not true. Until yesterday, we had no accidents for a full year.'
- Keep talking – it stops the interviewer from asking another difficult question. Keep promoting, in a general way, the good things about your company. Say, 'Safety is always uppermost on our minds, and we have a safety committee which is meeting as we speak…'
- Concentrate on the steps you're taking. 'We have drafted in a team of 20 people to clean up the mess … We're recalling all the faulty products … I've spoken personally to the family …'

KEEPING THE PRESS INFORMED

The company should keep giving information to the media. Otherwise, the media will resort to inventing its own news, because a journalist's job is to file stories. When an oil tanker went aground off the Shetlands, and nothing newsworthy happened for several days, journalists started writing apocalyptic stories about dead otters. In fact, the only otter to die had been run over by a TV crew. Providing the media with information sets the agenda and keeps the company in control.

SUMMARY: STEPS TO TAKE IN CRISIS PR

* Stop the problem. This could mean ceasing production of the product or turning off a valve.
* Instigate emergency procedures quickly – institute the emergency plan. Collect faulty stock from customers, or start mop-up operations.
* Liaise with media and customers. Set up a hotline if appropriate. Be honest with people.

Re-starting the business: after the crisis

After the crisis, the company should learn from its mistake, and aim to prevent it from re-occurring. It should investigate how the problem occurred, and take steps. This might involve staff training or the adoption of new procedures.

The company also has to rebuild confidence, and to ensure that sales are maintained. It may need to re-launch itself, to tell the world that it is back. Activity which attracts headlines is useful. After its benzene scare, Perrier re-launched its product as new Perrier, and organized a photo opportunity, showing the old bottles being crushed and recycled.

Those affected may be threatening litigation. In some cases, litigation is inevitable, but where possible it is better to settle out of court. Legal action is slow and therefore expensive. Juries in some countries can also hand out swingeing fines. The company should demonstrate contrition to those affected, and should speak to them in person. One building firm sends flowers to customers who complain, and then sends a sales manager to visit the person. The customer is usually more conciliatory after receiving the flowers.

DEALING WITH THE AFTERMATH: POST-TRAUMATIC STRESS SYNDROME

After an incident involving explosion, fire or flood, the survivors may need medical attention, food, clothing and warmth. They may then need help to reach a destination, or financial compensation.

Post-traumatic stress is now recognized as a serious problem. The company may provide the victims of major incidents with trained counsellors who help them come to terms with their experience. Survivors feel a mixture of emotions, including depression, fear and guilt at having survived while their colleagues or friends did not. Counsellors may encourage survivors to re-live their experience a sufficient number of times to reduce its intensity.

The company must be able to locate counsellors in a hurry: this will need to be planned in advance.

Useful links

Business Continuity Institute
www.thebci.org

Business Continuity magazine
www.kablenet.com

Contingency Planning World
www.business-continuity-world.com

Disaster Recovery journal
www.drj.com

Disaster Resource.com
www.disaster-resource.com

Federal Emergency Management Authority (FEMA) checklist for business recovery
www.fema.gov/ofm/bc.shtm

Global Continuity.com
www.globalcontinuity.com

Institute for Crisis Management
www.crisisexperts.com

Sample contingency plan
http://web.mit.edu/security/www/pubplan.htm

Sungard – continuity and workplace recovery
www.availability.sungard.com

Survive (business continuity association)
www.survive.com

UK government – business continuity management
www.ogc.gov.uk/sdtoolkit/reference/deliverylifecycle/bus_cont.html

Risk assessment – business continuity

By answering the questions below, you can assess the company's vulnerability to breaks in business continuity. Score one point for each box ticked. Note, the scale in this assessment is the reverse of those found in most other risk assessments.

Topic	Question	
Scenario planning	Has the business conducted scenario planning in the last 12 months?	☐
Emergency planning	Does the business have an emergency planning manager or contingency manager?	☐
	Is there an emergency response plan?	☐
	Has the emergency plan ever been tested?	☐
	Do you have a documented system for notifying management outside work hours?	☐
	Has the business the guaranteed use of alternative premises it could occupy in a crisis? Or does it have a mirror data site, with its own standby desks for mission-critical activities?	☐
Media training	Has the business carried out media training?	☐
Ethics	Is the business free from any secrets that, if disclosed, would cause major embarrassment?	☐
History	Has the industry been out of the media spotlight for the last 12 months?	☐
Industry	The industry is *not* one of the categories shown in Table 16.2	☐

Total points scored

Score: 0–3 points: high risk. 4–6 points: moderate risk. 7–10 points: low risk.

The appendix contains a summary of all the checklists in this book. By entering the results of this one, you can compare the scale of breaks in business continuity against other categories of risk.

17 *Introducing a Risk Management System*

In this chapter, we consider:

- *What is a management system*
- *Benefits of a risk management system*
- *Disadvantages of a risk management system*
- *Accounting for the unexpected*
- *Assessing risk*
- *Origins of the standards*
- *A review of the major risk management systems*
- *A plethora of standards*
- *Documentation*

What is a management system?

A management system is a framework of structures and procedures that ensure the organization can carry out the tasks required to achieve its objectives. In some areas it is also known simply as a 'framework'.

The most well-known management system is ISO 9000, the quality standard. Contrary to its title and popular belief, ISO 9000 is not really about quality. It is actually concerned with *consistency*. Its routine and predictable audits ensure that jobs are done the way they're supposed to be done. For example, if a bakery uses ISO 9000, its cakes are more likely to flow smoothly along the production line, every one alike in taste, consistency and appearance.

Similarly, a risk management system seeks to identify the major risks, and manage them systematically. Like ISO 9000, a risk management system should mean 'no surprises'. The principles involved in a risk management system are shown in Table 17.1.

When asked to explain what ISO 9000 is, experts have a summary which could be translated into risk management, as follows:

1 *Say what you do*: Write down your important risks, and specify how you will control them
2 *Do what you say*: Have written procedures for every risk, so that staff know what is expected of them
3 *Show that you've done it*: Keep records showing that you managed your risks in the way you planned, and audit the business to check that people are doing what they are supposed to.

As we will see later in this chapter, different organizations have come up with different systems. For example, the Australian Standards model differs from the US COSO model. But they all work on the same principle, as shown above. To be effective, a risk management

Table 17.1   Elements of a risk management system

Task	Effect
Understand your risks	Discover what risks the organization is prey to, and measure their likely impact
Set a risk policy	Decide on the business's attitude to risk
Decide how to deal with them; write procedures to manage risks	This ensures that there is an agreed method for managing the company's risks
Assign roles and responsibilities	Determine who will take responsibility for managing risks
Train staff; communicate effectively	Make sure that people are engaged in managing risk
Keep records	This allows you to see when or if important areas are moving outside the area of safety
Conduct regular internal audits	Audits ensure that every risk is regularly checked
Regularly review audit findings	This makes sure that management examines the audit findings, and takes corrective action
Institute a contingency plan	The plan aims to guide the business through a period of crisis
Engage external assessors	The system should be examined by independent outsiders, who are free from internal politics or culture

system must detail all the company's major risks, ranging from environmental to corporate governance.

Benefits of a risk management system

As we saw in Chapter 1, it is better to tackle risk in an integrated and systematic way rather than work on individual elements. Working on isolated problems means that you may overlook some risks, and fail to control other ones.

A risk management system (RMS) may also be a good defence in law. If you can show that the company had a system in place for managing risk, and that it was therefore taking reasonable steps to prevent a crisis, the judge is likely to look more favourably on the business in the aftermath of a crisis.

An RMS has many other benefits: It reduces the company's exposure to risk, leads to greater profits, and helps ensure a better use of resources. It makes the organization alert to changes in the market and society, and helps make sure that it doesn't become a laggard.

Disadvantages of a risk management system

People opposed to management systems usually have two complaints:

1 The system is unwieldy and bureaucratic.
2 The company only installed the management system because a major customer required it.

These two problems are not the fault of the management system, but of the management that implements it. Nevertheless, it is important to guard against such problems. Implementing a risk management system should be done with a light touch, and done in a way that everyone learns from it.

There is a third danger that the risk management system becomes routine and ossified – that it will fail to anticipate new dangers. Management can be lulled into a false sense of security, never dreaming that a problem could arise from an entirely unexpected direction. So management has to stay alert to new risks over time.

In addition, companies can write fine-sounding policies that are routinely ignored by the workforce. To be credible, therefore, a risk management system must be verifiable by a respected independent authority. In other words, a certification body must audit the system to check that it is in operation on a daily basis. Furthermore, the system must conform to a recognized standard. This yardstick tells stakeholders that the system is set at a meaningful level.

Accounting for the unexpected

As Figure 17.1 shows, some risks are largely manageable. These include fire, product quality and IT viruses. But many other types of risk are hard to predict – a new competitor, a new technology, or even terrorism.

A good risk management system must allow – and encourage – 'blue sky' thinking (not restricting yourself to the limitations of your present condition). It must avoid being mechanistic and being overly focused on the company's internal processes.

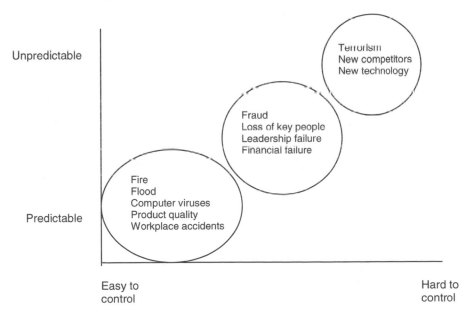

Figure 17.1   Predictability of risks

Assessing risk

How to assess risk was briefly examined in Chapter 2. Figure 17.2 expands on that. It shows that an organization's success or failure is set by its values, attitudes and culture; and these are set by senior management. It is also the task of top management to set policies and strategies, which will define how the company develops and uses its assets. These assets form the basis of the company's risk, and in the well-managed business there are systems, audits and controls in place to regulate them and provide feedback.

But it is often the interaction between the company's assets and external factors that create risk. For example, a computer virus designed by an 18-year-old in Lithuania can wreak havoc with the company's internal IT system. And an arsonist in the company's warehouse could burn the business down. Thus the risk management team needs to assess both the company's assets and systems, and the external factors that impinge on them.

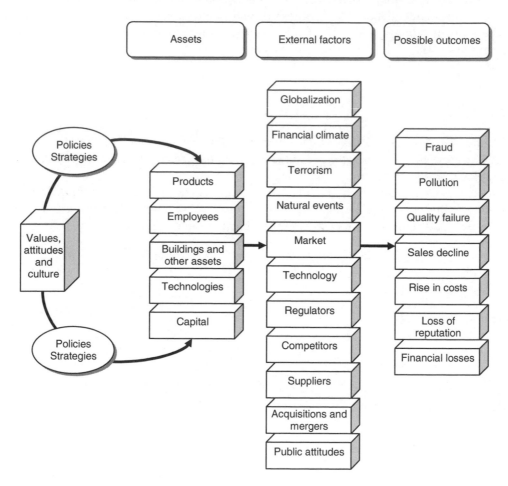

Figure 17.2   How risks are developed from corporate values, through the interaction of company assets and external factors

Origins of the standards

You can choose from several different systems when setting up your own risk management system. In the next section, we examine the competing ones.

There are various emerging standards and protocols produced by different organizations, and these arise from different traditions. Their origins include:

1 *Quality standards*, notably ISO 9000.

2 *Health and safety*, such as BS 8800:2004 and OHSAS 18001. These are concerned mainly with workplace risks.

3 *Corporate social responsibility* (CSR), notably the Quality Standard scheme (CSRR-QS) and SA8000. CSR involves voluntary actions above the minimum legal standards that lead to good corporate citizenship. CSR is concerned with environmental, workplace and social issues.

   Similar to CSR is 'triple-bottom line' (TBL), whereby a company adopts environmental, social and financial goals, and duly measures and reports on them. A TBL report would demonstrate environmental, social and economical value added or destroyed.

4 *Environmental management*, which includes ISO 4001 and BS 8555.

5 *Business continuity management* (BCM), including PAS 56 and NFPA 1600. BCM relates to disaster recovery and crisis management. So, while this involves assessing and managing risk, it focuses on keeping the company going after a catastrophe happens.

6 *Accounting control and reporting*, such as Basel II, COSO (discussed later in this chapter) and the Operating Financial Review, discussed in Chapter 13.

7 *IT issues*, such as data protection, security and software development. They include Tickit, BS 15000-1:2002, ISO-17799 and IEEE 1540.

8 *Project management*, such as BS-6079-3:2000.

You will find Internet links for many of these systems at the end of this chapter and in the Resources list at the end of the book.

A review of the major risk management systems

There are several risk management standards. They include:

- Australian Standard 4360
- PAS 56 (for business continuity)
- IRM's 'risk management standard'
- COSO Integrated Framework
- Canada's CAN/CSA-Q850-97 (R2002).

In the following section, we look at these systems, and consider their strengths and weaknesses.

AS/NZS 4360:2004, RISK MANAGEMENT STANDARD

Of the competing standards, the Australian Standard 4360 (see Figure 17.3) is the most recognizable management system that companies can implement. In other words, it contains requirements that a business can conform to. This means that a major customer or shareholder could be reasonably assured that a supplier with AN/NZS 4360 would be risk-free. However, as we shall see, few companies are undertaking external assessments for this or other standards.

4360 has the advantage of brevity and is written in a straightforward style. But it sometimes loses the crisp prescriptive tone found in 9000 (*Procedures should ensure that…*), and moves into narrative ('Selecting the most appropriate option involves balancing the costs of implementing each option against the benefits derived from it.') Like other risk standards, it is laboured and cumbersome when examining risks and deciding what to do about them. It has too many steps, and these could cause paper mountains and repetition (not to mention swearing) in factories around the world. Its five steps (identify, analyse, evaluate, treat and monitor) could be reduced to three: identify, treat and monitor.

The standard has eight main elements, seven of which are as shown in Figure 17.3. They are as follows.

1 *Communicate and consult*: The organization should consult with internal and external stakeholders throughout the risk management process.

2 *Establish the context*: The business should understand its external context (which includes its strengths and weaknesses, its key business drivers, and the business environment). It should also grasp the internal context (meaning the organization's culture, structure, capabilities and goals). It also needs to understand the 'risk criteria'; that is, the criteria against which decisions will be made, including operational, technical, legal and environmental criteria.

3 *Identify risks*: This step requires the business to write down the risks that it needs to plan for.

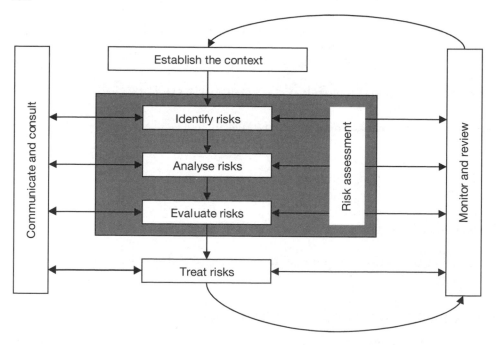

Figure 17.3   An overview of AS/NZS 4360

4 *Analyse risks*: The organization should consider the positive and negative consequences of the risks, and their probability. The analysis could be qualitative (an initial screening); semi-quantitative (ranking risks on a scale, rather than assigning numbers to them); and quantitative (assigning numerical values to risks rather than describing them). Quantification could be financial, technical, or in terms of numbers of humans affected.

5 *Evaluate risks*: This is the point at which management must decide which risks can be tolerated, and which options should be pursued.

6 *Treat risks*: The organization may decide to do any of the following:
   • Avoid the risk by discontinuing the activity
   • Change the likelihood of risk, perhaps by adding controls
   • Changing the consequences of loss, such as reducing the amount of stock in a warehouse, or by prescribing protective clothing
   • Sharing the risk, for example a joint venture rather than going into a market alone
   • Retaining the risk – after all risks have been evaluated, some will remain.

7 *Monitor and review*: This means repeating the risk management cycle regularly. It also means reviewing events, treatment plans and their outcomes.

8 *Record the process*: Each stage of the risk management process should be recorded. This should include assumptions, data sources, analyses, results and reasons for decisions. Decisions should take into account the legal requirements, cost of maintaining records and benefits of reusing information.

The standard finally bolts on additional material designed to establish risk management within the organization. It might have been neater to incorporate them into the standard, but it covers them under the following headings.

A. Evaluate existing practices and needs
This section recognizes that you may have existing elements of a risk management strategy in place, such as ISO 9000 or a business continuity programme.

B. Risk management planning
This section calls on management to develop a risk management plan, which will define how risk management is to be conducted throughout the organization. It also suggests a risk management policy, and reminds the reader that the support of senior management is essential. Companies, it says, should establish accountability and authority, by nominating those responsible for particular tasks or risks. Finally, it looks to the organization to allocate sufficient resources to risk management.

PAS 56

PAS 56 stands for Publicly Available Specification 56. It is a guide issued by the British Standards Institution (BSI) and the British Continuity Institute. Launched in 2003, it is not a formal standard, though this may develop in time. The standard focuses on business continuity – the disaster area of risk management – and is therefore less relevant to this chapter in so far as we are looking for a holistic system that will cover all aspects of risk management.

The disadvantage of concentrating on business continuity management (BCM) is that many business risks will not physically halt a company, but they are nevertheless severe. For example, a major accounting scandal would not interrupt the business, but it would be just as damaging as a temporary computer failure. However, BCM would not include a scandal as being within its ambit. Copies of the guide are available from the BSI.

IRM'S RISK MANAGEMENT STANDARD

The Institute of Risk Management (IRM) has developed a risk management standard (Figure 17.4), with help from the Association of Insurance and Risk Managers (AIRMIC) and ALARM, the National Forum for Risk Management in the Public Sector. The standard is linked to the Registered Risk Practitioner qualification, which will give it further salience. It contains the following steps:

Source: AIRMIC

Figure 17.4   Risk management process diagram

1 Analyse the risk. The document splits risk into five categories:
   • Strategic (capital availability, political risks and so on)
   • Operational (the day-to-day issues)
   • Financial (management of the organization's finances)
   • Knowledge management (intellectual property, competitive technology and so on)
   • Compliance (health and safety, environmental, and other regulatory issues).

2 *Describe the risk*: IRM's risk management standard recommends using a table format (such as in Table 17.2).

Table 17.2 Risk description

1 Name of risk	
2 Scope of risk	Qualitative description of the events, their size, type, number and dependencies
3 Nature of risk	For example, strategic, operation, financial, knowledge or compliance
4 Stakeholders	Stakeholders and their expectations
5 Quantification of risk	Significance and probability
6 Risk tolerance/appetite	Loss potential and financial impact of risk Value at risk Probability and size of potential losses/gains Objective(s) for control of the risk and desired level of performance
7 Risk treatment and control mechanisms	Primary means by which the risk is currently managed Levels of confidence in existing control Identification of protocols for monitoring and review
8 Potential action for improvement	Recommendations to reduce risk
9 Strategy and policy developments	Identification of function responsible for developing strategy and policy

Source: *A Risk Management Standard*, published by IRM

3 *Estimate the risk*: Organizations should evaluate the probability of each risk, separating them into high, medium and low probability risks. They should do the same for consequences – both in terms of threats and opportunities. In other words, a course of action, if successful, could bring big financial gains, but if it fails could bring big losses.

   This leads the business to produce a ranking for the different risks. This in turn allows the organization to see where more controls need to be put in place.

4 *Evaluate the risk*: After the risks have been enumerated, management can then decide whether and how to accept each risk. It will do this according to the risk criteria it has established, such as costs and benefits, and concerns of stakeholders.

5 *Report the risk*: Next the standard considers how to communicate the risk management process to the board, to business units, and individuals. It also considers the need for external reporting to stakeholders.

6 *Risk treatment*: The standard briefly touches on how organizations should manage their risks. This includes establishing the cost of implementing the controls.

7 *Monitoring and review*: The standard reminds the reader that risks must be monitored, especially as conditions are dynamic.

8 *Structure and administration of risk management*: The standard suggests that organizations will need a corporate policy, followed by board involvement, and active engagement by business units. It also indicates that a risk manager or risk department will be required, depending on the size of the business. Internal auditors will also be needed, and sufficient resources will be needed to manage the system.

THE COSO INTEGRATED FRAMEWORK

COSO refers to the Committee of Sponsoring Organizations of the Treadway Commission, a private-sector initiative set up in 1985 to investigate the causes of fraudulent financial reporting. The Chairman was James C. Treadway, hence the committee's name.

In 2004, COSO launched a document called 'Enterprise Risk Management – Integrated Framework'. This was designed to explain to businesses how to integrate risk management into their day-to-day controls. In the Framework, COSO identified eight principles:

1 *Internal environment*: This concerns the values and culture of an organization.
2 *Objective setting*: The organization must set objectives that are consistent with its risk appetite (the level of risk it wants to be exposed to). Objectives should be set for four categories:
   – Strategic: high-level goals, aligned with the organization's mission
   – Operations: effective and efficient use of its resources
   – Reporting: reliability of reporting
   – Compliance: compliance with applicable laws and regulations
3 *Event identification*: The Framework expects organizations to identify the risks it might face.
4 *Risk assessment:* Organizations should analyze its risks, considering their likelihood and impact.
5 *Risk response*: Management should set up actions designed to avoid, accept, reduce or share risk.
6 *Control activities*: This involves internal auditing, to ensure that the actions above are carried out.
7 *Information and communication*: The organization needs to capture relevant information that lets people carry out their responsibilities. It also needs to communicate generally throughout the business.
8 *Monitoring:* The organization must monitor its risks, and modify its response as time goes by.

The COSO Framework arose from the need for better corporate governance and financial reporting. As such, it is oriented to the needs of quoted businesses and regulated industries such as the financial services industry. It also seems more at home with the finance department than production or operations. Thus it sees 'internal auditors' as accountants rather than quality managers.

As with the IRM's Standard, the Framework sets out guidelines rather than instructions, which means that no organization can get audited against it. In the following section, we will examine its main tenets. But to avoid duplication we won't go into detail unless it deviates significantly from the methodologies discussed above.

COSO structure

In Figure 17.5, the four objectives are shown across the top, with the eight components shown in the horizontal rows, and the organization's units represented by the third dimension. According to the Framework, 'this depiction portrays the ability to focus on the entirety of an enterprise's risk management'.

This structure, it could be argued, places undue prominence on the organization's objectives, and insufficient weight on the allocation of roles and responsibilities, training, contingency planning and external auditing. The Framework also lacks, as we have seen, instructions or a formal system against which external assessors could measure the company's performance.

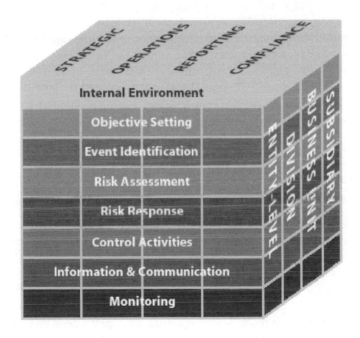

Source: COSO

Figure 17.5   COSO Framework: objectives and components depicted in a three-dimensional matrix

CSA GUIDELINE CAN/CSA-Q850

The Canadian Guideline is intended to help decision-makers to effectively manage all types of risk issues, including injury or damage to health, property, the environment, or something else of value. The Guideline describes a process for acquiring, analysing, evaluating, and communicating information that is necessary for decision-making. It describes the major components of the risk management process, and their relationship to each other, in a step-by-step process.

However, it does not provide a specification for risk management; or specific technical tools for risk analysis, evaluation and control. The Canadian Standards Association has also developed guidance documents to address risk analysis (CSA Standard CAN/CSA-Q634) and environmental risk assessment (CSA Standard Z763).

A plethora of standards

In the last decade, the average business may have gained ISO 9000, the quality standard, and possibly ISO 14000, the environmental standard, if its products had environmental effects. It may also have had to conform to new financial reporting standards.

Now along comes risk management, business continuity and CSR; and management asks itself, 'how do we manage these conflicting systems? Do we develop several different systems, or have just one bloated system? Or do we just give up and go down the pub?'

A single system is coordinated and uses a common methodology. But it risks being too cumbersome. With several different systems, the company risks overlap and duplication.

Some experts believe that businesses' problem areas (such as risk, quality and environment) can be put together in one neat package. Others think that companies' risks vary too widely, in contrast to ISO 9000's production issues.

The Institute of Internal Auditors (IAA) believes that a business should manage its risks as a portfolio. 'You don't slice an organization into four pieces and look at risk at each level,' says Dominique Vencinti, IAA's Vice President of Global Practices. 'Rather, you [should] have an integrated view of risk that allows companies to see how certain levels of risk impact and contribute to other risks, and how risks translate from one operation to another.'

Each business will have to decide on how it tackles risk management. However, the concept of the management system is right in principle – it helps the company tackle its issues in a coordinated and methodical manner.

CASE STUDY: VIEWS FROM A REGISTRAR

'We ask companies to identify their biggest risks and opportunities,' says one certification body (also known as a registrar). "Then we focus on those areas in our audit. As with ISO 9000, we look at their processes. The audit is tailor-made to each customer, and helps them control their risks.

'Risk management is still evolving,' he continues. 'ISO 9000 took many years to develop, and so we don't necessarily want an international standard before everyone agrees to what is needed.

'With risk management, different firms face different risks, and each industry is very different. By contrast, ISO 9000 is very broad and meets the needs of most industries. But even with ISO 9000, some industries, such as automotive, are developing their own variants of the standard.

'It's also worth remembering, that a risk-based assessment can take five times longer than a straightforward ISO 9000 one. We want to be of use to companies as their needs change, rather than imposing undue burdens.

'Another major issue we get involved with is "triple bottom-line reporting": often it's not financial problems that bring companies down but social or ethical issues.'

Documentation

You need to document the system; that is, keep proper records. But where possible the data should be kept to a minimum and be put on an intranet. Given the breadth of the system, from corporate governance to slippery warehouse floors, the system could easily turn into an unresponsive, unwieldy beast. The documentation should include the following:

- Organization charts
- Descriptions of roles and responsibilities for risk
- Risk register, describing major risks
- Policies
- Operating procedures; namely, a description of how the most important risks are controlled
- Process flowcharts
- Key performance indicators
- Results of audits
- Results of reviews.

Communication

The standards we have examined above refer to the need to communicate with stakeholders. This is essential, because the best policy in the world is useless if no one knows about it. However, different stakeholders need different communications. These can be summarized as follows.

- *Board and senior management*: information to help them make policy decisions, set priorities and allocate resources
- *Workforce*: information to help them avoid suffering physical harm
- *Management*: help in managing the company's risks
- *Local residents*: reassurance about corporate social responsibility issues, such as environmental matters
- *Investors and stockholders*: Information about the company's ability to survive the uncertainties of the market
- *Customers*: reassurance about the company's and brands' integrity; information about the products' safety or environmental credentials.

METHODS OF COMMUNICATION

Some of the best ways to communicate with stakeholders are as follows:

- *Team briefings*: Used to trickle policy and priorities down through an organization.

- *Intranet*: Good for communicating with employees. Some companies provide incentives on the intranet, such as free or discounted tickets to events. This is used as a means to get people to visit the intranet, and in so doing see the company's policies and news. The intranet could provide a risk portal, containing lists of the company's known risks, categorized by region, plant, process or market. The risk portal could encourage staff to suggest new risks, perhaps using a content management system that allows users to post material to the site.

- *Internet*: A good way to communicate with shareholders, pressure groups, young people, the local community and potential employees – in fact just about everyone.

- *Annual report*: As we saw in Chapter 3, analysts are unimpressed with companies' reporting of their risks in financial statements, with 53 per cent rating them 'fair' to 'poor'.

- *Email*: Most people are overwhelmed with email, so it is a less effective method of communication than it once was. Nevertheless, it gets to every desk; so at the very least you can use it defensively to demonstrate that you have, for example, disseminated corporate policies to staff.

- *Noticeboards*: Another good way of communicating news to employees.

- *Newsletters*: A solution often used to communicate with employees in an informal way.

- *Mail*: Since shareholders receive financial news by post, this can be a good time to explain how the company tackles risk. Mail is another option for firms who communicate routinely with customers by post, such as utilities.

- *On-pack information*: A good way to communicate with end users.

THE NEED FOR TWO-WAY CONVERSATIONS AND DIALOGUE

Much risk management communication tends to be one-way, for example telling people what to do. But the business should also engage in a dialogue with stakeholders. The very act of talking to stakeholders is in itself a risk – you don't know whether admitting risk could lead to shareholders taking fright. But unless you start a dialogue with the workforce, local community and advisors, you will be reliant on just your own knowledge. This means that the risk manager should liaise closely with the PR and marketing departments, so that the risk management message is regularly explained.

REPORTING TO SHAREHOLDERS

When investment analysts were asked about the quality of information contained in companies' financial statements, 53 per cent rated it as 'fair' or 'poor' (see Table 17.3). Yet this information is clearly important. In the same survey, 78 per cent of investment professionals said they frequently analysed companies' top hazards.

Table 17.3   Evaluating the quality of information on potential hazards in financial statements

Quality of information	%
Excellent	2
Good	45
Fair	31
Poor	22
Total	**100**

Source: Global FM

In a test by PriceWaterhouseCoopers (PwC), one group of analysts was given an abridged set of accounts relating to Danish firm Coloplast, while another group was given the full report complete with non-financial information. According to PwC, the results were startling. Those with the full report were overwhelmingly in favour of buying the stock, whereas those with only the financial data made the decision to sell.

Useful links

AS/NZS 4360:2004
www.standards.com.au

BSI (for PAS 56, ISO 9000, BS 8800:2004 and OHSAS 18001, Tickit, and BS 15000-1:2002)
www.bsi-global.com

Canadian Standards Association (for CAN/CSA-Q850-97 (R2002))
www.csa.ca

COSO
www.erm.coso.org

CSR Standard
www.csrr-qs.org

IEEE (for IEEE 1540)
http://standards.ieee.org

Institute of Risk Management (for Risk Management Standard)
www.theirm.org

ISO (for ISO 9000, ISO 14000 and ISO-17799)
www.iso.org

Social Accountability International (for SA8000)
www.cepaa.org

Triple Bottom Line
www.sustainability.com

UK government CSR
www.societyandbusiness.gov.uk

18 *Minimizing Risk in Major Projects*

In this chapter, we consider the following:

- *Nine steps for managing project risk*
- *Risk/reward contracts*
- *Risk in IT projects*
- *How to avoid problems when launching a new IT project.*

Nine steps for managing project risk

Projects take many forms – from road building to databases, from new products to overseas factories, and from corporate acquisition to drug research. But projects also have much in common: a big investment, a complex mix of people and assets, an uncertain outcome, and a high risk of failure.

Many businesses are wholly project-based, whether management consultants or film studios. So their entire existence is routinely at risk. And failed projects have a devastating effect on corporate success.

Whatever format they take, projects routinely overrun on cost and time, and don't work as they should. In many cases, the project is shelved.

Ford spent four years and millions of dollars developing an Oracle e-business procurement system called Everest before abandoning it and reverting to older technology. Sources blamed complexity, poor performance, and suppliers' unwillingness to use Everest to compete online for work.

Common to many major projects is the cost. A semiconductor plant costs up to $1 billion. This level of investment makes even the largest and most profitable firms nervous. As a result, many books have been written on the subject of project risk.

This is not the place to go into exhaustive detail, but the principles of managing project risk are worth enumerating here. Companies can minimize risk in major projects by adopting the nine steps shown in Table 18.1. They are as follows:

1 OBTAIN ADEQUATE INFORMATION

The company needs to collect proper market research and technical data, including information about similar projects undertaken by other firms. This is not always possible because the data is a commercial secret. The information should be quantified, showing how much money is at stake at different stages of the project. And it should include a sensitivity analysis, showing the results of different outcomes.

A decision often has to be made about building a new factory, depot, store or call centre. This may be because the current plant is operating at maximum capacity, or because

Table 18.1   Project management – nine steps

Planning for risk
1 Obtain adequate information
2 Examine all the options
3 Carry out a risk assessment
4 Allocate experienced staff
5 Create a project plan
Risk control
6 Invest one step at a time
7 Build in flexibility
8 Review progress regularly; review external information
9 Spread the risk

management wants to invest in a new opportunity. The company needs to know what the total demand in the market is, what share of the market it has, and what is likely to happen to demand over the life of the plant.

If several companies decide to build new plants at the same time, there will be excess capacity in the market. On the other hand, if the company does not invest in the new plant, it may be at a disadvantage, and perhaps be left with higher production costs in the old plant.

Information is vital at all stages of the project, especially information about costs and timing. Regular review meetings should ensure that data is shared. However, beware of putting too much faith in complex models such as Monte Carlo simulations. Their results often prove only what their authors want to show.

2 EXAMINE ALL THE OPTIONS

It is rash to undertake a major project without considering the options. Rather than building new stores abroad, the company might buy an existing chain. Rather than building its own computer system, it might outsource its computing facilities. Rather than launching a new product nationally, it could opt for a test market or regional launch. Rather than spending $2 million on a new plant, it could make the existing machines produce more products.

3 CARRY OUT A RISK ASSESSMENT

The risk assessment should examine the project's sensitivity to various factors. These factors might include a five per cent rise in raw material costs, a ten per cent downturn in demand, or a catastrophe (such as fire or explosion).

Companies often fail to identify the threats to the project. As a result, they are ill-equipped to fight back if these threats appear on the horizon. Businesses should be ready to expect problems so they don't turn up as surprises. With a little forethought, many could have been foreseen.

To identify the risks, management can set up a brainstorming session or involve experts from different disciplines. The risks should then be logged in a register. The business should also consider whether it is financially and managerially equipped to carry out the project.

The risk measurement should be done by the people who will be held accountable for the project.

4 ALLOCATE EXPERIENCED STAFF

Projects often go wrong because of the inexperience of the project manager. The company should appoint a manager who has previously carried out a similar project. If consultants are used, they should have worked on similar activities in the past.

5 CREATE A PROJECT PLAN

The business can now create a project plan. This will contain all the necessary costs, milestones and other data needed. Using project management software and a database can help. Software that allows different members of the project to input and review the information is especially useful.

Then the company should modify the design, the plan (people and money) and the contract, according to the likely risks.

6 INVEST ONE STEP AT A TIME

It is often possible to avoid committing the company to the entire costs of investment. For an engineering project, the phases of development might be as follows:

- Market research
- Engineering design
- Site preparation
- Order equipment
- Install and commission equipment.

At any one of these investment points, a decision can be made to go ahead or stop the project. The decision to proceed will only be given if the current stage is successful. This is common in oil and gas companies, where extraction comes after a long process of geological surveys and exploratory wells.

Once equipment has been ordered, most companies have passed the point of no return. However, capital projects with long lead times may be cancelled (as is the case of defence contracts for aeroplanes).

7 BUILD IN FLEXIBILITY

When creating a new plant, vehicle or plane, the company can build in flexibility so that the plant can produce more than one kind of product. Then, if the market forecasts are incorrect, the plant won't become a white elephant. While increasing flexibility can increase costs (because it may involve more expensive equipment), the company may decide that the reduction in risk will be worth it.

Building a smaller plant which can be expanded is an option for some companies. Retro-fitting is often unsatisfactory; but where output can be increased by, for example, adding more injection-moulding machines, this is a sensible option.

8 REVIEW PROGRESS REGULARLY

The company needs to continually reassess whether the facts that prompted it to develop the project remain true. This will allow the company to either alter the project or halt it. Management should review the 'business case' – the reasons behind the project – to see whether it is still valid. The company should also compare the milestones – progress against target – and identify where problems may be occurring.

9 SPREAD THE RISK

The cost of the project can be shared with other partners. Although this reduces the company's profit, it also means that the potential losses will be equally reduced. Moreover, the other partners may have skills or assets which the company does not possess, whether in political contacts, experience of similar projects, or marketing skills.

Another way of spreading the cost is to lease the equipment. This helps to delay payment and minimizes the effect on cash flow. Where insurance can be obtained, this is a good idea.

Risk/reward contracts

Risk/reward contracts give the supplier a stake in the successful outcome of the project. Whereas some conventional contracts either have penalty clauses for failure, and most have none, the risk/reward contract offers the supplier an incentive to meet the objectives. These include providing a workable solution, on budget and within the agreed timeframe. For example, an IT project might be worth £1 million. The client can offer to pay 90 per cent of this as normal, but will pay an additional 20 per cent if the supplier meets the objectives. Thus the supplier stands to earn 110 per cent of the contract if they deliver on time.

Companies often put 10–40 per cent of the value into the risk/reward element of the contract.

Such contracts are harder to manage than normal ones, and are at risk of dispute. For example, what happens if the client changes the specifications halfway through the project, as so often happens, to meet changing circumstances?

If you find it hard to get suppliers to agree to a risk/reward contract, it means they are unsure of meeting your requirements. This should signal a warning, and you should consider changing the parameters of the contract until suppliers are willing to shoulder some of the risk and reward.

In projects designed to achieve savings, and where the project contains uncertainties, the company might share both the costs and the rewards with the supplier. For example, doctors may receive incentive payments if they inoculate a specified number of older patients against flu, or if they conduct a certain number of 'well woman' consultations.

In another case, a health authority wanted to incentivize pharmacists to reduce the cost of treating diabetic patients, based on the cost per patient in the previous year. However, this risks a conflict of interest with the patients' needs, an issue discussed in Chapter 5. In other words, it might encourage pharmacists to offer patients cheaper but less effective treatments.

Risk in IT projects

Installing a new computer system or database is often expensive, with major systems costing millions of pounds. Management may have no experience of introducing IT systems, which is why so many go wrong. According to the Standish Group's 'Chaos' research, a staggering 31 per cent of IT projects will be cancelled before they get completed, and 53 per cent of IT projects will cost over 189 per cent of their original estimates.

The public sector is well known for its failed IT projects. This may be because of civil servants' lack of IT skills. But other factors are at work too. The nature and size of public-sector activities means that its IT projects are more complex and larger than those of the private sector. Moreover, private sector IT failures can be quietly buried, which isn't the case with public money.

Examples of major IT failures include the following:

- In 2004, only one in eight single parents awaiting government payments were receiving them, because of failings in a £456 million computer system designed by EDS for the UK's Child Support Agency. At one point, single parents were owed £750 million and were waiting four to five months for maintenance payments. More than half of cases entered into the new computer system were delayed by 'major problems', though this was subsequently reduced to 10 per cent. Staff were 'breaking down in tears of frustration' as they were reduced to calculating cases on paper. Glitches in the system meant they had no way of correcting on-screen errors and had to start files again from scratch every time a mistake was made.

- The London Stock Exchange spent five years and £300 million on a paper-free settlement system called Taurus. The system did not work and had to be abandoned.

- The Performing Right Society (PRS), which collects artistes' royalties, lost £8 million, one-third of its annual income, on a computer which failed to work. A report blamed the prevailing attitude of staff and managers in the PRS, whose attitude, it said: '... was not conducive to the successful conduct of large-scale computer projects. This requires the managers and staff to be open about mistakes, to learn from them, to expose their work to review by peers, to welcome criticisms, and to accept responsibility.'

- Wessex Regional Health Authority lost £20 million on its computer system.

There is no shortage of horror stories where computers are involved. The UK public sector spent an estimated £12.4 billion on software in 2003. But only around 16 per cent of its IT projects can be considered truly successful, according to a report by the Royal Academy of Engineering and the British Computer Society.

A typical private-sector failure is the management information system (MIS). Finance directors regularly demand one because it should, in theory, bring together data from production, sales, and purchasing. The goal is to show, on neat, interlinked screenfuls of information, how the company is doing. In practice, MISs often fail because the design is wrong. They don't show the information that they should, or they are too complicated to use. Eventually, managers give up and start to rely on the old information methods. The computer department, meanwhile, grumbles that management doesn't know what it wants.

THE MAIN PROBLEMS

Enough prominent IT failures have been reported to indicate the main problems to be avoided.

- *Lack of involvement by line managers*. Information technology, like accounting, is a subject which managers often don't understand and leave to experts. When the project finishes, the managers are given a system which they don't want or comprehend.

- *Consultants who don't understand the client's business*. Consultants sometimes win business on the strength of contacts with the chairman or chief executive. They may not take the trouble to understand how the business works. Understanding the business process is central to the success of the project. And this is where the analysts' time must be invested.

- *Box-shifting suppliers*. Some firms are uninterested in whether their computers meet the client's needs.

- *Over-ambitious projects*. It is dangerous to try to build a Tower of Babel. Any project which is 'state of the art' is risky. The consultants may be learning on the job, because they have never worked on this kind of project before.

HOW TO AVOID PROBLEMS WHEN LAUNCHING A NEW IT PROJECT

Though IT projects share similarities with other types of project, they also have their own special problems. Below we discuss how to overcome them.

- *Ask whether you need a bespoke solution*. If a standard software package will do the job, this is a safer option.

- *Formally assess the risks*. This should, at the very least, ensure that the risks are openly discussed and forecast. Responsibility will then be shared throughout the organization, rather than being laid at the door of a single IT manager, when perhaps it was caused by a board decision.

- *Involve line management* in drawing up the brief, and in approving the project's stages. The project must include detailed conversations with users, to understand how their departments work, the information that is needed, and any other criteria. Most end-users want to switch on a machine and find the information on the screen. They don't want to memorize computer protocols, or get involved with technical details.

- *Do not become too dependent on consultants*. Gain knowledge talking to vendors and consultants and by reading about the subject.

- *Be aware that vendors are not independent*. Vendors want to sell their system.

- *Don't underestimate the costs of the project*. As the Standish Group research shows, you should double any cost estimate, and perhaps the time too.

- *Beware of selecting a system that is too advanced*. Leading-edge technology is more likely to fail. A tried and tested system with many users will have had its bugs removed. Many computer consultants are in love with new technology; anything a few years old is boring to them.

- *Break big projects into manageable steps*. This will make the project easier to control.

- *Send tenders for any major project to several competing consultants*. The same applies to hardware and software specifications.

- *Choose consultants who demonstrate an understanding of your business*. The consultants must have implemented a similar system elsewhere. Let someone else pay for their learning curve. Get references, and take them up. Remember that consultants' fee rates vary enormously; the bigger the practice, the bigger the day-rate.

- *Consider using a TickIt-registered software house* (see Useful links at the end of the chapter). This ensures that the company has systems in place for managing the project professionally.

- *Undertake extensive trials before the system goes live.* The old and new system should continue to operate in parallel until the new system works flawlessly. Do not set tight deadlines, and don't allow your business to become dependent on the new system until it is working properly. Allow time for resolving the problems in the new system.

    In one recent project, making an order-processing database work properly cost an extra 60 per cent on top of the original cost. Ultimately, the system doubled the speed of processing orders, and was well liked by staff. But when it was first delivered, staff complained that it was full of bugs and hard to use. This shows that software can be delivered on time, on budget and to the right specification – but then requires more effort to make it work properly. It is rare for a software project to work first time.

- *Give managers and users formal training* in the system. Put money into the budget for this purpose. Some experts recommend spending a third of the budget on hardware, a third on software, and a third on training.

- *Have a disaster recovery plan.* This may mean paying a disaster recovery contractor.

- *Be aware of changes* that could alter the outcome of the project. If change occurs, check to see if it alters the risk.

- *Build in flexibility.* Ensure that the system is upgradeable. Consider using an 'open system' that uses industry-standard hardware and software. Don't become dependent on a single supplier's proprietary system.

- *Hold regular reviews.* Don't sit back and wait for the contractor to deliver a complete solution.

CASE STUDY: PROJECT RISK – FROM THE CONTRACTOR'S VIEWPOINT

One major electronics corporation admitted to difficulties over a recent project. The company had wanted to break into the food processing market. It aimed to prove its credentials to the client and to the other companies in the industry. Determined to win the project, it bid a low price.

The project required the company to install manufacturing controls in food factories around the world. Disadvantages included unfavourable payment terms; a lack of familiarity with the client's industry; and having to sub-contract some of the engineering work to an overseas subsidiary. When the project was 20 per cent complete, the contractor found that the costs were much higher than expected.

Originally, it had hoped to gain additional work from the client, but this is now a poisoned chalice. The client is now familiar with what needs to be done, and this makes it difficult for the contractor to raise the price of future contracts. And so the contractor may be destined to carry out more projects for the client at a marginal profit, in order to recoup some of its losses. Equally, the contractor can't cut corners because of the risks that this would entail.

This case study highlights the risks of pitching for work with several unknowns – in this case working in an unfamiliar market, in overseas operations, at low prices, and dealing at arm's length with a sub-contractor.

Useful links

Association for Project Management
www.apm.org.uk

International Project Management Association
www.ipma.ch

Project Management Institute
www.pmi.org

State of Texas project risk management
www.dir.state.tx.us/eod/qa/risk/

Tasmanian State Government – project risk guidelines
www.projectmanagement.tas.gov.au/

TickIt
www.tickit.org

19 *What Risks will the Future Bring?*

In this chapter, we consider the major changes that will occur in the next 10–20 years, and the risks and rewards that will flow from them.

- *Linear and cyclical change*
- *Political change*
- *Social change*
- *Job growth and job losses*
- *Technological changes*
- *Climate and weather risks.*

For a time traveller arriving in the early twenty-first century from the 1970s, most things would look reasonably familiar. Supermarkets may be bigger and there is more fresh food, but the products are broadly similar. Petrol stations look familiar. Shoes are still shoes. Men's suits haven't changed much. So for many markets, change is slow.

In other markets, however, the world looks different. Mobile phones and the Internet were simply unimaginable 30 years ago (though laptops have been around since 1981).

So the question is, which things will change in the future, and how will that affect your market?

Some changes are catastrophic, such as civil war, nuclear war, or a sudden new ice age. These apocalyptic changes are virtually impossible to plan for.

For the purposes of this book, we have to assume a reasonably consistent future. We have to presuppose that political change in the West will be consensual, and that no 1930s-style financial meltdown will occur. It is equally probable that some countries (notably in the developing world, and especially parts of Africa) will suffer famine and civil war. The rest of the world will continue to develop, albeit with upheaval in many markets and companies. The question is, therefore, what changes are we likely to see? If anticipating change keeps the business safe, how can we know what the future holds?

Changes in technology are reasonably safe to forecast, because most of the changes that will take effect in the next ten years are already in existence. Political, social or economic change is much harder to guess. But the changes will undoubtedly reflect certain patterns, specifically *linear change* and *cyclical change*, and we discuss these next.

Linear change

Some change is linear: that is, it goes in a straight line. For example, product quality gradually improves. And year by year the population is getting fatter.

Maslow's 'hierarchy of human needs' (Figure 19.1) reveals how linear change works. Maslow believed that people's most basic need is for shelter and food – this was caveman's main agenda for each day. When these needs are met, people need safety, followed by affection and the esteem of others. Finally, people opt for self-actualization. They look for ways to express themselves, whether by writing a novel or becoming assertive.

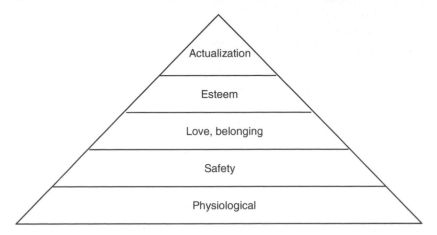

Figure 19.1   Maslow's hierarchy of human needs

The theory is unproven. But it can be seen in the holiday market where, as affluence rises, people tire of popular holiday resorts and begin to seek out more exclusive destinations. Or else they choose holidays where they learn new skills. Similarly, when people have all the electrical goods they need, such as a fridge or a radio, they seek experiences instead (Figure 19.2).

But products will continue to be important. People in the West will aspire to products associated with exclusivity, luxury or even celebrity. The success of companies such as Moët Hennessy Louis Vuitton (LVMH) demonstrates that people want exclusive brands in wine, fashion, perfume, watches, jewellery and retailing.

Thus as long as living standards continue to rise, people will seek better quality products, experiences and services. For example, as food takes a smaller share of people's budget, consumers will experiment with new, more exotic foods, such as olive oils. And they will seek higher quality food rather than the cheapest brand. Thus supermarket own-label brands, once the cheapest, are sometimes more expensive than the conventional brand leader.

Meanwhile, people living in the developing world will still aspire to products that they associate with the rich West. So the quality of products will vary throughout the world, while also increasing.

Some western markets are unlikely to see much change. Gardeners, for example, will still want watering cans and plants (albeit ones offering more added value , such as tough or fast-growth grass seed). Even in markets such as the automotive industry, change appears to be incremental rather than revolutionary. Unless governments decide to outlaw the internal combustion engine, there will be a gradual improvement in safety and fuel economy, allied to styling changes dictated by fashion. There is an outside chance that we will see a major change, with the introduction of revolutionary propulsion or energy (as heralded in the Toyota Prius, powered by petrol and electricity).

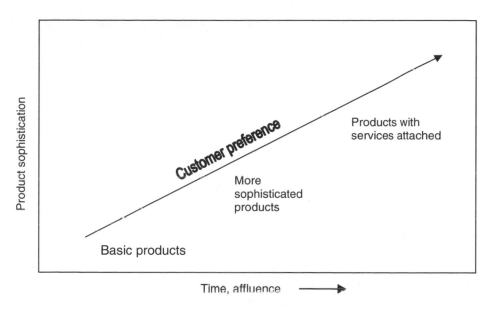

Figure 19.2   Linear change

Cyclical change

The second type of change is cyclical. If people like cars with rounded outlines today, in five years' time they will want cars with sharper lines. This thirst for change applies not only to hemlines and other fashion items, but also to many other areas of life, including politics (where people vote first for socialist politics and then for conservative ones). Thus politicians introduce greater control over businesses (for example the Sarbanes-Oxley legislation), and when these controls begin to mount, the population votes in new politicians who want to relax those constraints.

In economics we are subject to cycles, from growth to boom and bust and back again (Figure 19.3). There are cycles in exchange rates, the UK housing market, and investors' behaviour (where people hop from equities to property and then to government bonds). There are also many non-economic cycles, a few of which are shown in Figure 19.3.

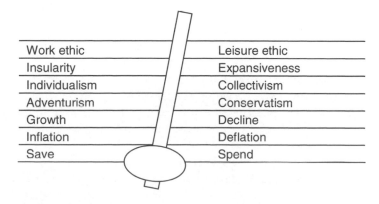

Figure 19.3   The swing of the pendulum: cyclical change – some themes

A business that is unaware of where it is in its particular cycle risks falling sales, or being unable to manage its sales peaks and troughs. When the number of house sales reduce towards the end of the business cycle, estate agencies with multiple offices find that they have too many offices and too many staff. Being aware of the cycle will help them plan; for example, it is better to restrict investment and recruitment at the peak of the market, because sales might slump thereafter.

Major socio-economic changes

Many factors are at work in the economy and in people's behaviour. Here are some of them:

- *Rising wealth*. As society moves forward, household wealth rises year by year, There is a possibility that the growth in affluence will be interrupted by the implosion of China or the USA, rising oil prices, stock market decline, inflation, a loss of consumer confidence, bank failures, and job losses. But these are unlikely scenarios.

  Increased affluence will lead people to seek better quality goods and services. Within the population as a whole, there will be wide variations – not everyone wants to engage in self-actualization, and people's purchasing behaviour will continue to be affected by their age and social class. In addition, some of the population will be affected by redundancy or other factor that reduces their spending power.

- *Continued globalization*. The loss of jobs in the West will be accompanied by the rise of China as the biggest economy in the world. As we have seen in Chapter 11, offshoring of jobs will mainly affect manufacturing and clerical work, plus some professional and management work. Services will be much less affected.

- *Increased proportion of older people*. On the one hand this will boost demand in some markets (for example, healthcare), and on the other hand it will have negative effects, such as making recruitment harder and increasing government expense.

- *Innovative new products, boosted by technological advance*. As we see later in this chapter, there will be new opportunities in nanotechnology and molecular engineering that will lead to new products in healthcare, personal services and other markets.

We will also learn to live with threats. They include:

- *Continued terrorist activity*. While this may continue, it is equally possible that this will abate. There are precedents for this, such as the fading away of the Baader-Meinhof gang in Germany in the 1970s.
- *Risk of chemical, biological, or nuclear disaster* (the so-called bioterror and bioerror).
- *Risk of nanotechnology error* (which we discuss later in this chapter).
- *Breakdown of law and order* due to income disparities and global instability.
- *New forms of infectious diseases* in the ways that AIDS and SARS have affected many populations.
- *Risk of environmental disaster*, associated with climate change.
- *Military adventures* by either the West or Islamic countries, leading to a clash of cultures.

Political change

Political changes are both linear and cyclical. Over time businesses become subject to ever more stringent rules. On the other hand, voters oscillate between laissez-faire and dirigiste governments.

Thus it is difficult to predict whether governments will choose to effect social change, such as:

- reducing the gap between rich and poor
- extending the rights of employees
- increasing consumerist legislation (for example, banning products or requiring greater transparency).

In the West there are two main types of economic model:

1 The Anglo-Saxon model which is a frontier-spirit type of economy that provides fewer safeguards for the sick, weak and the old. This has led the USA through decades of growth, but whether the population will continue to want this remains to be seen.
2 The European model that provides more support for its citizens, possibly to the detriment of growth and entrepreneurialism.

It is unclear which route western nations will choose in the future, and it is possible that populations will vacillate between the two. It is also likely that supranational groupings will continue to strengthen, such as ASEAN and the EU, while at the same these groups will be vulnerable to implosion and nationalist/separatist breakaways.

It is safe to say, however, that rising living standards will lead to higher standards of living and more regulation being imposed on business; but these are unlikely to affect the best-run businesses. Indeed, they can wipe out marginal, sweat-shop type businesses, to the advantage of larger or better-run organizations.

Social change

There has been a longstanding trend in the West towards individualism and social freedom. We have seen a loss of deference, and a loss of satisfaction with church and monarchy, allied to a decline in church going (but not in the USA). There has been a similar fall in membership of established political parties, and a fall-off in voting.

But people still have their *spiritual and emotional needs*. People are keen to belong – to identify themselves as being part of a movement, a spiritual organization or community. This poses a problem for established churches, and opportunities for new political parties and religions.

The same loss of deference can be seen in the loss of trust in established medicine, and a reaching out for complementary and alternative medicine.

As politicians preach the importance of choice, people expect to have choice in their children's education, in medicine, housing, planning and other government functions. This can lead to dissatisfaction if those choices are unavailable, limited perhaps by the population's unwillingness to vote sufficient funds to meet their expectations. All this poses challenges for government organizations, and the businesses they contract with to provide the services. It also means that consumers want to be treated as an individual when they buy goods and services in both the private and public sector, and to have their needs met by a personalized service.

In the recent past, people have been more mobile, moving distances to attend university or change jobs. This means they are less rooted, and less bound by the conventions of their upbringing. They also have greater emotional needs. In the future, however, people may try to stay in their community.

Another factor is people's *dissatisfaction at work*, and their need for a better *work–life balance* and an enhanced private life. This can take the form of working fewer hours or down-shifting. Employers may more easily satisfy their employees by providing greater flexibility rather than extra money. Mid-career breaks or sabbaticals may grow in popularity. If outsourcing and offshoring continue, companies will have a smaller pool of full-time employees, bolstered by freelancers, part-timers and seasonal workers, and with the majority of non-customer-facing labour taking place in the developing world. But a gulf between growing corporate profits and reduced labour compensation could lead to unrest, higher taxes, protectionism, or other government legislation.

Population change is something we have alluded to. This takes the form of the post-1945 baby-boom generation getting gradually older, resulting in a larger and more affluent group of people in later life, who are also more active and adventurous than their parents had been. This is an attractive market for many businesses. It also means reductions in the size of the workforce as the baby boomers retire, which will create problems for some companies.

In the West, *obesity* will continue to be a problem. This, together with smoking, is a class-based phenomenon, with fewer professionals and managers overweight. Obesity (and its ugly offspring diabetes and heart disease) is likely to be a growing problem for healthcare providers. It also requires new solutions for airlines and restaurants (wider seats), and new opportunities for other industries, such as gyms and pharmaceuticals.

Forecast job growth and decline

We will now look at forecasts of job growth and decline. A small growth in industries that employ many people can produce the same increase as explosive growth in new industries. So the impact is the same economically, but the underlying story is different.

The data below is from the US Bureau of Labor Statistics. What happens in the US may be different from the UK or other countries, for example, the timing of government investment in teacher training can be different in each country. But the forecast sheds some light on future trends.

The US Bureau of Labor Statistics expects the biggest increase in employment to be in the following occupations, as shown in Table 19.1.

- Teachers (a big employment group)
- Health (a big employment group, but with increased employment due to the ageing population – note the growth of home health aides)
- IT occupations
- Packers and packagers
- Truck drivers and delivery services: we will order more goods online, and people will be needed to deliver them
- Retail salespersons and cashiers, except gaming: will grow but at below average rates
- Food preparation and serving workers, including fast food and waiters and waitresses: eating out and food preparation will grow

- General and operations managers (these are growing at about the same rate as the total for all occupations)
- Security guards are projected to increase by 35.2 per cent, making it the fastest growing occupation on this list that is not computer or health related (our pre-occupation with security is highlighted in the growth of these workers)
- Among building and grounds cleaning and maintenance occupations, janitors and cleaners will inrease the most (this indicates the growth of people who are time poor and too affluent to do their own cleaning)
- Customer service representatives and receptionists and information clerks are projected to increase rapidly.

Table 19.1 USA occupations with the largest forecast job growth, in thousands, 2002–2012

Postsecondary teachers	603
Elementary school teachers, except special education	223
Teacher assistants	294
Secondary school teachers, except special and vocational education	180
Waiters and waitresses	367
Combined food preparation and serving workers, including fast food	454
Food preparation workers	172
Nursing aides, orderlies, and attendants	343
Home health aides	279
Medical assistants	215
Registered nurses	623
Personal and home care aides	246
Retail salespersons	596
Cashiers, except gaming	454
Customer service representatives	460
First-line supervisors/managers of retail sales workers	163
Janitors and cleaners, except maids and housekeeping cleaners	414
General and operations managers	376
Truck drivers, heavy and tractor-trailer	337
Truck drivers, light or delivery services	237
Receptionists and information clerks	325
Office clerks, general	310
Security guards	317
Sales representatives, wholesale and manufacturing, except technical and scientific products	279
Landscaping and grounds keeping workers	237
Maintenance and repair workers, general	207

continued

Table 19.1   *concluded*

Accountants and auditors	205
Management analysts	176
Computer systems analysts	184
Computer software engineers, applications	179

Source: US BLS.

Remember that a big profession like teaching is likely to be at the top of this list because of the scale of the profession, and its constant need for new blood. That aside, Table 19.2 paints a picture of a society taking on:

- Manual labour, to wait at tables, prepare food, and guard our homes
- More shop staff, to cater for our retail needs
- Computer people, as IT continues to grow
- Teachers, because it's a big profession
- Health workers, to support an ageing population and a medical industry that has ever more ways to heal people
- Managers, to keep the whole thing going.

A different view is provided by the greatest increase in percentage terms, which is shown in Table 19.2. This shows new jobs coming to the fore, such as self-enrichment teachers, and fitness trainers and aerobics instructors.

Table 19.2   Fastest growing occupations, 2002–2012 (Increase in numbers in thousands of jobs)

	Employment		Change	
	2002	*2012*	*Number*	*Per cent*
Medical assistants	365	579	215	59
Network systems and data communications analysts	186	292	106	57
Physician assistants	63	94	31	49
Social and human service assistants	305	454	149	49
Home health aides	580	859	279	48
Medical records and health information technicians	147	216	69	47
Physical therapist aides	37	54	17	46
Computer software engineers, applications	394	573	179	46
Computer software engineers, systems software	281	409	128	45
Physical therapist assistants	50	73	22	45
Fitness trainers and aerobics instructors	183	264	81	44
Database administrators	110	159	49	44
Veterinary technologists and technicians	53	76	23	44
Hazardous materials removal workers	38	54	16	43
Dental hygienists	148	212	64	43
Occupational therapist aides	8	12	4	43
Dental assistants	266	379	113	42
Personal and home care aides	608	854	246	40
Self-enrichment education teachers	200	281	80	40

continued

Table 19.2   *concluded*

	Employment		Change	
	2002	*2012*	*Number*	*Per cent*
Computer systems analysts	468	653	184	39
Occupational therapist assistants	18	26	7	39
Environmental engineers	47	65	18	38
Postsecondary teachers	1581	2184	603	38
Network and computer systems administrators	251	345	94	37
Environmental science and protection technicians, including health	20	38	10	37
Preschool teachers, except special education	424	577	153	36
Computer and information systems managers	284	387	103	36
Physical therapists	137	185	48	35
Occupational therapists	82	110	29	35
Respiratory therapists	86	116	30	35

Source: US Bureau of Labor Statistics

DECLINING OCCUPATIONS

Other occupations will decline, for various reasons. They are shown in Table 19.3.

• The majority of the declines are in occupations where computers or automation will reduce the demand for many jobs. This includes typists, loan interviewers, switchboard operators; and other office and administrative support occupations.
• The jobs of many production workers will disappear due to advances in technology, such as faster machines and automated processes.
• Electronic business will automate other jobs such as parts salespersons; procurement clerks; order clerks; wholesale and retail buyers; postal service mail sorters, processing machine operators; dishwashers; railroad operators; and meter readers.
• Farmers and ranchers will be affected by farm consolidation.
• In other cases, jobs will be reduced by the industry being in decline, such as sewing machine operators and railway conductors.
• In some cases there will be structural unemployment, for example butchers and meat cutters, whose work will shift from the retail trade to food processing plants.

Table 19.3   Occupations with the largest job decline, 2002–2012

	Employment		Change	
	2002	*2012*	*Number*	*Per cent*
Farmers and ranchers	1158	920	-238	-21
Sewing machine operators	315	216	-99	-31
Word processors and typists	241	148	-93	-39
Stock clerks and order fillers	1628	1560	-68	-4
Secretaries, except legal, medical and executive	1975	1918	-57	-3
Electrical and electronic equipment assemblers	281	230	-51	-18

continued

Table 19.3   *concluded*

	Employment		Change	
	2002	*2012*	*Number*	*Per cent*
Computer operators	182	151	-30	-17
Telephone operators	50	22	-28	-56
Postal service mail sorters, processors, and processing machine operators	253	226	-26	-10
Loan interviewers and clerks	170	146	-24	-14
Data entry keyers	392	371	-21	-5
Telemarketers	428	406	-21	-5
Textile knitting and weaving machine setters, operators and tenders	53	33	-20	-39
Textile winding, twisting and drawing out machine setters, operators and tenders	66	46	-20	-30
Team assemblers	1174	1155	-19	-2
Order clerks	330	311	-19	-6
Door-to-door sales workers, news and street vendors, and related workers	155	137	-18	-12
Travel agents	118	102	-16	-14
Brokerage clerks	78	67	-11	-15
Eligibility interviewers, government programs	94	83	-11	-12
Prepress technicians and workers	91	81	-10	-11
Fishers and related fishing workers	36	27	-10	-27
Sewers, hand	36	29	-8	-21
Textile cutting machine setters, operators and tenders	34	26	-8	-23
Textile bleaching and dyeing machine operators and tenders	27	19	-8	-29
Announcers	76	68	-8	-10
Meter readers, utilities	54	46	-8	-14
Chemical plant and system operators	58	51	-7	-12
Mixing and blending machine setters, operators and tenders	106	99	-7	-7
Credit authorizers, checkers and clerks	80	74	-5	-7

Source: US BLS

Technological changes

We have grown accustomed to the changes brought about by the Internet, but there are other changes on the horizon. Many of these changes are being facilitated by the growth in computing power, something we turn to next.

MOORE'S LAW – THE CONTINUED GROWTH IN COMPUTING POWER

The changes in technology will be driven by Moore's law, which states that computer power will double every 18 months (shown in Figure 19.4). This means that computing power becomes cheaper and more powerful every day, and that it will have hitherto unexpected uses.

Formulated by Gordon Moore of Intel in 1965, this law has held true for over 30 years, and shows no signs of tailing off. The associated technologies such as lithography (for printed boards) are likely to give way to others, which will enable computing power to continue its growth. Some believe that the law is a self-fulfilling prophecy – in that companies like Intel put huge efforts into making the law come true. Whether or not this is true, the outcome is a continuing race to develop ever more powerful processing power, which in turn makes technological advances possible.

Transistor count – Intel microprocessor

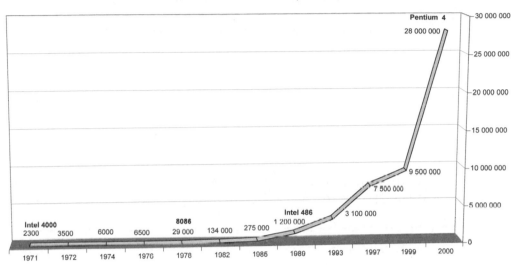

Source: Intel

Figure 19.4   Moore's law as demonstrated in Intel microprocessors

Although computing power has grown in a linear manner, the changes created by new technology will be neither gradual nor linear. History suggests that technical change is discontinuous. Things will seem to be steady or moving forward gradually, and then take off in a new direction. Such changes are hard to predict. For example, no one realized that mobile phones would be heavily used for texting – using a primitive twelve-key telephone keypad.

Computing power will also become embedded in everyday objects, giving us feedback and control that isn't possible today. According to Paul Sappho, the Director of the Institute of Future Thinking, there is more computing power in the average electronic watch than existed in the entire world before 1960.

OTHER TECHNOLOGIES

Continued growth of the Internet is expected, leading to new forms of association and networking, and giving people instant information. The network provided by the Internet will also lead to almost free phone calls and other forms of communication between objects and people.

However, we have failed so far to produce breakthrough transportation technologies such as teleportation or new methods of extreme propulsion such as anti-gravity.

Nanotechnology is the technology of very small things, which involves building products by moving atoms around. This makes it possible to manufacture anything at low cost. It includes:

- very small objects, such as nanorobots, which perform surgery, kill cancer cells, or remove pollutants from water
- conventional objects made from nanotechnology, including food made from atoms, and self-healing materials.

According to Foresight Technology, nanotechnology will bring about a revolution in manufacturing. This technology may allow things to be made for not much more than the cost of their raw materials. It is also likely to converge with other sciences and technologies, just as computers and telecoms did in the 1990s. Nanoscience, biotechnology, information technology and cognitive science (NBIC) promises innovative new products.

- *Robotics* will remove the need for much physical labour. Already this can be seen in self-guiding vacuum cleaners. According to Hans Moravec of the Robotics Institute at Carnegie Mellon University, robots will, fuelled by the growth in computing power, become more intelligent than human beings later this century. However, many experts believe that it will take many years before robots will be walking around the home. John Petersen, founder of the Arlington Institute, says that programming computers to behave like a human is very difficult. Tasks that humans regard as second nature, such as going upstairs, is a complicated process.

- *Molecular engineering and biotechnology* will extend people's lives and improve their quality. We are moving into an era where people can choose their babies' gender and other attributes. Stem cell technology will create new treatments from curing cancer to ending baldness. We will have a greater understanding of the role of individual genes (or groups of genes), particularly in triggering disease. We will see the development of tailored drugs that will manage cancers and other diseases more effectively. Using drugs and subcutaneous sensors and motors, we should be able to conquer diseases such as Parkinsons.

- *Carbon nanotubes* will be the likely successor to silicon in computing, monitors, batteries and other products.

- *Fuel cell cars* herald the end of the internal combustion engine, as well as a means of powering other objects such as laptop computers.

- *Flexible displays and memory devices* will be integrated into clothing, or rolled up and stuffed into a pocket (organic light-emitting diodes, OLEDS, and plastic transistors).

- Voice over internet protocol (VOIP) is with us today. This lets people make phone calls over the Internet, at a fraction of the cost of traditional phone calls.

- *Wearable computers* will monitor the individual's health, and allow more portable music or satellite navigation devices.

- *Haptic devices*: 'Haptics' refers to transferring a user's movement into action by a machine, and are already in use in some video games. Surfaces are likely to be full of haptic sensors, which will respond to our arm movements across them. These devices will replace the mouse.

TECHNOLOGIES THAT WON'T DISPLACE CURRENT INDUSTRIES

Many up-and-coming technologies merely enhance or supersede existing products. These include cars that guide themselves, the fridge that warns you when food is past its sell-by date, or biosensors that monitor your health.

While companies need to adopt these new technologies to stay in business, they won't cause a step-wise change in the market. Thus new forms of cryptography or computer grid networking will make life easier and more flexible but won't change the way the consumer does things. And the factory that produces silicon-based memory will merely switch to making plastic ones. Such technology includes radio frequency ID tags (RFID).

And while molecular machines will allow doctors to perform nanosurgery, repairing arteries and removing clots, this will still require a surgeon with the knowledge of the body, prescribing and controlling the nanobots in the patient's body. So even this most radical of technologies will in some cases merely give additional armentarium to existing technicians.

Some experts believe that the keyboard will still be everywhere, since it's the perfect device for inputting large amounts of text very quickly. Voice-activated systems will also be common, but in the office they may not be very practical.

THE RISKS ON SOCIETY OF NEW TECHNOLOGIES

Cellular telephones and the Internet have given people unprecedented ability to communicate. However, there is also an opposing trend. New technology allows the state or corporation to exert greater control over the individual. For example, the police can use tracking devices to restrict an offender's movements, and keep them in a geographic area. The same technology can let an abusive husband track his wife, and identify where she goes and for how long. In time, therefore, there may be calls for democratic controls on the technology, as we have already seen with genetically modified organisms (GMOs) and stem cells.

There is also a risk that the new technologies – for example, powerful new diseases or new military technologies – could be stolen and misused by malevolent or mad individuals to wreak havoc on civil society. Even self-replicating machines pose dangers. This means that there may have to be more stringent controls.

Biological technologies are evolving so fast that many scientists are unaware of their consequences, in the same way that nuclear scientists in the 1950s could not foresee the dangers of nuclear proliferation, miniaturization of nuclear hardware, and the theft of nuclear devices. As Bill Joy, co-founder of Sun Microsystems, points out, we are moving 'from wet to dry', no longer working with test tubes but instead clipping lengths of DNA to alter life forms.

Similarly, the arguments over genetically modified (GM) food demonstrated that the scientists had not thought sufficiently about the risks of GM crops. These include the possibility that crops would become resistant to pests or herbicides, or wipe out or harm wildlife. It could also mean biotechnology companies taking an increasing control of the world's agriculture.

Climate and weather risks

Global warming creates changeable weather patterns, with an increase in mean temperatures in some areas, and violent weather in others. Rising sea levels are another development. These new weather patterns can alter markets. For example, increases in temperature could:

- increase the demand for one type of product while hampering another – for example, we could see increased sales of soft drinks, salads and light clothes, and reducing sales of heaters
- change crop production, with British farmers discovering that their land is more able to grow Mediterranean crops.

More unpredictable or hostile weather could have the following effects:

- make sales harder to predict, leading to swings in demand in weather-related industries
- make logistics less reliable, with more hold-ups occurring
- stop normal sales activity, as in the case of tropical storms
- damage or destroy property and other assets.

Organizations can adapt to changing weather patterns by:

- altering their products to suit changed markets
- reducing dependency on suppliers and customers in geographical areas that are at risk from bad weather
- learning to predict and adapt to a new seasonality, for example the annual arrival of a stormy season
- making their buildings and other assets more storm-proof
- ensuring that staff are able to cope with weather emergencies, for example by practising emergency drills.

Meanwhile some low-lying coastal areas may get engulfed by the sea as the years progress, leading to the loss of property and tourist businesses. Conflicts will grow between residents desperate to save their livelihoods and governments reluctant to fight a losing battle with the weather.

Since weather affects many markets, directly or indirectly, each business will have to assess the likely impact of weather on their products, markets and suppliers; and take practical steps. The Swiss are building new resorts on higher alpine slopes, to counteract the loss of snow in traditional resorts. This, meanwhile, has led to outcries by environmentalists.

Finally, changing weather patterns can bring big rewards to companies that see risk as an opportunity.

Useful links

Bureau of Labor Statistics (USA)
www.bls.gov/EMP

Foresight Technology
www.foresight.org

Millennium Project
www.acunu.org/index.html

Nanotechnology
http://science.howstuffworks.com/nanotechnology.htm

Santa Fe Institute
www.santafe.edu

Appendix: The Final Risk Checklist

The checklist below summarizes the checklists located at the end of chapters. To complete the assessment, mark in the risk factor for each. This identifies the organization's greatest areas of risk.

Given the range of organizations and the differing risk in each, this checklist can provide only a broad assessment. You can adapt it to your own purposes.

Chapter	Title	Low risk	Medium risk	High risk
3	Risk organization			
4	Operations and production			
5	Purchasing			
6	Health and safety			
7	Environment			
8	Fire			
9	Security			
10	Fraud			
11	Finance			
12	IT			
13	Legal			
14	Marketing			
15	People and ethics			
16	Business continuity*			

*Note: for this assessment, the scale is the reverse of those found in most other risk assessments.

Resources

This is a selective list of useful organizations and websites focused on business risk management. Updates for this list of resources can be found at www.inst.org/risk.

Organizations

AIRMIC, Association of Insurance and Risk Managers (UK insurance)
www.airmic.com

Business in the Community
www.bitc.org.uk

FERMA, Federation of European Risk Management Associations (insurance related)
www.ferma-asso.org

GARP, Global Association of Risk Professionals (financial)
www.garp.com

Institute of Chartered Accountants in England and Wales
www.icaew.co.uk/risk

Institute of Internal Auditors
www.iia.org.uk

Institute of Risk Management (insurance related)
www.theirm.org

IOSH
www.iosh.co.uk

PRMIA, Professional Risk Managers International Association
www.prmia.org

RIMS, Risk & Insurance Management Society (insurance North America)
www.rims.org

SRA, Society for Risk Analysis
www.sra.org

Survive, a business continuity association
www.survive.com

PUBLIC POLICY, PUBLIC SECTOR ORGANIZATIONS

ALARM, National Forum for Risk Management in the Public Sector
www.alarm-uk.com

PRIMA, Public Risk Management Association (USA)
www.primacentral.org

Public Entity Risk Institute
www.riskinstitute.org

Risk World
www.riskworld.com

SRA, Society for Risk Analysis (global public policy)
www.sra.org

Portals

Riskinfo
www.riskinfo.com

Standards

AIRMIC
www.airmic.com

BSI
www.bsi-global.com

COSO
www.coso.org

ISO
www.iso.org

Standards Australia
www.riskmanagement.com.au

Newspapers (to be searched for risk topics)

Financial Times
www.ft.com

Wall Street Journal
http://online.wsj.com

Journals

Foresight (insurance focus)
www.rirg.com

Risk Management
www.rmmag.com

Risk Reports
www.riskreports.com

SRA Newsletter
www.sra.org

Search engines and news

Google (sign up for news on risk)
www.google.com

Universities and colleges

Some universities hold risk management courses.

Caldeonian Business School
www.cbs.gcal.ac.uk

Georgia State University
www.gsu.edu

Monash, Australia
www.monash.edu.au

Southampton University
www.management.soton.ac.uk/risk

University of Calgary
www.ucalgary.ca

University of Pennsylvania, Wharton School
www.upenn.edu

Training courses

Business Forums International
www.bfi.co.uk

Insight
www.insight.co.uk

Institute of Risk Management
www.theirm.org

Key Skills
www.prince2.com/riskman.html

Silicon Beach Training
www.siliconbeachtraining.co.uk

Standards Australia
www.riskmanagement.com.au

Emergency notification systems

247i
http://247i.co.uk
3online
www.3nonline.com

Enera
www.enera.com

Software

Erisk (a risk portal)
www.erisk.com

Methodware
www.methodware.com

Paisley Consulting
www.paisleyconsulting.com

Picnet
www.picnet.com.au/pols/prmt

RisGen
www.ris3.com

Risk Register
www.incom.com.au

Strohl LDRPS
www.strohlsystems.com

Sungard Paragon
www.availability.sungard.com

Further reading

AS/NZS 4360:2004-10-28 Standards Australia, 2004.

Bernstein, P., *Against the Gods. The Remarkable Story of Risk*, Wiley, 1998.

Chapman, C. and S. Ward, *Project Risk Management – Processes, Techniques and Insights*, John Wiley & Sons, 2003.

DeLoach, J.W., *Enterprise-wide Risk Management, Financial Times*, Prentice Hall, 2000.

DeMarco, T. and T. Lister, *Waltzing with Bears: Managing Risk on Software Projects*, Dorset House Publishing Co, 2003.

Good Practice Guidelines, Business Continuity Institute, 2002.

Grose, V.L., *Managing Risk: Systematic Loss Prevention for Executives*, Longman, 1988.

Hiles, A. and P. Barnes, *Definitive Handbook of Business Continuity Management*, John Wiley & Sons, 1999.

Hoffman, D.G., *Managing Operational Risk: 20 Firmwide Best Practice Strategies*, Wiley Finance Editions, 2002.

Lam, J., *Enterprise Risk Management: From Incentives to Controls*, John Wiley & Sons, 2003.

Managing Risk, Briefing Note 13, Institute of Internal Auditors – UK and Ireland, 1998.

McNamee, D., *Assessing Risk*, Institute of Internal Auditors, 1996.

Murray, B., *Defending the Brand: Aggressive Strategies for Protecting Your Brand in the Online Arena*, 2003.

Peters, T., *In Search of Excellence*, 2004.

Regester, M. and J. Larkin, *Risk Issues and Crisis Management: A Casebook of Best Practice* (PR in Practice Series), Kogan Page, 2001.

Wideman, R.M. (ed.), *Project and Program Risk Management: A Guide to Managing Project Risks and Opportunities*, PMIC, 1998.

Glossary

In risk management the meaning of some words is different from that of other specialisms. For example, the word 'control' differs from its use among research scientists. Even the various risk standards don't always agree on the definition of the words.

The definitions below have been taken from various sources, including COSO, AS/NZS 4360 and the Institute of Internal Auditors, and in some cases have been adapted by the author to improve clarity. For more detail, the ISO/IEC Guide 73:2002 provides a standardized vocabulary for risk.

Appetite	See *Risk appetite*.
AS/NZS 4360: 2004	Australian risk management standard.
Assurance	An element of *corporate governance* that provides feedback on the effectiveness of operations, compliance with laws and regulations, and accuracy of financial information.
Business continuity	Avoiding interruptions to the business, for example through computer viruses, fire or PR crisis.
BCM	Business continuity management also aims to recover quickly from any interruption. It emphasizes the need for disaster planning.
Business risk	The organization's operational risks. This contrasts with *credit risk*.
Compliance	Conforming to laws and regulations, a standard or a management system.
Consequence	Outcome of an *event*.
Control	A process or practice that minimizes or prevents negative consequences. Some kinds of *procedure* are controls.
Corporate governance	The rules by which companies are run, as regulated by government. The board is responsible to shareholders.
COSO	The Committee of Sponsoring Organizations of the Treadway Commission. An influential US private-sector organization that has produced a framework for risk management.
Credit risk	For a financial services organization, the risk that a borrower or bond issuer may default and be unable to pay their debt or the interest.
CRO	Chief risk officer

CSR	Corporate social responsibility. Relates to a company's economic, social and environmental impacts.
Denial-of-service attack	Occurs when a cyber criminal uses an automated process to deluge a company with fake emails or repeatedly interrogates a company's database. This clogs up the company's server and prevents customers from using the company website.
D&O	Directors and Officers; relates to liability and insurance.
ERP	Enterprise resource planning. Software that links a company's purchasing, inventory, and order tracking.
ERM	Enterprise risk management. Managing business risk in a planned way across the organization. The word 'enterprise' reminds the reader that we aren't referring to the risks commonly debated in the banking or insurance industry, such as client reliability, liquidity or stability.
Event	A set of circumstances leading to a *consequence*.
HACCP	Hazard analysis and critical control point. A safety methodology for food processors.
Hazard	Source of potential harm.
HAZOP	Hazard and operability studies. System for managing safety and reliability in the design of plant, especially in the chemical, oil, food and water industries.
Impact	Result or effect of an *event*.
Intellectual property	Trademarks, patents and copyright.
Internal control	A process designed to assure managers that policies are being met (such as compliance with laws or regulations).
ISO	International Organization for Standardization. A network of national standards' institutes. The source of ISO 9000, ISO 14001, and other standards.
Market risk	For financial companies, the risk that price of stocks or other investments will fall, usually caused by outside forces such as recession or inflation. Also known as *systemic risk*.
OFR	Operating financial review. A UK regulation designed to give shareholders better information on quoted companies.
PAS 56	Guide to *Business Continuity Management* (BCM), published by the British Standards Institution.
Probability	The likelihood that an event will occur. A number between 1 and 0, which represents how likely some event is to occur. A probability of 0 means the event will never occur, while a probability of 1 means that the event will always occur.
Procedure	Written instructions, in a series of steps, for carrying out a *process*.

Process	An activity that is repeatedly carried out within the enterprise.
Residual risk	Risk remaining after *risk treatment*.
Risk	The chance of something happening, usually with negative consequences.
Risk analysis	Systematic process to understand the nature and scale of risk.
Risk appetite	How much risk the organization is willing to bear.
Risk assessment	The overall process of identifying, analysing and evaluating risks.
Risk management	The process of identifying, controlling and minimizing the impact of uncertain events.
Risk retention	Accepting the burden of loss, or benefit of gain, from a specific *risk*.
Risk sharing	Sharing the burden of risk with another party, such as an insurance company or joint-venture partner.
Risk treatment	Measures that modify *risk*.
Sarbanes-Oxley Act	US Act that places controls on annual reports and directors' behaviour. Also known as *SOX* and *Sarbox*.
Sarbox	See *Sarbanes-Oxley Act*.
Scenario planning	Looking at a range of outcomes and their effects.
Sensitivity analysis	A 'what if' analysis.
Six sigma	A movement designed to improve business processes. Six sigma relies on statistical techniques to measure success. Most experts emphasize incremental process improvement. Six sigma equates to fewer than 3.4 defects per million in manufacturing or service operations.
SOX	See *Sarbanes-Oxley Act*.
Stakeholders	People interested in or affected by the organization's risks.
SCM	Supply chain management. Procurement, fulfilment and shipping.
Systemic risk	see *market risk*.

Index